PRIVATIZATION IN CHILE

Since 1985 the International Center for Economic Growth, a nonprofit organization, has contributed to economic growth and human development in developing and post-socialist countries by strengthening the capacity of indigenous research institutes to provide leadership in policy debates. To accomplish this the Center sponsors a wide range of programs—including research, publications, conferences, seminars, and special projects advising governments—through a network of more than 230 correspondent institutes worldwide. The Center's research and publications program is organized around five series: Sector Studies; Country Studies; Studies in Human Development and Social Welfare; Occasional Papers; and Working Papers.

The Center is affiliated with the Institute for Contemporary Studies, and is headquartered in Panama with the administrative office in San Francisco, California.

For further information, please contact the International Center for Economic Growth, 243 Kearny Street, San Francisco, California, 94108, USA. Phone (415) 981-5353; Fax (415) 986-4878.

ICEG Board of Overseers

PRIVATIZATION IN CHILE
AN ECONOMIC APPRAISAL

Dominique Hachette and Rolf Lüders

An International Center for Economic Growth Publication

ICS PRESS

San Francisco, California

Publication signifies that the International Center for Economic Growth (ICEG) believes a work to be a competent treatment worthy of public consideration. The findings, interpretations, and conclusions of a work are entirely those of the authors and should not be attributed to ICEG, its affiliated organizations, its Board of Overseers, or organizations that support ICEG.

The research presented here was managed at the World Bank and was financed by a grant from its Research Committee, Research Project 673-31. The findings, interpretations, and conclusions in this publication do not necessarily represent the views and policies of the World Bank or its Board of Directors or the countries they represent. The World Bank does not guarantee the accuracy of the data included in this publication and accepts no responsibility whatsoever for any consequences of their use.

Inquiries, book orders, and catalog requests should be addressed to ICS Press, 243 Kearny Street, San Francisco, California 94108, USA. Telephone: (415) 981-5353; fax: (415) 986-4878; to order call toll-free in the continental United States: **800-326-0263**.

Editor: Heidi Fritschel.
Indexer: Shirley Kessel.
Cover designer: JPD Communications and Design.

Library of Congress Cataloging-in-Publication Data

Hachette, Dominique.
    [Privatización en Chile. English]
    Privatization in Chile : an economic appraisal / by Dominique Hachette and Rolf Lüders.
       p.   cm.
    "An International Center for Economic Growth Publication."
    Includes bibliographical references and index.
    ISBN 1-55815-208-3
    1. Privatization—Chile 2. Government business enterprises—Chile. I. Lüders Schwarzenberg, Rolf. II. Title.
HD4098.H3313 1993   92-22670
338.983—dc20

CONTENTS

PREFACE

Since the mid-1970s Chile has undergone a massive privatization program, transferring more than 550 state-owned enterprises from the public to the private sector. *Privatization in Chile* is the first study to provide a detailed and rigorous account of the economic impact of this unprecedented wave of privatization. Here Dominique Hachette and Rolf Lüders examine exactly what privatization has meant for efficiency, employment, government revenues and expenditures, the capital market, and savings and investment in Chile.

Privatization may be an idea whose time has come, but its net effects are often difficult to determine and obscured by preconceived notions and biases. On the one hand, critics of privatization claim that it causes unemployment and leads to disparity in capital ownership. On the other hand, proponents claim that it increases economic efficiency and strengthens capital markets. In this volume Hachette and Lüders take on both sets of assumptions, showing that ultimately the effects of privatization depend on how the process is carried out.

Based on Chile's experience with privatization, unique in its scope, Hachette and Lüders extract policy lessons that are essential for anyone who works on or studies the privatization of state-owned enterprises around the world.

Nicolás Ardito-Barletta
General Director
International Center for Economic Growth

Panama City, Panama
November 1992

vii

ACKNOWLEDGMENTS

We owe a special debt of gratitude to José Martínez, who made generous use of his time to guide us through the intricacies of the administration of privatization and to provide basic information. We also wish to acknowledge the skillful collaboration of Angel Cabrera in Chapter 5, Sebastián de Ramón in Chapter 7 and Appendix C, and Jorge Kaufmann in Appendix E. Cecilia Cifuentes, Angélica Jaramillo, and Tomás Fernández were invaluable for their patient gathering and presentation of information. Representatives of the Investment Steel Company of the Pacific (CAP), the State Development Corporation (CORFO), the National Electricity Company (ENDESA), and other enterprises consulted were extremely helpful. Finally, we wish to thank Jorge Cauas, Bruno Philippi, and Gert Wagner for their careful and detailed comments. Of course, we remain responsible for all errors and misinterpretations of facts.

We are especially grateful to Thomas Connelly, who diligently edited our English, and to Marily Morales, who carefully reviewed the various drafts. We owe special thanks to Myriam Abarca and Ana María Saguez, who bore the burden of typing.

The research upon which this book is based was made possible through the generous support of the World Bank, CORFO, CAP, and the National Science and Technology Fund (FONDECYT).

D. H. and R. L.

LIST OF ABBREVIATIONS

AFP	administradora de fondos de pensiones (pension fund administration company)
CAP	Compañía de Acero del Pacífico (Steel Company of the Pacific); after 1981, Compañía de Acero del Pacífico S.A. de Inversiones (Investment Steel Company of the Pacific)
CAPM	capital assets pricing model
CCNI	Compañía Chilena de Navegación Interoceánica (Chilean Interoceanic Navigation Company)
CCU	Compañía de Cervecerías Unidas (United Breweries Company)
CGEI	Compañía General de Electricidad Industrial S.A. (Industrial Electric Company)
CHILECTRA	Compañía Chilena de Electricidad S.A. (Chilean Electric Company)
Chile PAC	Red Pública de Transmisión de Datos (Public Network for the Transmission of Data)
CHILGENER	CHILECTRA Generación (CHILECTRA Generation Company)
CHILMETRO	CHILECTRA Metropolitana (Metropolitan CHILECTRA)
CHILQUINTA	CHILECTRA Quinta Región (CHILECTRA–Fifth Region)
CIDCOM	Compañía de Telefonía Móvil (Mobile Telephone Company)

CIEPLAN	Corporación de Investigaciones Económicas para Latinoamérica (Latin American Economic Research Corporation)
CMET	Complejo Manufacturero de Equipos Telefónicos (Telephone Equipment Manufacturing Complex)
CNE	Comisión Nacional de Energía (National Energy Commission)
CNT	Compañía Nacional de Teléfonos (National Telephone Company)
CODELCO	Corporación Nacional del Cobre de Chile (National Copper Corporation of Chile)
CONAF	Corporación Nacional Forestal (National Forest Corporation)
COPEC	Compañía de Petróleos de Chile (Petroleum Company of Chile)
CORA	Corporación de la Reforma Agraria (Agrarian Reform Corporation)
CORFO	Corporación de Fomento a la Producción (State Development Corporation)
CPI	consumer price index
CTC	Compañía de Teléfonos de Chile (Telephone Company of Chile)
CTM	Compañía de Teléfonos de Manquehue (Telephone Company of Manquehue)
DFL	decree with the force of law
DL	decree law
ECA	Empresa de Comercio Agrícola (Agricultural Trading Company)
ECOM	Empresa Nacional de Computación e Informática Ltda. (National Computer and Information Company)
EDELAYSEN	Empresa Eléctrica de Aysén (Electric Company of Aysén)
EDELMAG	Empresa Eléctrica de Magallanes (Electric Company of Magallanes)
EMEC	Empresa Eléctrica Coquimbo S.A. (Electric Company of Coquimbo)

EMEL	Empresa Eléctrica de Melipilla, Colchoque, y Maule S.A. (Electric Company of Melipilla, Colchoque, and Maule)
EMELIG	Empresa Elétrica La Ligua (Electrica Company of La Ligua)
EMELMA	Empresa Eléctrica Maule (Electric Company of Maule)
EMPREMAR	Empresa Marítima del Estado (State Maritime Corporation)
ENAEX	Empresa Nacional de Explosivos (National Explosives Company)
ENAMI	Empresa Nacional de Minería (National Mining Company)
ENAP	Empresa Nacional de Petróleo (National Petroleum Company)
ENDESA	Empresa Nacional de Electricidad S.A. (National Electricity Company)
ENTEL	Empresa Nacional de Telecomunicaciones (National Telecommunications Company)
FFCC	Ferrocarriles del Estado (State Railway)
FONDECYT	Fondo Nacional de Ciencia y Tecnología (National Science and Technology Fund)
GDP	gross domestic product
GISP	General Index of Share Prices
GNP	gross national product
IANSA	Industria Azucarera Nacional (National Sugar Industry)
INFORSA	Industrias Forestales S.A. (Forest Industries)
ISAPRE	Institución de Salud Previsional (Social Security Health Institution)
ITT	International Telephone and Telegraph Corporation
JAC	Junta de Aeronáutica Civil (Civil Aeronautics Board)
LADECO	Línea Aérea del Cobre (Copper Airlines)
LAN Chile	Línea Aérea Nacional–Chile (National Airline of Chile)
LIBOR	London Interbank Offering Rate

MRP	stock market risk premium
ODEPLAN	Oficina Nacional de Planificación (National Planning Office)
PEM	Programa de Empleo Mínimo (Minimum Employment Program)
POJH	Programa de Obras para Jefes de Hogar (Program of Employment for Heads of Families)
SAESA	Sociedad Austral de Electricdad S.A. (Austral Electricity Company)
SEBI	Sistema de Estadísticas Básicas de Inversión (Investment Basic Statistics System)
SIC	Sistema Interconectado Central (Central Interconnected System)
SIIC	Standard International Industrial Classification
SING	Sistema Interconectado del Norte Grande (North Interconnected System)
SOE	state-owned enterprise
SOQUIMICH	Sociedad Química y Minera de Chile (Chemical and Mining Society of Chile)
TELECOM–Chile	Telecommunications Chile S.A.
UF	unidad de fomento (production unit)
VTR	Vía TransRadio

ONE

Introduction

After the 1930s, the economic systems of many countries of the world were characterized by growing government intervention and, in particular, by a spectacular increase in public ownership and management of economic activities. Supporters of state intervention usually justified this trend using the concept of market failure, an explanation that became fashionable after the Great Depression and received strong intellectual support from John Maynard Keynes. They argued that several factors made government involvement necessary, including natural monopolies for the production of socially valuable services, the technological characteristics of those services, and capital market imperfections in the presence of large economies of scale. They also argued that public enterprises could be used to stabilize employment and to improve the lot of the poor through subsidized prices and wide distribution of certain social services.

Serious and superficial arguments were mingled, but the available empirical evidence could not justify growing government involvement. In most cases, these arguments were ingeniously used to support power-hungry individuals and political parties in the name of improving social conditions, a peculiarity of the post-Depression period that was most pronounced after World War II in many developing countries.

Over time, however, events have revealed serious weaknesses in public enterprises (and in government intervention in general). Public

1

firms are often mismanaged, and they frequently contribute to high public deficits and inflation. The market failure argument also loses force in the face of not only technological changes that reduce the importance of natural monopolies but also the strengthening of capital markets and of the private sector in general, which allows the latter to carry out projects even vaster than those of the traditional public sector. Furthermore, gross inefficiency in the distribution of public services resulted in flagrant contradictions with redistributive objectives, while management inefficiencies prevented public enterprises from attaining either internal efficiency or allocative efficiency, although in some cases they achieved technical efficiency, which, for some reason, many considered sufficient and even saw as an object of pride during the 1970s.

A reaction against the widening grip of state enterprises set in both in developed countries such as England and Spain and in developing countries like Bangladesh and Chile. This book tells the story of the Chilean process of privatization. Our main objective is to explain in some detail why privatization occurred, how divestitures were carried out, what difficulties were encountered, and what conditions were imposed to ensure efficiency in both private and public enterprises. We will also describe other aspects of the preparation of state-owned enterprises (SOEs) for privatization and the effects of privatization on government revenues and wealth, savings and investment, the capital market, employment, distribution of property, and management. This account emphasizes the role of the major structural changes carried out by the military government that came to power at the end of 1973, in particular those designed to shift economic functions to the private sector, which would become the main—though not exclusive—actor in the new strategy for development.

This is neither a theoretical nor an ideological book. Our intention is to present as candid and objective a study of the divestiture process as possible, in the hope that the views and experiences narrated here will benefit other countries that are either pursuing or considering SOE privatization. It is not a recipe book or a do-it-yourself divestiture manual. We have aimed for a positive rather than a normative approach, to reduce the scope of value judgments, which have usually colored the general issue of private versus public property. In so doing, we hope to clear up some misconceptions on the subject.

The Significance of the Chilean Experience

The case of Chile is particularly interesting, given the large share of public enterprises in gross domestic product (GDP) when the process of privatization began and the depth of the process itself; with the divestiture of about 550 enterprises between 1973 and 1988, SOE participation in GDP fell from 39 percent to 16 percent (Tables 1.1 and 1.2).

Until the Great Depression of the 1930s, state enterprises played a limited role in Chile. After the depression, however, and until the military takeover in late 1973, most Chilean administrations intervened heavily and increasingly in the economy. Part of that intervention took the form of the creation and management of state enterprises. In this respect, the State Development Corporation (CORFO, a state-owned development bank) became an important instrument. During its initial years, it created several large corporations related to the steel industry (the Steel Company of the Pacific, CAP), the sugar beet industry (the National Sugar Industry,

TABLE 1.1

State-Owned and State-Managed Enterprises in Selected Years, 1970–1989 (number of enterprises)

	1970	1973	1983	1989
Enterprises related to CORFO	46	571	24	24
Subsidiaries	46	228	23[a]	24[b]
State-managed enterprises	0	325[c]	0[d]	0
Banks	0	18	1	0
Other state-owned enterprises	20	22	21	18
Other financial institutions	2	2	2	2
CODELCO	0[e]	1	1	1
Total	68	596	48[f]	45

NOTE: See Appendix A for a list of enterprises included in the different categories of this table. CORFO is the State Development Corporation. CODELCO is the National Copper Corporation of Chile.

a. In 1979, two enterprises in which the state participated were created: Compañía Chilena de Litio and Télex-Chile.

b. Between 1983 and 1989 the following fourteen new SOEs were formed as a result of the breakup of existing companies: Empresa Eléctrica de Aysén, Empresa Eléctrica Colbún-Machicura, Empresa Eléctrica del Norte Grande, Empresa Marítima del Sur, Empresa de Servicios Sanitarios de Tarapacá, Empresa de Servicios Sanitarios de Atacama, Empresa de Servicios Sanitarios de Coquimbo, Empresa de Servicios Sanitarios del Libertador, Empresa de Servicios Sanitarios del Maule, Empresa de Servicios Sanitarios del Bío-Bío, Empresa de Servicios Sanitarios de la Araucanía, Empresa de Servicios Sanitarios de Los Lagos, Empresa de Servicios Sanitarios de Aysén, and Empresa de Servicios Sanitarios de Magallanes.

c. Excludes state-managed enterprises (compañías intervenidas) in which CORFO had a minority interest, which are included in the group of subsidiaries.

d. After September 1973, 350 state-managed enterprises were returned to their owners, most of them during 1974.

e. Although CODELCO did not exist, the state owned 50 percent of the big copper companies. It acquired this percentage when it invested in foreign-owned companies during 1970 as a result of the Chileanization process.

f. This does not include more than fifty "odd sector" enterprises indirectly managed by the state, which fell into government hands during 1983 as a result of government intervention in some financial institutions and which were privatized before 1989 (see Chapter 4).

SOURCE: CORFO.

TABLE 1.2

Share of State Enterprises in Sectoral GDP, 1965–1988 (percentage)

Sector	1965	1973	1981	1988
Mining	13.0	85.0	83.0	n.a.
Industry	3.0	40.0	12.0	n.a.
Utilities	25.0	100.0	75.0	n.a.
Transportation	24.3	70.0	21.0	n.a.
Communications	11.1	70.0	96.3	n.a.
Finance	0.0	85.0	28.3	n.a.
All state enterprises and public administration	14.2	39.0	24.1	15.9

n.a. = not available.
SOURCES: C. Larroulet, "Reflexiones en Torno al Estado Empresario en Chile," *Estudios Públicos* (Winter); Embassy of the United States in Chile, (Santiago, 1985); authors' estimates.

IANSA), the energy sector (the National Electricity Company, ENDESA), and others. Later, CORFO took over several privately owned corporations that could not service the large CORFO credits they had received.

During the 1930–1973 period, other large state enterprises were also created, including the Agricultural Trading Company (ECA), the National Mining Company (ENAMI), the National Petroleum Company (ENAP), the State Maritime Corporation (EMPREMAR), and the National Airline of Chile (LAN Chile). In 1970, sixteen of these "giant" SOEs were functioning. In addition, the government engaged in a large-scale land reform program toward the end of the 1960s, expropriating and managing many farms. At the same time, it "Chileanized" (purchased a 50 percent share of) existing large copper companies.

Tables 1.1 and 1.2 show the number and scope of state enterprises toward the end of the 1960s. In 1965, the SOEs produced 14 percent of GDP, although in some sectors—utilities and transportation—they produced up to 25 percent of sectoral GDP. The total number of state enterprises (excluding the expropriated farms and the Chileanized mines) in 1970 stood at sixty-eight, still a rather limited number.

Until the late 1960s, despite growing opposition, the expansion of the state enterprise sector had not become an issue, although the land reform was a point of contention. The election of Salvador Allende, a Marxist-socialist, in 1970 changed that climate. Nevertheless, the nationalization of the remaining shares of the big foreign copper companies still received unanimous legislative support. The reaction against the large state enterprise sector began when the government accelerated the land reform program, intervened in the management of industrial enterprises—legalized by a never-used decree law issued in the 1930s during the 100-day "socialist" government[1]—and purchased a controlling interest in most of the wholesale distribution and financial firms of the country.

Between 1965 and 1973, the number of companies controlled by the state grew from 68 to 596, excluding the expropriated farms. Of these enterprises, 325 were state-managed industrial firms (*compañías intervenidas*) and 18 were banks;[2] they included the most important industries in the country and almost all the financial institutions (Table 1.1). The expropriated farms included more than 60 percent of irrigated land. The relative share of the state enterprise sector exploded to 39 percent of GDP in 1973, encompassing 100 percent of utilities and more than 85 percent of mining and financial services (Table 1.2).

Chile's privatization experience has been unique in both scope and diversity. In a First Round of divestitures (1974–1979), nontraditional public enterprises were divested. Many of these firms, however, returned to public control in the midst of a major financial crisis and depression (1982–1983), only to be privatized again in 1984 and 1985. In a Second Round (1984–1989), the large traditional public enterprises were privatized. Other unusual aspects of the Chilean experience include, first, its new rules for public firms, which not only stimulated efficiency, but also served as preparation for divestiture, and second, the ingenious variety of privatization modes.

Main Conclusions

Although our conclusions will be explicitly detailed and supported in every chapter of the book, it may be useful to highlight here what we consider to be the main results of our analysis of the Chilean divestiture process. On the whole, the process of privatization was successful in distributing property ownership; it stimulated the private sector to improve efficiency; it opened new investment opportunities and created new responsibilities for the private sector; and it helped reduce practical and psychological dependency on the powerful and pervasive public sector. The process was also successful in converting critical and antagonistic groups, convincing them of the benefits of privatization. In doing so, it reduced the risk of reversibility despite significant changes in the political setting when the military government transferred power, after elections, to a democratic government. The latter recognized the validity of the privatization process and is even following in the steps of its predecessor, though at a more modest pace.

Errors were committed in the process of privatization. Some were predictable; others were unavoidable; and still others, put forward by some critics, were nonexistent. The most repeated error—though not unique to Chile—appears to be the lack of transparency in divestitures. Although we do not believe this affected the fiscal impact of privatization in any relevant way, it raised eyebrows, to say the least, and provided ammunition to groups that felt they were not given fair access to SOE stock being divested and ideological groups opposed to any notion of privatization. This lack of transparency appears to have been, in retrospect, the main shortcoming. The authorities, however, learned from their experience and, even with respect to this issue, made improvements that had some bearing in the later divestitures.

The success of privatization in Chile resulted from the political and economic environment and from the diversity of divestiture modes. A president who held power for seventeen years and was firmly convinced of the economic and political significance of privatization ensured the relative constancy of the process. Although the presence of a military government may appear to have been favorable for maintaining constancy, it should not be forgotten that critical views were voiced within the military establishment: autarkism and interventionism were two favorite war-horses. The views of the president, General Augusto Pinochet—that democracy could be strengthened only with widespread property ownership, a strong private sector, and a public sector in a subsidiary role—ultimately prevailed.

The economic situation in the early stages of privatization and through the 1970s was favorable to the process. The large fiscal deficit and high inflation inherited from the socialist government, caused partly by public enterprise losses, were convincing factors. Then, structural changes carried out by the new authorities strengthened competition, stimulated the capital market, freed prices and interest rates, improved resource allocation, and raised investment levels, creating a propitious environment for divestitures. The financial crash and deep depression of 1982–1983, with its concomitant reversal in privatization, was largely overcome by the beneficial impact of the institutional changes implemented in the 1970s, which came to maturity in the 1980s when the largest divestitures occurred.

Finally, the diversity of modes of privatization ensured that objectives as varied as maximizing government revenues and spreading property ownership—two important goals favored by both supporters and opponents of privatization—were met. A price had to be paid to spread property; however, it does not seem high, given the extent of property distribution obtained so far and the growing political support the process of privatization has earned.

Principal Merits and Shortcomings of This Study

From our biased point of view, this book presents some distinctive features while also suffering from obvious limitations. Among its merits are the following: First, it covers the main issues that are discussed among professionals and politicians and that are of some importance from a theoretical perspective. Second, it attempts to achieve objectivity and to avoid normative statements. Third, it uses novel methodologies, consistent with the empirical approach, which can be replicated usefully in other countries. Fourth, this is a timely moment to reexamine the implications of the structure of ownership, given technological and structural changes in areas where public property has traditionally been concentrated and the growing interest in privatization around the world.

The main limitations, and by no means the only ones, include the following: First, the evidence provided does not allow for proving or disproving some of the basic statements proposed in the book; it only supports them. Relevant information has not yet accumulated, given the novelty of the privatization process. Our main source of information has been the Normalization Unit of CORFO, which was especially generous in making available to us the data we required. Many other institutions, including CAP, ENAP, and the Santiago Stock Exchange, also contributed requested information to the study. Unfortunately, we could not carry out a description and analysis of the privatization of the enterprises composing the "odd sector"—private sector enterprises controlled and managed temporarily by the government as a consequence of the 1983 commercial banking intervention—because the most significant institutions in charge of implementing those privatizations were not willing to provide information such as transaction prices, dates, and purchases. Second, we tackled the classical issue of differences in efficiency among private and public firms only tangentially; unfortunately, its analysis will have to be deferred.

Structure of This Study

This book contains nine chapters and five methodological and statistical appendixes. Chapter 2 presents the framework of economic trends, institutional changes, and main events of the 1973–1989 period, during which divestitures took place. It highlights the strategy of economic liberalization, within which privatization logically fit and without which it could not have been successful. Appendix A presents a detailed list of enterprises in which the state participated between 1970 and 1989.

The objectives of privatization are analyzed in Chapter 3, in both political and economic terms. Although the promotion of individual rights and the decentralization of economic power were the bases for divestitures during the period of military government, specific economic justifications varied over time. The chapter provides the full array of reasons put forward in support of privatization and the discussions that took place concerning some of them. During the First Round, objectives included returning control of the previously state-managed private enterprises to their legitimate owners and reducing fiscal deficits. In the Second Round, they included the normalization of the firms taken over by the public sector in the depression of the early 1980s and the generation of public funds to finance social and capital expenditures. There were also the obvious desire to improve efficiency, which came as a logical aftermath of decades of inefficient public enterprise operation, and the desire to spread stock ownership in order to strengthen the capital market and, especially, the market orientation of the development strategy.

In Chapter 4, we present a synthesis of the evolution of the privatization process. The chapter first describes the wide scope of Chilean privatization, which covered agricultural land; social services such as pension funds, health care, education, and housing; and mining, industrial, commercial, and service firms (in this book we are mainly concerned with the latter categories). The chapter next examines the many modes of divestiture adopted, their advantages and shortcomings, and the institutions involved in divesting public firms. Finally, it covers the overall achievements of the process.

The privatization of public enterprises implies a transfer of public assets to the private sector, which can affect both the income statement and the balance sheet of the public sector. Both aspects are covered in Chapter 5, which analyzes the fiscal impact of privatization. Studies of privatization usually fail to measure wealth transfers or long-run fiscal effects of divestitures; they are measured here to obtain a complete picture of the impact of privatization on the income statement of public accounts. Another special contribution of this chapter is the proposal of a methodology to measure the market price of SOEs, which, applied here, allows us to quantify the price gap that favored the private sector in the divestiture of SOEs, a topic for hot debate wherever privatization is carried out. Appendix B includes a firm-by-firm estimate of that price gap.

The effects of privatization on the capital market, ownership distribution, savings and investment, and employment are discussed in Chapter 6. We argue that both divestiture successes and the strengthening of the capital market reinforced themselves, at least after 1984. Ownership distribution, which intensified political support for privatization, was stimulated by the development of the capital market. We also advance the hypothesis that different modes of privatization may have had different effects on savings and investment. Although the possibility of privatization's having a negative effect on employment is theoretically high, we investigate other contemporaneous factors that may largely explain the changes in employment. Differences between the rules established for public and private firms may in the short run be more important than mere transfers of property, although in the medium and long run the distribution of property may exercise a decisive influence.

In addition, it is to be expected that "the allocation of property rights does matter because it determines the objectives of the owners of the firm (public or private) and the systems of monitoring managerial performance. Public and private ownership differ in both respects. As a result, changes in property rights will materially affect the incentive structures, and hence, the behavior, of managements" (Vickers and Yarrow 1988:3). Therefore, Chapter 7 presents the results of our detailed analysis to determine whether significant differences can be found in the management of private, privatized, and public firms. We use discriminant and canonic analysis, two powerful tools, to discover the extent of differences based on financial ratios. The competitive and regulatory environment, while not the main actor in this analysis, nevertheless plays a significant role in explaining the results obtained. Chapter 7 is supported by two appendixes, one methodological (Appendix C) and one statistical (Appendix D).

Not all public enterprises were divested by the straightforward methods described. The transfers of two SOEs, CAP (steel industry) and ENDESA (electricity generation), involved unorthodox procedures that were strongly criticized at the time and still raise numerous objections. These cases are analyzed in detail in Chapter 8, not only to put the delicate issues they raised into proper perspective, but also to give a more realistic picture of the process of privatization. Appendix E describes the institutional, competitive, and regulatory environment that many SOEs faced at the moment of their divestiture and summarizes some of the major achievements of the military government in liberalizing the economy and in improving resource allocation.

Finally, Chapter 9 summarizes the main lessons to be drawn from the privatizations carried out in Chile between 1974 and 1989.

TWO

The Economic Framework, 1973–1989

The successes and failures of privatization in Chile are closely related to certain features of the country's general economic development. In fact, the two rounds of privatization discussed in this book were clearly tied to two different phases of Chilean economic evolution.

The First Round, which began with a major recession in 1975 and ended with an even deeper one in 1982–1983, took place during a period of substantive institutional adjustments, a major drive to reestablish macroeconomic balances, and painful stabilization efforts. During the two years of recession that followed that hectic period, about fifty of the most important previously privatized firms came back under the control of the government in the wake of a massive disruption in the financial sector. A period of recovery, adjustment, consolidation of the main institutional developments of the 1970s, and even a boom followed immediately, starting in 1984 and lasting until the present. Firms that had been managed by the state during the downturn returned to the private sector and a Second Round of privatization took place, which ended when a new president took office early in 1990.

This chapter will situate the privatization process within its economic context, beginning with the conditions faced by the new military government at the end of 1973. The principal quantitative information necessary to illustrate the descriptions and judgments proposed in this chapter appear in Table 2.1.

TABLE 2.1

Economic Indicators for Chile, 1971–1989

	1971	1972	1973	1974	1975	1976	1977
Real sector							
GDP growth rate (%)	9.0	–1.2	–5.6	1.0	–12.9	3.5	9.9
Gross investment/GDP (%)	14.7	12.4	8.0	21.5	13.6	13.2	14.8
National savings/GDP (%)	12.4	8.3	5.2	20.7	7.9	14.5	10.7
Unemployment rate (%)	5.5	3.8	4.6	9.7	16.2	16.8	13.2
Prices							
Inflation rate (%)	26.7	108.3	441.0	497.8	379.2	232.8	113.8
Real wages index (1970 = 100)	123.0	96.0	80.0	64.8	62.1	63.0	71.1
Short-term real interest rate (lending rate, %)	n.a.	n.a.	–76.1	–36.9	16.0	64.3	56.8
Real exchange rate (1977 = 100)	71.1	71.2	90.2	87.9	149.7	114.0	100.0
Terms of trade (1977 = 100)	150.6	145.3	163.6	172.9	103.6	111.7	100.0
Monetary and financial sector							
Total change in monetary base (% GDP)	n.a.	n.a.	22.2	7.5	7.2	8.0	5.3
M2/GDP (%)	n.a.	n.a.	22.3	11.1	11.2	11.7	13.0
Consolidated banking credit to the private sector/total credit (%)	28.5	22.2	18.6	15.2	15.9	15.6	37.7
Public sector							
Public sector expenditures (% GDP)	31.1	31.2	44.9	32.4	27.4	25.8	24.9
Fiscal deficit of the central government (% GDP)	10.7	13.0	24.7	10.5	2.6	2.3	1.8
Foreign sector							
Export growth in constant prices (%)	8.6	–13.0	–0.4	49.4	7.9	25.4	7.4
Current account surplus/ exports (%)	–17.8	–48.1	–19.7	–12.9	–27.1	5.4	–21.8
Annual change in external debt (US$ millions)	73	406	446	726	80	–134	481
Annual change in foreign reserves (US$ millions)	–231	–87	92	–73	–223	237	165
External debt service/exports (%, medium and long term)	36.8	15.6	11.9	15.1	31.2	39.4	43.9

TABLE 2.1 continued
Economic Indicators for Chile, 1971–1989

1978	1979	1980	1981	1982	1983	1984	1985	1986	1987	1988	1989
8.2	8.3	7.8	5.5	-14.1	-0.7	6.3	2.4	5.7	5.7	7.4	10.0
18.3	18.4	21.7	23.9	11.3	9.8	13.6	13.7	14.6	16.9	17.3	18.2
12.6	12.4	13.9	8.2	2.1	4.4	2.9	5.4	7.7	12.6	16.3	16.9
14.0	13.6	11.8	11.1	22.1	22.2	19.2	16.4	13.5	12.3	11.0	9.8
50.0	33.4	35.1	19.7	9.9	27.3	19.9	30.7	19.5	19.9	14.7	17.0
75.7	82.0	89.4	97.5	97.1	86.4	86.7	82.9	84.5	84.3	89.8	91.5
42.2	16.6	11.9	38.7	35.1	15.9	11.5	11.0	7.5	9.2	7.4	11.8
106.9	97.2	88.4	79.1	83.7	100.1	104.8	128.8	141.8	146.9	157.3	151.7
97.0	103.6	87.4	73.7	70.2	76.5	71.2	66.3	74.8	77.4	94.2	94.0
3.4	2.5	2.3	0.0	-1.3	-0.1	0.5	0.6	0.9	0.8	1.1	0.8
16.0	17.4	19.3	23.4	25.4	18.8	18.2	18.4	18.2	19.5	20.3	25.5
50.6	54.7	68.1	81.1	83.0	80.8	79.8	83.4	84.1	82.9	83.7	n.a.
23.8	22.8	23.1	24.9	28.5	28.4	28.8	32.5	30.0	28.3	30.7	n.a.
0.8	-1.7	-3.1	-1.7	2.3	3.8	4.0	6.3	2.8	0.1	1.7	n.a.
6.2	-2.8	18.5	1.5	4.7	0.6	6.8	6.9	9.8	8.8	5.5	9.2
-37.8	-26.1	-33.9	-88.4	-62.2	-29.2	-56.4	-34.9	-27.1	-15.5	-2.5	-9.3
1,463	1,820	2,600	4,458	1,611	278	1,446	441	70	-180	-1,559	-1,396
785	1,256	1,244	67	-1,165	-541	17	-99	-228	45	-732	n.a.
44.6	41.2	39.6	64.2	64.4	65.7	60.9	65.4	57.1	36.5	36.5	37.5

n.a. = not available.
SOURCES: Central Bank of Chile, *Indicadores Económicos y Sociales* (Santiago, various years); Joseph Ramos, *Neoconservative Economics in the Southern Cone of Latin America, 1973–1983* (Baltimore: Johns Hopkins University Press, 1986); Rolf Lüders, "Lessons from the Financial Liberalization of Chile: 1974–1982" (Santiago: Pontifical Catholic University of Chile, 1986, processed); Sergio de la Cuadra and Dominique Hachette, "The Timing and Sequencing of a Trade Liberalization Policy" (Santiago, 1986, processed); Ministry of Finance, *Exposición sobre el Estado de la Hacienda Pública* (Santiago: various years).

Initial Conditions

As part of its effort to implement its political agenda, the Allende government tried to revamp the Chilean economy. Among the measures it took were significant income redistribution and extensive state control of the means of production. By the end of 1973, however, Allende had created a legacy of deep macro- and microeconomic disequilibria.

That this should occur was inevitable: massive wage and social benefit readjustments, greatly broadened subsidies, significant expansion of public employment, and the nationalization and expropriation of private firms all required financing that the government was unable to obtain through taxes, because the Chilean parliament was opposed to at least part of Allende's revolutionary program. Nevertheless, the government persisted with its plans, even opting for fiscal deficits financed by central bank credit to the extent that, in 1973, the deficit exceeded 20 percent of gross domestic product (GDP). At that time, in order to avoid runaway inflation, generalized price controls were imposed, which led to long lines for shoppers and a black market for consumer goods, disrupting channels of distribution even more and further eroding the tax base. In August, official inflation was an unprecedented 300 percent per year; only two months later, it rose to around 1,000 percent.

Since the sources of revenue necessary for control of the means of production were dwindling, nationalization and expropriation were soon replaced by government requisition or outright seizure of firms. Fair compensation was awarded only in a few instances.

As a result of these developments, production declined precipitously in 1972 and 1973; decapitalization rose rapidly in numerous sectors; foreign reserves dwindled; real income gains achieved in 1971 were eroded; the drain of technical and managerial expertise and of capital was accelerated; and labor productivity diminished significantly as labor conflicts escalated. The economic decline was exacerbated by a drop in world prices for copper, Chile's main export, in 1971 and 1972, although the price rose spectacularly in 1973, and by a withdrawal of international credit from traditional sources.

Major Objectives of the New Authorities

The elimination of serious and pressing macroeconomic disequilibria was a primary objective of the new government that took control after September 1973. Its long-run objectives, however, concerned the correction of structural disequilibria that had long characterized the Chilean economy and the concomitant reorganization of the economic system.[1] Thus, there were three main goals:

1. to secure a high and stable rate of economic growth, which, in the government's view, had been seriously jeopardized in previous decades by a combination of a faulty development strategy (based on import substitution) and an inadequate choice of instruments (tariffs, prohibitions, and price and exchange controls, among others)
2. to eradicate extreme poverty and achieve full employment through highly productive activities
3. to achieve both price and policy stability

All economic objectives, whether imposed by necessity or chosen as explicit policy, were to respect individual rights to property and equality of opportunity in education, health, and social security. Effective economic decentralization was also a goal, since it was considered a precondition for effective political decentralization and the basis for efficient democratic organization.

These objectives were to be attained through a combination of means:[2]

1. restoration of the market as the principal instrument of economic decision making
2. restoration of the private sector as the main agent of development,[3] a condition that implied not only a revision of public sector responsibilities, but also a drastic reduction in that sector's size and involvement in economic activities; divestiture of public enterprises would be a logical step in this endeavor
3. greater openness to foreign markets, in order to exploit comparative advantages, reap the benefits of greater specialization, and improve efficiency by facing foreign competition
4. nondiscriminatory treatment of all productive sectors in order to improve resource allocation
5. development of an efficient financial market (previously nonexistent) to enhance savings and investment allocation
6. use of general economic tools, such as exchange and interest rates and the money supply, to help achieve these goals

Policies and Results: 1974–1981

Stabilization and development were the two main policy concerns during the 1974–1981 period. However, efforts to reduce extreme poverty through well-focused social programs and to improve access to opportunities (such as education and health) that would alter income distribution in the long run were also carried out.

Stabilization policies

The goal of restoring price stability was pursued through a combination of restrictive fiscal and monetary policies and use of the exchange rate to control expectations for most of the period, along with mandatory wage adjustments in the first few years to hinder the growth of aggregate demand. Fiscal efforts were aimed at eliminating deficits, reducing the size of the public sector, and making it more efficient. In 1974 a comprehensive tax reform program introduced a value-added tax (20 percent) in place of a progressive sales tax, improved the taxation of undistributed corporate earnings, eliminated exemptions, and increased real estate assessments and income tax rates. Public enterprises were allowed to raise their prices significantly, and most of those firms were subjected to the rules of self-financing and marginal cost pricing. Expenditures were reduced by cutting personnel (close to 2.5 percent of the national labor force was laid off between 1974 and 1977), while the government eliminated several programs and reduced public investment, at least as a percentage of GDP.[4]

As part of its drive for fiscal restraint, consistent with the subsidiary role to be played in the future by the public sector, the government transferred more than 500 state-controlled firms to the private sector (either by auction or by unrequited transfer) or dissolved them. The transferred firms had accounted for a disproportionate share of overall public sector deficits—one-third in 1973. As a result, the deficit of the consolidated public sector disappeared in 1976 and that of the central government in 1979, reappearing as "equilibrium deficits," limited in size both in 1982 and 1983.

The most important monetary policies to stabilize prices were, first of all, the prohibition of central bank lending to public sector entities other than the central government and, second, the prohibition of central bank lending to the public sector as a whole, a provision that was even incorporated into the 1980 Constitution. Central bank credit to the public sector diminished in nominal terms between 1979 and 1981 despite an average annual inflation rate of more than 20 percent, while consolidated private bank credit to that same sector, which represented 84.4 percent of total credit in 1976, was reduced to only 18.9 percent in 1981. At the same time, indexed Treasury securities were issued in the capital market.

Although the government considered the exchange rate a relevant price control mechanism for redirecting resource allocation while maintaining balance of payments equilibrium, the stabilization policy had some bearing on exchange rate management. After early 1976, it became clear that the combination of fiscal, monetary, and exchange rate policies implemented in 1975 had produced a drastic turnaround in the balance of payments, which had been severely strained after the sudden fall in the price of copper earlier that year, but that the same combination of policies would not reduce the rate of inflation as rapidly and as substantially as desired. Thus, the government decided to lower inflationary expectations through exchange rate management. Consequently, adjustments in the exchange rate were lower than inflation between 1976 and June 1982, except when used to support tariff reductions. The government used an announced sliding peg until 1978, followed by scheduled adjustments until June 1979. Then, after a devaluation, it fixed the rate until July 1982 in an attempt to further link domestic and international inflation.

The real exchange rate shrank almost steadily between 1976 and mid-1982, stimulating imports and trade balance deficits. The nominal exchange rate, deflated by the consumer price index (CPI), fell by about 60 percent between the first quarter of 1976 and the last quarter of 1981.

Finally, wage adjustments between 1975 and 1978 were meant to keep pace with expected inflation so as to reduce inflationary expectations. Later, the combination of declining inflation, booming economic activity, and the 1978 Labor Plan—which established a wage floor equal to the previous wage package, indexed by the CPI—stimulated real wages, which soared until 1982.

The package of stabilization policies, with the exception of wage policy after 1978, seemed adequate for bridling prices. It took several years, however, for inflation to come down to international levels. Even when the nominal exchange rate was fixed (June 1979–July 1982), the rate of inflation still varied between 10 and 30 percent—considerably higher than international inflation. This apparent contradiction can be explained by consumers' extremely optimistic expectations for future wealth and income and the significant inflows of foreign credit stemming from the gradual creation of a Chilean capital market and the expansion of foreign liquidity available to Chile.

Initially, optimistic expectations were repressed, to a degree, by stringent monetary policy. After 1978, however, they were fed by inflation-producing inflows of foreign debt and reduced domestic savings, putting severe pressure on prices of nontradables, which kept rising at rates far greater than international inflation. Hence, high domestic inflation, despite a fixed exchange rate and a continuous decline in the real exchange rate, prevailed. In fact, to the extent that the fixed exchange rate was instrumental in stimulating capital inflows that fueled aggregate demand and, through it, nontradable price increases, the exchange rate policy was invalidating itself as an instrument of stabilization. However, that policy was certainly not alone in inciting capital flows between 1978 and 1982: the implicit deposit insurance that existed until 1982 convinced would-be borrowers that the combination of greater world liquidity with a more open Chilean account was, simply, manna from heaven.

At any rate, inflation fell from a level of about 1,000 percent at the end of 1973 to about 20 percent in 1981, and even to 10 percent the following year, although it rose again later for reasons explained below.

Development policies

Policy makers' efforts toward price stabilization should not overshadow the significant institutional adjustments they implemented between 1974 and 1981, changes that built on past development and were to have a major impact on the future as well.

Chilean authorities had assumed that improved resource allocation and increased investment and savings stimulated by an efficient capital market would, when combined with deeper domestic integration in the world economy, be enough to raise and stabilize the growth rate and to mend income distribution through increased use of labor, the country's relatively most abundant factor.

The measures taken to rectify resource allocation are too numerous to mention in full. A few may suffice:

1. The authorities eliminated price controls[5] and multiple exchange rates.[6]
2. They progressively increased and ultimately ended the legal ceiling on interest rates and at the same time liberalized the capital market.
3. They eliminated most taxes, subsidies, and prohibitions that had fostered discrimination among sectors, and they gradually did away with special central bank credit lines to the private sector. By 1978, the only remaining credit lines were for reforestation and housing.
4. They undertook a major liberalization of trade, of paramount importance for benefiting more fully from Chile's comparative advantages and for entering foreign markets, far wider and more dynamic than domestic ones. All foreign commerce prohibitions were eliminated in 1973 and 1974.[7] Between 1974 and July 1979, tariffs, ranging from 0 to 750 percent, were set at a single flat rate of 10 percent for all items. At the same time, the impact of this tariff reduction on the trade balance was compensated for by a higher real exchange rate than that which had prevailed in the 1960s. Thus, on both counts, exports were effectively stimulated, and, although the traditional antiexport bias did not disappear, it was significantly reduced.

As a result, exports increased steadily at an average annual rate of 13.2 percent at constant prices between 1973 and 1981, a good performance. Exports also diversified so significantly that copper fell from 82.2 percent of total exports in 1973 to less than 50 percent in 1981. This result is even more remarkable given that the exchange rate trend, as part of stabilization policy, did not favor export diversification for part of the period (1976–1981), although auspicious external conditions were an important growth factor.

Saving and investment were encouraged by a more stable environment for private enterprise, a more efficient capital market, and a foreign investment code attractive to investors.

Authorities developed the domestic financial market principally by (1) freeing interest rates; (2) eliminating or reducing qualitative and quantitative controls over credit; (3) reducing barriers against the establishment of new local banks, financial intermediaries, and foreign banks; (4) easing financial institution regulations with respect to minimum capital requirements, ownership, and reserve requirements; (5) establishing limits on equity participation in financial institutions (the limits were later eliminated in 1976); and (6) selling or auctioning to the private sector most of the banks under state control in 1973.[8]

Opening the Chilean economy to the outside world included the authorization of domestic bank accounts denominated in foreign currency and the reduction of quantitative limits on capital inflows. These limits, however, on capital flows into Chile for periods of less than two years continued to be prohibitive until mid-1981. On the whole, the rules governing capital inflows remained restrictive until 1978–1979, and those governing capital outflows remained so for the entire 1974–1989 period.

In July 1974 a new Foreign Investment Code, Decree Law 600, was promulgated. It was rewritten soon after Chile withdrew from the Andean Pact, in October 1976, because the government desired a more flexible and expansive code than Decision 24 of the Pact would allow.[9] The code greatly reduced the sectoral prohibitions on foreign investment and other discriminatory measures: foreign investors were to be treated as equal to national investors, except for access to domestic credit; limits on profit remittances were eliminated; a choice of tax regimes on profits was offered; foreign investors were allowed to repatriate their capital after two years; and the stability of the foreign exchange system was ensured.

A major institutional change was the replacement of the old system of social security, based on the principle of pay-as-you-go, with an obligatory personal savings and insurance program. Although this change was initially unrelated to the private financial market, it was to have a significant impact on that market's development, on the allocation of private savings and investment, and on the success of SOE (state-owned enterprise) privatizations. Since it was approved only in 1980 and implemented in 1981, its influence was not felt during the period under analysis here. Its main characteristics will be discussed in Chapter 4.

In practice, the effects of the new policies on development and distribution proved to be far different from what was expected. Average growth for 1974–1981 was only 3.7 percent, compared with the average of 3.8 percent between 1950 and 1970. Of course, this outcome should be seen in the light of a significant and systematic slide in the terms of trade after 1974 and a very deep recession (1975), two somewhat inter-related phenomena. The index of the terms of trade fell from 172.9 in 1974 to 73.7 in 1981, a loss of 57 percent (it continued to fall until 1987). The average for the 1974–1981 period was 99.7, compared with 132.5 for the 1950–1970 period. The depression of 1975, characterized by a 12.9 percent drop in GDP, cannot be fully explained by this slide. Instead, restrictive monetary and fiscal policies introduced in 1975 to achieve stabilization, together with foreign reserve shortages and lack of access to foreign financial markets, worsened the situation.

Gross investment rates, estimated at current prices as a percentage of GDP, performed better in the period 1974–1981 than in the 1960s—19.7 percent compared with 15.1 percent.[10] Since then, gross investment rates at current prices have dropped considerably. When expressed in constant 1977 prices, however, the volume of investment performed better in the 1960s than during the 1974–1981 period, because relative prices turned against investment goods during the 1970s. In other words, on the whole, gross investment rates did not experience major changes during the period under study when compared with the 1960s, although efficiency improved greatly. Annual GDP growth rates remained at extremely high levels between 1977 and 1981, although the rate of growth of investment did not follow.

While the government significantly reduced public investment during 1975–1981 to avoid crowding out private investment, the share of private investment in fixed capital rose only to about 10 percent of GDP, compared with 8 percent in the 1960s. This performance was slug-gish in the light of exaggerated expectations for a booming, dynamic private sector.

Why did investment rates not perform better? Apart from measure-ment problems (see note 10), one of the main reasons lies in the 1975 recession during which the gross investment rate fell to an average of 13 percent of GDP. However, higher than average figures (22.9 percent) were achieved during the rest of the period. These figures nevertheless mask the much higher-than-normal accumulation of inventories between 1979 and 1981, which reached up to 3 percent of GDP and was probably stimulated by the fixed nominal exchange rate and anticipation of devaluation. So, on the whole, the performance of fixed capital formation did not meet expectations. These conclusions, however, should be carefully revised when the new series of investment figures becomes available.

This evidence is even more discouraging when compared with the ever-increasing flow of foreign savings between 1977 and 1982, which was expected to bolster, or at least complement, domestic savings. Foreign savings were high for most of the period and reached unprecedented levels during 1979–1981, with an annual average rate of 10.3 percent of GDP, "financing" 64 percent of investment in 1981, at the peak of its volume. These foreign savings, attracted to the Chilean financial market by large interest rate differentials in a context of abundant world liquidity and a slowly opening local financial sector, behaved as partial substitutes for domestic savings during the years 1979–1981, while they seem to have complemented domestic savings only in 1977 and perhaps also in 1978.[11]

Furthermore, the performance of domestic savings was less than satisfactory. Authorities expected the development of the financial sector, together with numerous investment opportunities, to enhance domestic savings. However, three separate factors overpowered this optimistic perspective: recessions, inadequate financial market development, and consumer expectations related to permanent income. The relationship between savings and recessions is obvious and needs no further comment.

Authorities relied on financial liberalization to induce greater savings through at least two channels: higher interest rates and a wider range of longer-term credit and savings instruments.[12] Real interest rates, at the extremely high level of more than 25 percent per year during 1975–1976, far exceeding the low or negative rates of the 1950s and 1960s, did stimulate financial savings. However, since they were closely tied to economic fluctuations, domestic savings were not stimulated as expected. At the same time, the incipient financial market was still incapable of rapidly developing long-term instruments that would attract significant funds for financing a wider array of investment projects, because the demand for these instruments was limited by the exceedingly high interest rates. Moreover, the financial sector remained segmented throughout the period, a factor unfavorable for increasing saving rates.

Finally, the high GDP growth rates of the late 1970s and early 1980s, and the prevailing optimism with respect to income growth, reinforced by rapidly rising asset prices, raised expectations with respect to permanent income. This encouraged economic agents to increase consumption, particularly of durables, more rapidly than the growth of disposable income would seem to allow. In fact, agents went into debt to both domestic and foreign creditors, especially the latter, since foreign credit was more available and less expensive than domestic. As a result, domestic saving rates were significantly reduced.[13] Even if the purchase of durables is viewed as investment and saving, it adds only two percent-age points to the domestic savings levels of the 1960s. Thus, this factor does not alter the main conclusion that the saving rate was low between 1974 and 1981.

Income redistribution

Even though income redistribution in the short term was not a major concern of the government between 1974 and 1981, it did attempt to reverse progressive deterioration.[14] The stabilization efforts and major institutional adjustments undertaken had significantly worsened living conditions for many.

Two basic factors may explain the decline in living conditions: high unemployment and an unusual trend in domestic relative prices. Unemployment rose suddenly in 1974 as the high level of excess labor that had accumulated in the public sector during the Allende era was eliminated and as structural changes, in consequence of the policies men-tioned above, stimulated major sectoral and business firm adjustments. The recession of 1975 only deepened the problem.[15] Despite better than average employment performance later and a systematic reduction of the unemployment rate between 1977 and 1981, unemployment remained high by Chilean standards—11.1 percent in 1981 or 15.7 percent, if employ-ment in special public work programs is included—compared with 6 to 7 percent in the 1960s.

Liberalization policies and price flexibility were implemented and subsidies eliminated while there was an increased real exchange rate, causing a rise in the relative price of food. Given the importance of basic foodstuffs to lower income groups, the effect of these hikes was to severely worsen their status relative to that of other income groups.

To face this worrisome situation, the government increased social expenditures, focusing them more carefully on the absolute poor. More-over, it created a public work program, the Minimum Employment Program (PEM), which was the equivalent of a subsidy given the extremely low pro-ductivity of the participants and the low social value of the tasks ascribed to the program. Nevertheless, employment in that program fluctuated between 4 and 6 percent of the total labor force, a considerable figure.

To reduce inequalities and discrimination and to stimulate smoother functioning of the labor and capital markets, starting in 1974, special discriminatory benefits were eliminated; family allowances and retirement age requirements were made uniform; the social security tax rates were gradually reduced; and a major shake-up of the social security system was carried out.

The government had also predicted that both employment and income distribution would improve in the medium term as the labor market became more efficient. Major changes were introduced in the labor laws. The Labor Plan of 1978, and later the Social Security Reform of 1981, reduced labor costs to employers by reducing legal severance pay, granting the right to dismiss workers without naming the cause, limiting the application of minimum wage regulations, granting absolute freedom of worker association, eliminating the exclusive right of one union per firm and the legal distinction between blue-collar and white-collar workers, and establishing conditions for strikes in private firms and obligatory arbitration in the case of several public institutions. Furthermore, all negotiations were to take place at the firm level, with arbitration if desired. This labor reform[16] also established a wage floor equal to the previous wage package, indexed by the consumer price index (CPI). The only element of these changes that may have had an impact on income distribution in the short term was the wage floor, which allowed for an increase in real wages as inflation decreased.[17]

Crisis and Stabilization: 1982–1984

During 1982–1983, that is, after the end of the First Round of privatization, Chile underwent a deep economic and financial crisis. Although the depressed international economy may have sparked this recession, domestic management of the exchange rate and certain features of the financial market (including the ties between producers of goods and services and financial institutions) only worsened the situation.

The most immediate causes of the crisis were the gradual loss of access to international markets and a drop in the terms of trade. These factors raised doubts about the economy's capacity to maintain the same accelerated spending rate as in the previous years. They brought about a reduction of domestic demand and, consequently, of overall economic activity.

The productive sectors, especially of tradable goods (exportables and importables), had serious difficulties withstanding, on the one hand, the double effect of this demand shift and, on the other, the rapid loss of competitive capacity. The latter was the result of the significant reduction of the real exchange rate between 1980 and 1982 and the labor "floor" derived from the new labor laws imposed in 1980. In fact, these phenomena are two sides of the same coin. In effect, demand for Chilean tradables was increasingly curbed internationally by the ongoing recession and domestically by the growing substitution of ever-cheaper foreign goods for domestic products.

Enterprises turned increasingly to debt, encouraged by the financial liberalization, the significant flow of foreign loans, the pushy behavior of financial institutions looking for clients in the midst of abundant liquidity stemming from extremely high capital inflows, and, last but not least, the belief that the world recession would be brief.

This belief was shared by the authorities, who gave signals that corresponded with those expectations and stimulated further foreign indebtedness. But suddenly, at the end of 1981, foreign flows stopped, as external and internal conditions worsened. Heavily indebted and unable to gain additional credits, many productive enterprises went bankrupt, carrying along several prestigious financial institutions in what can be described as a huge financial disaster, inadvertently produced by the ambiguity and laxity of the regulations designed to implement the financial liberalization.

The mode of privatization used before 1982 accelerated the negative impact of the crisis by permitting financial institutions to be, in effect, holding companies with high leverage in their affiliates, which experienced, as did all firms, a sharp drop in the demand for their products. Furthermore, insolvent banks worsened their situation by (1) rolling over unrealized loan losses (distress borrowing) and (2) engaging in moral hazard and making generous use of the existing contingent subsidies for exchange and interest rate risk offered by the authorities during 1981 and part of 1982.[18]

As a consequence of this crisis, GDP fell at the rate of 14.1 percent in 1982, the hardest shock to the Chilean economy since the Great Depression. As foreign reserves quickly diminished, export growth lagged, and external debt service nearly doubled in two years in proportion to exports, imports had to be reduced significantly, adding yet another blow to economic activity. Moreover, the government carried out regulatory takeovers of sixteen financial institutions, some to be liquidated and others to be restored to financial soundness and reprivatized later on. Among these were the main commercial banks (such as Banco de Chile and Banco de Santiago), the major pension fund administration companies (AFPs, such as Provida, Santa María, and Luis Pasteur), and large commercial and industrial enterprises (such as the Petroleum Company of Chile and Forest Industries). This action reversed the previous privatization process. Since most of these institutions were owned by holding companies, this intervention once more gave the state direct or indirect management of a large number of enterprises that "belonged" to the private sector. Because this intervention blurred the ownership of all these enterprises, they came to be known as the "odd sector." Reprivatization of these enterprises, as well as of the traditional SOEs (or significant percentages of their ownership), constituted the second large privatization effort of the period under study here.

During 1983, the productive sector's crisis worsened, because the country was obliged to adjust to external restrictions that had become even more acute than during 1982. GDP fell again, but by a modest 0.7 percent. Open unemployment reached its highest level in decades—22.2 percent. At the same time, the existing public work program—PEM— had to be complemented by another one, the Program of Employment for Heads of Families. The labor absorbed by both programs rose to 15.1 percent of the total labor force by October 1983. Social unrest became widespread. Meanwhile, investment fell to its lowest level in decades— and remained low in 1984—while total and per capita consumption fell for the third consecutive year. Within this context, investment decisions may have been postponed because of high interest rates and the ambiguity about property rights that arose from the major state intervention in financial concerns and conglomerates.

The government took several steps to face the simultaneous shocks of the increased cost of foreign debt and the closing of the foreign capital market. Exchange rate policy was regeared toward encouraging exports and limiting imports. Tariffs on imports were doubled from 10 percent to 20 percent, and other measures were taken to put financial institutions and other enterprises back in solid positions. As a result, in 1984 there was a fundamental shift in the trend of the main aggregates, and the economy began to recover.

From Recovery to Boom: 1984–1989

During the Second Round of privatizations, initiated in 1984, the economy continued to recover from the 1982–1983 crisis and began a steady, extended boom.

When privatizations were resumed in 1984, recovery from the crisis was far from complete. Unemployment was still high, at 16.6 percent of the labor force; real wages were at their lowest point of the decade; gross national savings and gross investment did not exceed 5.4 percent and 13.7 percent of GDP respectively, figures well below the average of the 1960s and 1970s; and per capita consumption was still 21.7 percent below its 1981 level.

At the same time, the terms of trade continued to worsen and the gravity of the foreign debt crisis became evident in Chile and other debtor countries. The situation in 1985 was especially disquieting. Social demands for improved welfare were difficult to meet in the short term because of acute constraints in foreign credit and would become serious medium- and long-term problems if the extremely low saving and investment rates were not increased. Confronted with these difficulties, the authorities decided to "redouble the structural reform efforts, within the framework of a structural adjustment geared to emphasize increased exports, investment and savings" (Büchi 1988).

Reduction of foreign credit constraints

In the mid-1980s Chile found itself with a need for additional foreign exchange to service its debt but unable to obtain foreign credit. To reduce this foreign credit constraint, it adopted a combination of switching and restrictive expenditure policies and renegotiated its foreign debt. Improved terms of trade after 1987 also certainly helped.

To encourage the use of resources for the production of tradable goods, both to transform exports into an engine for growth and to curb imports, the government initiated polices to establish a realistic exchange rate. After 1983, the exchange rate was adjusted in relation to a currency basket of Chile's principal commercial partners. In real terms, it rose by more than 60 percent between the 1982–1983 period and 1989.

At the same time, the authorities avoided stimulating domestic spending, thus preventing strong inflationary pressures that would reduce the competitiveness of exports, which, in turn, would create improper pressures on the commercial balance. To this end, moderation guided both fiscal and monetary policies from 1985 until 1988, although those policies became expansive in 1989 in anticipation of the end-of-the-year referendum on General Pinochet's candidacy in the 1990 presidential election. The consolidated deficit of the nonfinancial public sector dropped from 4.4 percent of GDP in 1984 to 0.8 percent in 1987, and a large surplus was recorded in 1988. Simultaneously, monetary policy was designed to meet the needs of a recovering and expanding economy in ways consistent with the restrictions on foreign trade and a generally declining rate of inflation.

In order to alleviate the cost of its foreign debt, Chile renegotiated the debt with its creditors. In mid-1987, it signed the last agreement with creditor banks to restructure foreign bank debt maturities, to extend the availability of short-term credit lines, to modify the frequency of interest payments, and to reduce interest rates. In addition, the maturities of government credits were renegotiated through the Paris Club.

To reduce the foreign debt, the authorities implemented two mechanisms contained in Chapters XVIII and XIX of the Foreign Exchange Law. By the end of 1989, accumulated redemptions amounted to US$5,701 million, making it possible to reduce the total stock of foreign debt to its 1981 level, despite the subsequent use of new credits.[19] These measures also brought about a significant improvement in foreign solvency indicators. Debt service was reduced from 65.4 percent of exports in 1985 to 37.5 percent in 1989, while the ratio of total foreign debt to exports dropped from 5.1 in 1985 to 2.0 in 1989.

Finally, Chile experienced fortuitous relief from foreign constraints from a rise in the price of copper and reductions in the price of oil and the international lending rate (LIBOR). The impact of the terms of trade on disposable income was positive for the first time in years in 1988 and again in 1989, mostly because of the significant improvement in the price of copper.

The success of the policies designed to relieve foreign constraints is undeniable. Exports of goods and services, representing 25 percent of GDP in 1983, rose to nearly 30 percent by the end of 1989, in terms of 1977 prices. On the other hand, this trend permitted sustained growth of imports, which had been the main tool of adjustment to foreign restrictions during the crisis. Today, imports represent more than 28 percent of GDP, compared with 21 percent in 1983. This combination of events, together with relatively stable financial servicing, made it possible to reduce both the negative balance of the current account and the need for additional credit to the extent that, even with a modest inflow of capital, Chile was able to accumulate foreign exchange reserves in the late 1980s. Likewise, some recent policy measures tend to reduce the risk of a new tightening of foreign constraints. On the one hand, the reduction of tariffs to 15 percent in 1987 helped correct the bias against nontraditional exports, which today represent more than a third of total exports,[20] while a Copper Stabilization Fund, designed to freeze part of the increase in the price of copper since 1988, will help reduce the negative impact of world cycles. At the same time, large investments from private foreign concerns and a reduction in the relative importance of foreign debt in terms of overseas liabilities will lead to more procyclical debt service.

Stimulating saving and investment

Shortly after the crisis, the authorities recognized that it was necessary for investment to recover in order to maintain high, sustained growth and so improve the welfare of the general population. They also knew that national savings were going to have to finance this effort. Both variables were stimulated, after the crisis, by the recovery of general economic activity, by the solution of business and bank decapitalization problems, and by the institutional strengthening of the capital market.

GDP grew at an annual average rate of 5.7 percent between 1984 and 1989. This is both a cause and a consequence of increased investment, which rose from 13.6 percent of GDP in 1984 to 20.4 percent in 1989. Even though the private sector assumed an important role in the investment boom once the crisis of 1982–1983 was over, public investment represented a higher share of GDP in 1988 than in the 1979–1981 period—6.8 percent compared with 4.2 percent.

Since there had been a significant reduction in the foreign savings contribution after the crisis of the early 1980s, investment was increasingly financed by an extraordinary rise in national savings, which increased from 3.0 percent of GDP in 1984 to 16.9 percent in 1989. Domestic savings grew even more rapidly, the difference between the two being the net payment to foreign factors, which represented more than 7.7 percent of GDP in 1989. The saving effort was shared by both private and public sectors. In fact, the period 1985–1989 witnessed the greatest effort in domestic savings achieved in Chile to date: the annual average was 22.5 percent of GDP. During the 1965–1969 period, when the price of copper was at its peak, it had not surpassed 17.3 percent.

In spite of reduced deficits, the government maintained high levels of investment, thanks to significant saving efforts. In 1988, national savings reached 8.2 percent of GDP, a figure that includes those resources destined for the Copper Stabilization Fund. More severe controls on current expenditures explain this promising result. Government savings gradually lost importance in terms of GDP, allowing for greater private sector leadership in national economic development. The private sector was obliged to reduce consumption until 1987 in order to increase savings, but since then, both consumption and savings have increased at a rate above that of population growth. This trend in the consumption rate reveals a gradual recovery toward levels prevalent at the beginning of the decade, although per capita consumption surpassed its 1981 level only in 1989.

The strong recovery of the financial market explains, in part, the trends sustained in investment and savings, at least those of the private sector. In addition to increases of both deposits and loans in real terms, many other significant changes took place in this period. One was greater competition among institutions, which reduced the spread between active and passive interest rates and significantly increased profits. Another was the normalization of the financial system at the end of 1986, which put financial and ownership situations on a solid footing and was followed by the reprivatization of two of the country's most important banks in 1987. Third was an improvement in the quality of assets, together with the series of incentive mechanisms to inject capital into financial institutions—popular capitalism, foreign investment through Chapter XIX, central bank lines of credit, and others. All of these measures resulted in improvements in the net worth of financial institutions and, thus, their solvency. Various laws were modified to gradually reduce deposit insurance, to allow for the creation of bank subsidiaries, and, not least, to improve the regulatory framework for financial institutions, an important factor in the fragility of the financial system before 1982 and fuel for the fire of the 1982–1983 recession.

The normalization of the financial system was linked to the ever-improving situation of debtors, who were favored by the general growth of activity, the gradual reduction of the cost of credit, and government initiatives for debt reprogramming. Likewise, saving and investment were encouraged by the rapid development of institutional investors (AFPs and insurance companies) and foreign investors, who operated through DL 600 and Chapter XIX. Although contributions made through this last mechanism did not represent new investment in precise terms, they did allow enterprises to pay their debts immediately and thus strengthened the financial market, making saving more attractive. In addition, they allowed for a greater share of risk capital in foreign hands, which helped stabilize private savings. Finally, the tax reforms carried out after the crisis constituted an important and enduring factor for encouraging savings, because they reduced income taxation and increased the consumption tax.

These developments in the financial system are directly related to the privatization of SOEs, especially the price paid for those enterprises and the effects of this process on the entire financial system. These subjects will be discussed in the following chapters.

Reduced foreign constraints and surging investment, within the favorable institutional structure put in place during the 1970s, have both been instrumental in stimulating exports and general economic growth and in improving living conditions, employment, and overall income distribution. The volume of noncopper exports has been increasing at an annual rate of more than 11 percent since 1985, while the GDP growth rate established a new record in 1989, when it rose to 10 percent. The unemployment rate fell to 9.8 percent in September 1989, the lowest level since 1974, while the public work programs had completely faded away by that time. Unemployment has continued to decrease since then, with real wages increasing since 1985. Nevertheless, by 1989, they had not yet regained their 1981 level, which had been the highest since 1972. Given the stringency of the labor market, if growth and high investment continue real wages should maintain their upward trend, with positive repercussions on income distribution.

THREE

The Ideological and Economic
Objectives of Privatization

Within a coherent policy framework, privatization should be one element in a set of complementary actions designed to achieve both sociopolitical and economic objectives. In practice, this is not always the case; some countries adopt divestiture programs exclusively for the purpose of solving pressing fiscal problems. The Chilean case will serve to illustrate the complexities of this issue.

Privatization in Chile took place as part of a sweeping process of institutional reforms undertaken by the military regime, which was convinced that its goals of economic growth, full employment and the elimination of extreme poverty could not be achieved within the existing institutional arrangement. The regime further held that effective economic decentralization was a necessary condition for attaining efficient democratic organization. These convictions led it to favor individual rights, such as private property, and to adopt "liberal" principles: nondiscrimination, the market as the main instrument of economic decision making, the private sector as the fundamental agent for development, foreign trade as the principal means for exploiting the country's comparative advantages, encouragement of domestic efficiency, and others. Given this ideological perspective and the predominance of the state as entrepreneur under the previous government, the privatization process appeared to be consistent with political as well as economic goals and was strongly promoted from 1974 onward.

Public Enterprises and the Loss of Economic Freedom

Although the history of the state as entrepreneur in Chile begins in the eighteenth century, that role was amplified radically in this century with the creation of the companies related to the State Development Corporation (CORFO) and of others established by special laws.[1] Until the mid-1960s, however, care was taken so that their role within the economy was either "strategic" or complementary to the private sector, for example, in cases requiring otherwise unavailable investment resources. Even so, by 1965, the value added by state-owned enterprises (SOEs) reached 14.2 percent of gross domestic product (GDP), a figure significantly higher than Western Hemisphere or even world averages (Hachette and Lüders 1988).[2]

After 1965 this state of affairs changed rapidly and dramatically. Under the government of Eduardo Frei, a strong agrarian reform gave a new impulse to the state as entrepreneur, which then started to compete directly with the private sector by administering 60 percent of Chile's arable land. In addition, the large mining sector was first Chileanized by Frei and subsequently nationalized under the Popular Unity government of Allende.[3] Moreover, the Allende government either nationalized or intervened in many large and medium-sized industrial, commercial, and financial enterprises, so that the total number of these types of enterprises under public management increased from 68 in 1970 to 596 in 1973. In this way, the participation of SOEs in GDP reached 39 percent in 1973, while SOEs generated 100 percent of the product in the public services sector, about 85 percent in the mining and financial services sectors, and high percentages in the remaining sectors of the economy.

Central government subsidies to SOEs to finance their losses generated most of the enormous fiscal deficit during 1973 and were therefore the main immediate cause of the runaway inflation of the period. The nationalization and intervention policies of 1971–1973, which took place within a chaotic social and political context, generated an image of the state as an extremely inefficient entrepreneur, which only intended to use economic power to impose a totalitarian regime. This perception became the basis of the support for the military takeover and provided the government's fundamental political legitimacy, explaining to a large extent the speed and depth of the privatization process in Chile.

It is important to recall that the implicit mandate of the military regime to privatize enterprises managed by the public sector at the time of the takeover was universally recognized only with respect to the formerly private enterprises either managed or acquired by the Allende government. It could be argued that the military regime recognized this early in its administration when it drew up a list of enterprises that would remain in the public sector, and which included the National Copper Corporation of Chile (CODELCO), the Telephone Company of Chile (CTC), the Chilean Electric Company (CHILECTRA), and other large public utilities and SOEs created either by law or by CORFO.

There was always considerable public opposition to privatizing these large, "traditional" SOEs. In fact, the Constitution prevents the privatization of CODELCO and the state petroleum company, ENAP. Moreover, each time the Pinochet government began to privatize one of the other SOEs on the list, which it did after 1985 and especially toward the end of the 1980s, it drew significant public criticism, even from some of the nationalist supporters of the regime. Nevertheless, the privatizations of most of these enterprises were carried out and are today accepted. At least that is what the public debate during the 1990 national elections suggests.

This analysis calls attention to an interesting digression. Most people would have expected the military, accustomed to hierarchical forms of organization, to favor a relatively centralized economy, in which planning would have played an important role. Nevertheless, after a year of indecisiveness, the Pinochet government opted in favor of a market economy, that is, for deregulation and privatization. No doubt, the logical relationship between the historic task of restoration of democracy and the existence of a market economy must have played an important role in the option taken. The fact that market economies perform better than centralized economies in raising living standards, beginning to be accepted at the time and reinforced by the experience of the Allende years, must also have had considerable influence. However, the decisive factor in the policy decision in favor of a market economy was probably another one.

A group of liberal economists, led by the so-called Chicago Boys,[4] had articulated an economic plan during the early 1970s to be proposed to new authorities under the assumption of an eventual replacement of the Allende government by a more liberal group. This plan favored a market economy in which economic agents were to be stripped (through legal means) of any monopoly or monopsony power they might have. The breakup of monopoly power was to affect both enterprises and labor unions. This scheme, within the context of the Pinochet regime, which controlled not only the executive but also the legislature and the armed forces, actually strengthened the government by pulverizing most other sources of power within society. This power was further enhanced later on by the retention in government hands of a few key enterprises, such as CODELCO (generating about 50 percent of the foreign exchange of the country and financing a considerable proportion of the purchases of armaments through a special tax), ENAP (the petroleum-producing monopoly), and some transportation companies (such as railroads and an airline).

In summary, the divestiture of SOEs was an instrument of the military regime designed to decentralize and spread economic power in the country, an objective considered essential for establishing a viable democracy. At the same time, it may have played an important role in granting the government the power it found necessary to keep public order and at the same time produce revolutionary structural reforms. These reforms have contributed to a peaceful transition to democracy and, since the mid-1980s, a rapidly growing economy.

The Economic Objectives of Privatization in the 1970s

Although the Chilean privatization process, like the British process, pursued political objectives, in the final analysis, its main objectives were economic. Like privatizations everywhere, the Chilean privatizations during the 1970s were expected, above all, to help finance the public sector deficit. At the time of the military takeover, central government expenditures had reached about 50 percent of GDP, only half of which were financed through taxes and other income. The military government expected to eliminate the deficit of 25 percent of GDP by (1) raising tariffs of utilities and forcing the SOEs in the sector to become self-financing; (2) instituting a tax reform to increase revenues by 5 or 6 percent of GDP; and (3) using revenue from privatizations. Therefore, divestiture modes were chosen that would maximize public sector revenues. This decision turned out to have important, albeit unexpected, consequences during the economic and financial crisis of 1982–1983.

Of course, privatizations in Chile were also expected to contribute to economic efficiency. Officials stressed this point continuously, and they created an environment in which both public and private enterprises had incentives to be efficient.[5] In that sense, they were worried about the inefficiency of public enterprises only in the medium and long run, that is, under a different institutional setting from that created by the military regime. A new setting was, consequently, gradually developed during the 1970s and early 1980s, in which: (1) all enterprises were subject either to strong competition or to special regulations based on marginal cost pricing that would disallow monopoly profits and curtail efficiency; (2) public enterprises were obliged to become self-financing with no further subsidies and were allowed to charge market rates for their products; and (3) the government stopped interfering with SOE management.

Moreover, SOEs were obliged to distribute a high percentage of their profits to the state in dividends (during the 1980s the norm was 100 percent), and new investments were allowed only after a careful project evaluation. New indebtedness of SOEs was, for all practical purposes, prohibited, except in conjunction with a new investment project.[6] This arrangement raised the rate of return on SOE net worth during the early 1980s to close to that of enterprises in the private sector. This was a dramatic reversal of the huge losses of the early 1970s, while, at the same time, SOEs avoided the indebtedness problems that were to plague private enterprises (Hachette and Lüders 1988).

There are several important assumptions behind the notion that SOE divestiture will lead to a higher degree of economic efficiency. To discuss this, we must make a distinction between internal efficiency and allocative efficiency.[7] It has been shown that in a perfectly competitive world, given a complete set of markets and some other technical assumptions, a profit-maximizing private enterprise will pursue a welfare-maximizing allocation of resources; that is, both types of efficiency are maximized. The assumption behind Chile's privatization policy was that the other economic policy measures taken (such as the freeing of markets, the opening of the economy to international trade, and some sector-specific regulations in the case of natural monopolies) would allow the Chilean economy to resemble a perfectly competitive economy closely enough to assure a reasonably adequate allocation of resources once the privatizations were complete. Moreover, any costs in this respect would be more than offset by internal efficiency gains.

Although it is true that several of the most important Chilean SOEs were created as a result of important market imperfections, at least according to reasons given at the time, these imperfections either no longer existed during the 1970s or their importance had diminished significantly. The large CORFO-created enterprises, it has been argued, required either amounts of capital or technological know-how that could not be raised or found in the private sector. Without justifying some of the costly excesses of the 1950–1973 period, international economic conditions after the 1930s induced the country to substitute imports, which implied an industrialization process, which in turn required large investments in infrastructure. At that time, a well-functioning international capital market did not exist and available technologies were highly concentrated in the hands of a few private producers. At the same time, the local capital market was tiny and local technological know-how almost nonexistent. The state seems to have been the only actor capable of carrying out the necessary task. This is why and how ENAP, the National Electricity Company (ENDESA), and the Steel Company of the Pacific (CAP), among others, came to exist as SOEs.

International economic conditions changed rapidly after World War II, however, and the absolute size of the Chilean economy had expanded considerably by the end of the 1960s. The SOEs mentioned could probably have been privatized long before the 1970s, as was the original intention, and they would, in all likelihood, have flourished within the private sector. Moreover, assuming the existence of a stable, open market economy, the necessary capital and technological know-how for most economic activities could have been obtained by the private sector in the international and local capital markets and from foreign sources, respectively. Thus, especially in light of the experience of several Asian countries, the continued existence of SOEs did not seem to be justified.

Some of these SOEs were large public utilities, considered to be natural monopolies. These can, it is usually assumed, be induced to produce the ''optimum'' output levels (those which would be produced if the activity were to be competitive) either as government-owned monopolies or regulated privately owned companies. It is also usually assumed that in the latter case internal efficiency will be higher and that that arrangement is therefore preferable. This was the basis on which the Chilean privatization policy of this type of company was defined and made concrete through regulations put in place before the actual privatizations. In practice, the problem is rather more complex. Asymmetric information gives even the regulated monopolist the opportunity to obtain excess profits or, alternatively, to share monopoly profits with the regulator through bribes. In Chile, to minimize these problems, regulation was usually implemented by law, based on objective facts, thereby eliminating the intervention of authorities as much as possible.

Chilean privatization objectives had their origin in the widespread concept that firms with profit-maximizing owners will use resources within the enterprise in the most efficient manner. This is another reason why, during the second phase of the First Round of privatizations, majority control packages were divested.[8] Principal-agent theory clearly shows that under such circumstances, privately owned enterprises are internally more efficient than SOEs. Moreover, the same theory shows that this is not the case when ownership of a private enterprise is widely distributed (as in a corporation). In that case, the monitoring of the management contract becomes a public good and no individual shareholder (holding only a small percentage of the company) will be interested in spending time and resources on monitoring, since he might obtain the same benefits, at no cost, if some other shareholder does the monitoring. It is likely, therefore, that no one will monitor the managers, who will then seek their own objectives, which will probably not coincide with enterprise profit maximization. In other words, from a theoretical point of view, it is not clear that an SOE will necessarily be less efficiently managed than a private corporation.

There are, however, ways in which this problem can be solved, at least partially. Competition puts "bad" management in evidence, since the lower rate of return acts as a signaling device. Strict bankruptcy laws, which imply high costs for managers, induce them to avoid failure and, thereby, to generate profits. Laws that facilitate takeovers induce managers to be relatively efficient, since they might otherwise lose their jobs as a result of a takeover. In the Chilean case, all these measures have been taken, and it is therefore possible to assume that privatization, as carried out, has been consistent with the objective of achieving greater internal efficiency. Interestingly enough, with the partial exception of measures taken to increase competition, regulatory changes were made not to achieve this objective but for other reasons.[9]

During the First Round, therefore, privatizations in Chile were consistent with the overall policy objectives of the government; other policies that were necessary according to theory were implemented as needed. However, credit granted to purchasers of shares in SOEs divested to maximize government revenues proved, later, to have important undesirable effects. This point will be discussed in more depth in Chapter 4.

Lessons from the 1970s and New Objectives for the 1980s

The government learned several lessons from the First Round of privatizations that caused it to adopt new modes of divestiture from 1985 onward. As mentioned above, during the First Round, it mainly pursued medium-term revenue maximization, subject to efficiency maximization, and to this end it offered controlling stock packages to investors, expecting in this way to receive better prices per share than by spreading ownership widely. It provided credit, since it was aware that after the economic and social crisis of the first half of the 1970s the Chilean private sector was decapitalized and so had no working capital. It did not, for the same reason, require purchasers to prove ownership of any level of net worth. Finally, it was not concerned with the effects of the privatizations on property concentration. As a matter of fact, at the time, it was argued that the elimination of trade restrictions and other policies followed by the government probably required the existence of strong conglomerates to be able to compete in the international markets; that, for the same reason, they would not achieve monopoly power; and that high levels of indebtedness had not prevented Japanese and German companies from performing well and surviving over time.

Some of these ideas proved to be wrong. During the economic and financial crisis of the early 1980s, the highly indebted conglomerates failed and the enterprises they controlled fell again into the hands of the state, generating the odd sector.[10] The fact that the ownership of most of these enterprises was interrelated and concentrated probably aggravated the crisis, since insolvency in a few affected the others.[11] Moreover, the concentration of economic power (now in the private sector) resulting from the privatization process had given rise to strong political criticism. The government therefore restated its objectives for the privatizations.

The list of objectives, presented here with no intention of indicating priorities, was expanded in 1985 to include (1) the normalization of the financial and productive institutions of the odd sector; (2) the generation of resources for public debt repayment and necessary investment in public services and general economic infrastructure; (3) a strengthened financial position and increased investment in SOEs; (4) an increase in the availability of investment instruments, especially for the pension funds, and a strengthening of the capital market in general; and (5) the spreading of ownership, through the offering of favorable purchasing conditions. After 1985, this list of objectives did not change in any substantive way, although some aspects of it were spelled out in more detail.[12] To achieve these objectives and avoid the problems of the First Round, the government chose a wide variety of privatization modes. These will be described in detail in the next chapter.

Analysis of the relationship among these objectives suggests that some of them might be contradictory. For example, the objective of maximizing fiscal revenues might contradict that of spreading ownership because, as financial theory shows, widely distributed ownership weakens control of the company, resulting in lower net value. Some, however, have argued that widespread ownership might reduce the likelihood of reverse privatization at an arbitrarily low price, and therefore increase government revenues. This hypothesis was tested in the Chilean case and found to be true, eliminating this apparent contradiction of objectives. However, the achievement of the maximum efficiency objective can also contradict that of maximizing revenues, because, for example, encouraging competition eliminates monopolistic powers, which leads to a "high" sale price of shares. Chilean authorities, however, unlike those of many countries including Great Britain and Argentina, have always, even during the First Round, favored efficiency gains over revenue maximization.

The elimination of SOE deficits is, curiously, one of the objectives mentioned in the more detailed list presented by CORFO in 1988. This objective should be interpreted as a warning to the state to avoid the long-run costs of SOE deficits. It must be understood simply as a precautionary note. Although it is true that a few minor SOEs were still showing losses during the 1980s, most SOEs had transformed their losses (especially significant during the early 1970s) into profits. As mentioned earlier, from

1975 onward, SOEs in Chile were subject to the same economic criteria as private enterprises; that is, they aimed to maximize profits within a competitive (or regulated) environment.

The strengthening of the capital market, as a privatization objective, is directly related to the privatization mode chosen. The sale of small stock packages through the stock exchange may actually strengthen the capital market significantly, as in fact it did during the Second Round of privatizations, allowing greater diversification of investors' portfolios. Privatization, nevertheless, contributed less to capital market development during the First Round of privatizations, when most divestitures were made in large, controlling packages that did not get to the market. Other factors, however, have also recently contributed to the strengthening of the stock market, so not all the progress can be attributed to privatization. This point is discussed at length in Chapter 6.

The objective of financing public investment projects that have high social profitability with funds generated from privatization has been an important aspect of public debate. During the 1980s, the government argued that it had to carry out important infrastructure projects, without which the country could not grow. Others said that the funds gathered by privatizations should not be used to finance current expenditure, as this would cause a capital loss for the state. In fact, the objective of privatization should be to contribute to the generation of the largest possible present value from the existing SOEs for society, because the state must serve the common good.

In that sense, privatization generates a certain gain to society, which must be assigned. During the First Round of divestitures, the government tried to capture that benefit (plus the value of the SOE as such) to finance a budget that included an important component of social expenditures, which, in the absence of those revenues, probably would not have been carried out. In short, privatization financed social expenditures.[13] During the Second Round the government was willing to pay a price to be able to spread share ownership widely, and workers and taxpayers were able to buy shares in SOEs at subsidized prices. Except for that, however, the government continued to make an effort to receive the full value of the privatized SOE and used the revenues to expand public sector investments. Privatization subsidized the spreading of ownership and, indirectly, both capital market development and new investments in infrastructure.

The objective of increasing the supply of investment instruments deserves special attention. When, at the beginning of the 1980s, the government modified the social security system from a publicly managed pay-as-you-go to a privately run capitalization system, it intended to finance the payment of benefits to the beneficiaries of the old system from general tax revenues. However, the change of system coincided with the economic and financial crisis, and therefore the government initially financed those benefits to a large extent by selling debt instruments to the privately run AFPs. This implied, in fact, that from a financial point of view, the system had not changed, since those who were paying social security were providing the resources for those who received the benefits. As the economy recovered and the financial structure of private enterprises was normalized, the government began to finance its liabilities with the social security system in part through general tax revenues, as intended originally, and in part through the sale of stock of SOEs to the AFPs.[14] This system, known as "institutional capitalism," in addition to allowing the privatization of significant portions of the stock of large SOEs, spread the ownership of such stock (each pension fund, owned by thousands of workers, was allowed to buy only a limited proportion of the stock of any one enterprise) and provided a potential boost to the stock market (the AFPs were actively trading as part of their portfolio management activities).[15]

Implicit Privatization Objectives

As a rule, not all government objectives are expressed explicitly anywhere, and this apparently was the case with the privatizations under the military government. It is by definition difficult to identify implicit objectives, which can only be discerned through analysis of the corresponding actions.

Although the explicit privatization objectives of the Pinochet regime were always clearly stated, the constant modification of the government's goals regarding the percentage to be sold in the various SOEs during the Second Round was unexplained by the objectives expressed by CORFO and has been interpreted by some as a reflection of unstable and unclear privatization objectives. These modifications, however, probably reflect objectives that were not explicitly stated.

The facts are as follows: of the thirty-three enterprises that were in the process of privatization, twenty underwent one change in the goal of private participation, seven underwent two changes, three underwent three changes, and one (ENDESA) underwent four changes in its privatization goal (see Table 3.1). These changes created a lack of credibility in the announcements regarding the privatization percentages, which may ultimately have harmed the process. It is difficult to find an economic argument for continually changing the announcements of the private participation percentage.

TABLE 3.1

Evolution of Planned and Actual Private Participation in State-Owned Enterprises, 1985–1989 (percentage)

Company	Goal for private participation					Actual private participation			
	Sept. 1985	Dec. 1986	Dec. 1987	Sept. 1988	March 1989	Dec. 1986	Dec. 1987	Sept. 1988	March 1989
CAP	49	80	100	100	100	52	100	100	100
COLFOMAT	30	100	100	100	100	n.a.	n.a.	100	100
Colbún-Machicura	0	30	30	30	30	0	0	0	0
CTC	30	51	100	100	100	11	25	75	86
CHILMETRO	30	100	100	100	100	63	100	100	100
CHILGENER	0	49	100	100	100	35	65	100	100
CHILQUINTA	30	100	100	100	100	63	100	100	100
ECOM	30	100	100	100	100	100	100	100	100
EMEC	30	100	100	100	100	100	100	100	100
EMEL	30	100	100	100	100	100	100	100	100
EMELAT	30	100	100	100	100	0	100	100	100
ENCAR	30	49	49	49	49	0	0	1	8
ENAEX	30	100	100	100	100	0	100	100	100
ENDESA	30	30	49	55	100	0	20	51	90
ENTEL	30	30	51	75	100	30	33	51	72
IANSA	30	49	56	100	100	46	49	88	100
Laboratorio Chile	30	49	49	63	100	23	49	63	100
LAN Chile	30	33	60	60	100	0	0	16	16
Pilmaiquén	30	100	100	100	100	100	100	100	100
Pullinque	10	100	100	100	100	0	100	100	100
SOQUIMICH	30	65	100	100	100	55	82	100	100
Schwager	30	49	100	100	100	0	33	46	95
Telex-Chile	49	100	100	100	100	100	100	100	100
EDELNOR	0	0	49	100	100	0	0	2	4
EDELMAG	0	12	49	100	100	12	12	67	100
ISE	0	0	33	49	49	0	0	0	2
Chile Films	0	0	0	100	100	0	0	0	100
EMPREMAR	0	0	0	35	35	0	0	0	0
Pehuenche	0	0	0	50	50	0	0	0	2
EMOS	0	0	0	49	49	0	0	0	0
ESVAL	0	0	0	49	49	0	0	0	0
Metro de Santiago	0	0	0	0	100	0	0	0	0
EDELAYSEN	0	0	0	0	100	0	0	0	0

n.a. = not available.
SOURCE: CORFO annual reports and press information.

The explanation given by CORFO on this matter is the following: The authorized sales percentage started in most cases at 30 percent, because the small Chilean capital market, and the stock exchange in particular, did not permit large volumes of sales to be carried out in the short term. The problems mentioned as part of this argument, however, should not have prevented the announcement of the intention of privatizing 100 percent (or the percentage of the company that was finally transferred to the private sector), as small stock packages were being put on sale. This would have permitted the strategy of total transfer of control of SOEs to the private sector to have had its presumed favorable effects on prices from the beginning. It is worth noting here that, unlike some others, we have been unable to establish an econometric relation between variations in the prices of shares and the announced percentages of SOEs to be privatized (or the percentages actually privatized).

The explanation for these seemingly inconsistent announcements appears to be strategic-political in nature. From the beginning, the process of privatizating the large SOE public utilities and infrastructure enterprises was, to say the least, controversial, and the authorities had no way of knowing the force of the generalized negative reaction. The government may have believed that the favorable impact of these initially partial privatizations on the enterprises themselves, on the fiscal accounts, and on the economy in general might create a favorable climate for these measures and, consequently, make it possible to broaden privatization goals. The government might have acted, as well, on the idea that moderate changes would produce a weaker political reaction. It is important to bear in mind not only that the political opposition criticized privatization of these large SOEs but also that important political groups argued that the crisis that began in 1981 was the result of the failure of Chile's private economy. In addition, sectors connected to the government itself demonstrated a certain resistance to handing over to the private sector the ownership of companies that had in the past had enormous political influence, both because of their monopolistic nature and because, under certain circumstances, they had been used as income redistribution tools (Rosende and Reinstein 1986).

Stated differently, the variation in the privatization goals may reflect the fact that the government, after the crisis of the early 1980s, aware that it eventually might have to relinquish power to the opposition, tried to privatize the SOEs as fast as was politically possible, with the purpose of reducing the state's economic power to a reasonable minimum. The use of different forms of privatization was, among other things, an attempt to disperse economic power within the private sector. The objective of this dispersion of the nation's economic power was to create conditions that would make possible the real exercise of individual freedom.

Critical Analysis of the Objectives

It is important to distinguish criticism of privatization in itself from criticism of the specific privatization procedure adopted and the moment chosen to implement it. The description and analysis presented above lead to the conclusion that privatization was a policy consistent with the objectives of decentralizing economic power and implementing a market economy. Moreover, secondary objectives, such as increasing efficiency and maximizing public sector revenue during the First Round of privatizations, could also be enhanced by that policy, although in the case of the latter, the privatization modes chosen turned out to be inadequate.

Although privatization of commercial enterprises, which had fallen into public sector hands as a result of either bankruptcy or intervention, was generally accepted, as already mentioned, the deepening of the process to include the traditional SOEs was often criticized. For example, J. A. Allende's position is that the only motivations for the Chilean privatization process were political (Allende 1988). He suggests that the goals of the government were to increase the chances of President Pinochet's winning the plebiscite of 1988 and to complete and consolidate the capitalist foundations of the state. There is no doubt about the second motive mentioned, but it seems unlikely that a process that aroused so much negative reaction, even among supporters of the government, would increase the chances of winning the popular election. Monckeberg (1988) holds an opposite position that the privatization process was a political maneuver to maintain power in case the government lost the plebiscite.

Allende also criticizes the objective of efficiency, arguing that companies managed by the state could be internally efficient. Although this argument is theoretically correct, it is also true that SOEs, under democratic regimes, are subject to stronger political pressures than private companies. Even during the Pinochet government executives of the National Copper Corporation (CODELCO) were pressured to maintain excessive levels of employment.[16]

Marcel, another critic of the Chilean privatization process, also asserts that the origin of privatizations is political, and that the consolidation of the neoliberal movement was the main objective all along (Marcel 1989a). He acknowledges that privatization may accomplish increased efficiency if it is implemented within a competitive context, but he adds that it is not the best way to spread ownership.

Finally, we should point out that Chilean SOEs, especially the large ones, have shown political power of their own under every regime. They can exercise this power in ways inconsistent with the authorities' objectives and can use it to reduce and even to avoid regulations, thereby circumventing incentives designed to increase efficiency. This point should be considered before any decision is made to create a large new SOE in the mistaken belief that the private sector cannot fulfill certain broad functions.

Conclusions

The main objective of privatization in Chile has been to decentralize economic power in order to permit the emergence of a free and participatory society. Privatization was considered a necessary condition for the existence of an effective market economy. Secondary objectives have been to increase economic efficiency and, during the First Round of privatizations, to maximize public sector revenue. It can be debated whether privatization is, from a theoretical point of view, necessarily conducive to higher levels of efficiency. Nevertheless, given the particular conditions of the Chilean economy at the time of the privatizations, these political and economic objectives, including efficiency, were probably partially achieved by privatization. In this sense, privatization should have been considered a desirable policy by all those favoring a market economy, probably the vast majority of citizens. The main criticism was that privatization was used to further the political objectives of General Pinochet, but this criticism, as we have shown, is without merit.

FOUR

The Privatization Process

Two separate efforts characterize the divestiture process under the Pinochet government. We define these two efforts as the First Round (1974–1979) and the Second Round (1984–1989). During the First Round, the government returned almost all state-managed firms to their legitimate owners and privatized all nontraditional state-owned enterprises (SOEs). Still in the public sector were the large copper companies, the National Petroleum Company (ENAP), and the large, traditionally state-owned public services and infrastructure companies, such as electricity generation and distribution operations, telephone companies, steel companies, and railways. During the Second Round the government divested odd sector firms and transferred varying percentages of the equity of some of the large public enterprises to the private sector.[1]

In addition to enterprise divestitures, a high proportion of agricultural land was reprivatized during the late 1970s and significant privatizations took place in the social sector. Together with some regulatory and tax changes, these divestitures and privatizations revolutionized the economic structure of the country.

The First Round

Most of the structural changes in the Chilean economy took place during the 1970s and early 1980s. During that period, the management of about

550 of the largest enterprises in the country was transferred back to the private sector; land expropriated under the agrarian reform of the late 1960s and early 1970s was allocated to private owners (generally former agricultural workers); and market forces and decentralization were introduced into the education, housing, health, and social security sectors.

Divestiture of state-owned enterprises

Two stages marked the First Round divestiture effort: the first took place in 1974, when the control of state-managed firms was returned to their owners, and the second, from 1975 until 1979, when the onerous divestitures, involving cash payments from private buyers to the government, of the First Round took place. Also during the second stage, massive privatizations occurred in the agricultural and social sectors.

First Round, Stage One: 1974.   Immediately after the military takeover in September 1973, the government appointed representatives in every state-controlled enterprise for the purpose of normalizing their operations (Decree 88). In February 1974, Decree 333 allowed these enterprises to normalize their credit status within the financial system, in effect granting an interest rate subsidy to compensate for some of the losses generated during the 1970–1973 intervention period. At the same time, the State Development Corporation (CORFO) created an Enterprise Management Unit to help direct the development and management of its firms, to initiate necessary studies, and to negotiate the transfer of its property to the private sector. During the first stage of privatization, 325 state-managed enterprises, with a net book value of about US$1 billion, were returned to their owners on condition that they would formally agree not to litigate against the state. In special cases, additional conditions were imposed to ensure the maintenance of employment levels, competitiveness among related industries, and level of new investments. At the same time, the owners demanded special credit conditions, arguing that the state-managed enterprises had lost all their working capital. Apart from the implicit costs of these conditions, which have not been quantified, the return of these businesses to their owners was unrequited.

In practice, owner compliance with these conditions was not controlled very diligently (see the section called "Employment" in Chapter 6), while business naturally took full advantage of the special credit conditions provided. As a result, an additional transfer of resources to the owners of these enterprises occurred. This transfer, however, may have been justified because even with it the owners may not have recovered the full value of assets lost during intervention; this was especially true with respect to their working capital.

First Round, Stage Two: 1975–1979.   The second stage of the First Round consisted mainly of the costly transfer to private hands (for the equivalent of about US$1.2 billion) of 207 financial institutions, industries, wholesale distribution companies, and other corporations, which had been acquired by the public sector over the years, especially during the Allende government. Only a handful of CORFO subsidiaries were retained in the public sector for strategic reasons, along with most enterprises established by special law. Most of these enterprises were either natural monopolies or controlled a high percentage of the business in their field.

Although more than 80 percent of the existing state enterprises were privatized during the second stage of the First Round, the proportion of the net worth affected was a different matter. Unfortunately, no reliable estimate is available for the percentage of net worth of SOEs divested during this second stage. However, the share of the present value of payments related to divestitures between 1974 and 1982 in an estimate of the assets of SOEs in late 1979 (after most of the First Round divestitures had taken place) is 5 percent, a small share compared with the number of enterprises divested.

Tables 1.1 and 1.2 in Chapter 1 help illustrate the results of the privatization effort. Between late 1973 and the end of 1980, the number of public enterprises was reduced from 596 to 48; only two new SOEs were created. All banks, except the State Bank (Banco del Estado) and another small commercial bank with legal problems, had been transferred to the private sector.

Although the value added by state enterprises fell from 39 percent of gross domestic product (GDP) in 1973 to about 24 percent in 1981, it remained extremely high in several subsectors, such as communications (96.3 percent), mining (83.0 percent), and utilities (75.0 percent). Moreover, the value added by state enterprises in 1981 was still about 10 percentage points higher than the corresponding value at the end of the 1960s (before the Allende government).

Employment in the state enterprise sector decreased dramatically, from about 161,000 in 1973 to less than 90,000 in 1982, that is, from 5.6 percent of the work force to 3.2 percent. Only part of this reduction can be attributed to privatization; the remainder is due to other factors, especially to government attempts to increase public sector efficiency. The success of this effort is demonstrated by the significant increase in production in the National Copper Corporation (CODELCO) despite an approximately 20 percent reduction in personnel during this period. (See the analysis of the impact of divestiture on employment in Chapter 6).

The direct divestiture of SOEs was carried out in different ways during the 1974–1982 period. One method was liquidation. A number of enterprises were closed down and their assets auctioned when the government anticipated operational losses in spite of efficient management. Liquidation also occurred for firms for which even the best bid was not as high as the anticipated liquidation value. It should be noted that some of these companies were created when Chile had a completely different incentive structure (prices, customs duties, and subsidies) from both that prevailing at the time of the divestiture and that expected in the future. Under such circumstances, it is to be expected that the value of going concerns might in some cases be well below liquidation value and that, therefore, the rational decision was to liquidate the enterprises.

The most common form of divestiture during the second stage was bidding at auction, a process regulated by Decree 1,068. As a rule, the public sector would for a nominal price offer a package of information about the company to be divested and the detailed conditions of the auction. Bidders could usually pay for the divested enterprises either in cash or in installments. In general, the seller, CORFO or some other public institution, reserved the right to refuse all offers, as well as the right to negotiate better prices or conditions with the highest bidders. Negotiation between the two highest bidders eventually became the norm. It is probable that this often led bidders to lower the level of their first offers, especially in those cases with few bidders. This, in turn, may have resulted in lower final prices, since in the negotiation process the participant willing to pay the highest price could acquire the firm by offering only a little more than the highest offer of the following bidder.

The primary objective of the auction mode was to maximize the sale price of public sector assets. To this end, in most cases controlling packages (usually all the shares owned by the state) were sold. At the outset of the privatization drive, to ensure relatively broad equity participation in the financial sector, no one was allowed to purchase more than 1.5 percent (3 percent for corporations) of the equity of any financial institution, but this limitation was soon repealed. Even if formally followed, it was easily circumvented. In addition, influential government officials believed it only served to lower bids. Ownership of financial institutions thus became highly concentrated, and most commercial banks came directly under the control of a few conglomerates.

A related issue is the widespread use of credit to purchase these enterprises. At the time of divestiture, most enterprises, public and private, had lost their working capital. Moreover, Chileans, compared with citizens of other developing nations, did not have significant diversifiable assets abroad. Finally, an unfavorable foreign investment climate prevailed at the time. This meant that the Chilean private sector did not have significant liquid assets to exchange for shares of corporations being divested and that foreign resources could not be expected to replace them. This is one of the reasons, perhaps the most important, for public sector acceptance of the principle of payment by installment. Prices for the divested corporations would have been extremely low if they had been sold for cash. Even so, one of the criticisms leveled at the privatization process has been the low price the public sector obtained for its assets.

The scarcity of private liquid assets, the unfavorable foreign investment climate, and the revenue-maximizing practice of bidding at auction were among the factors instrumental in generating a particular pattern of enterprise ownership in Chile after divestiture. This pattern was characterized by the development of several "financial" groups, a few of which were relatively large, that were nothing more than highly leveraged conglomerates built around one or more financial institutions.

At that time in Chile, the process of creating and developing a financial group was simple. The public sector would offer a financial institution for sale. One person or a small group of people would buy those shares with a small down payment, financing the difference either with direct credit offered by the public sector as part of the divestiture process itself or with credit granted by the divested financial institution to one of their holding companies. In either event, the credit was guaranteed, at least in large part, by the shares being acquired. Next, encouraged by the capital gains realized, as share prices rose rapidly on the stock exchange, the same group would participate, perhaps through a holding company, in bidding for other enterprises being divested by the public sector. The controlling group would finance the required down payment in these cases with profits they had made from operating the financial institution acquired earlier or from other enterprises they owned, although they would, more often than not, complement those resources by using new credit granted by the financial sector to the holding company. The fact that the group controlled the financial institution evidently did not make it more difficult to obtain the credit. As before, the credit was guaranteed with shares—both the shares being purchased and that portion of the shares of the financial institution released, by then, from the guarantee provision. Important capital gains in the stock market provided the incentive and the necessary capital base for the purchase of additional firms on credit. Furthermore, conditions were such that an abnormally high level of "asset monetization" began, allowing greater expansion of the financial groups.

The process of asset monetization is quite simple and normal: someone buys assets (shares, land, other real estate) from a third party, financed with credit granted by a financial institution. The latter finances those loans by receiving deposits (in an aggregate equivalent of the sum of the sale price) from the sellers of the real assets. No savings are really necessary, since the process represents simply an asset transfer financed with a corresponding creation of credits and deposits of about the same value.

An abnormally high level of asset monetization, however, such as occurred in Chile in the late 1970s, requires relatively high and rapidly rising asset prices. The high prices entice many people to sell their assets, and the rapidly rising prices induce others to buy those assets in order to make a capital gain. Moreover, the process, once initiated, can fuel itself, and probably did during the 1970s. What triggered the process was probably a set of significant asset price hikes that occurred after 1976, owing to the generally perceived success of the economic policy being implemented and the growing influx of foreign resources.

While trying to maximize revenues from divestiture and to use its resources more efficiently, the government participated unwittingly in the monetization of assets. In fact, one could view a significant proportion of the second stage of privatizations as a monetization of assets. From 1974 to 1982, the government increased its financial investments rapidly, from a tiny proportion of its total investment to about 50 percent, thus providing some of the resources required by the financial system to finance the purchase of state-owned assets. Between 1974 and 1978, the public sector increased its assets in the financial system by about US$300 million while, during the same period, it received payments of US$582 million for the divestiture of SOEs.

During the 1970s and early 1980s, many investors, including some of the highly leveraged conglomerates, "capitalized" the interest payments on their debts. As mentioned, this debt often arose as the result of the purchase of SOEs and the process of asset monetization. The rate of return on the assets of Chilean corporations tended to be relatively low during 1974–1982. Interest rates in particular exceeded the level of rates of return, but the capital gains rate was very high through 1980, making the overall rate of return on equity holdings quite attractive, as shown in Table 4.1. These conditions induced most bankers to finance, and most purchasers of assets on credit to demand, the capitalization of interest. Often installment payments on credit purchases of SOEs were also rolled over by going into debt with the financial system.

In summary, offering controlling share packages at auction, while granting credit purchases, was the basic system used to divest SOEs during the second stage of the First Round of privatizations. The timing and mode of privatization contributed, together with other factors, to the emergence of a pattern of asset ownership in which relatively few highly leveraged conglomerates, headed by financial institutions, controlled a significant proportion of the country's largest enterprises. Other factors were the lack of capital among Chilean entrepreneurs; the unequal distribution of wealth; the small size of the private sector; the prevailing

TABLE 4.1
Rates of Return on Assets, 1975–1982 (accumulated values)

	1975	1976	1977	1978	1979	1980	1981	1982
Accumulated value of 1 peso invested at the implicit rate of return of the general index of real stock prices	1.000	1.193	2.468	4.092	5.721	8.233	5.672	4.198
Accumulated value of 1 peso of debt capitalized at the real short-term peso rate of interest	1.000	1.652	2.609	3.748	4.384	4.969	6.936	9.374

SOURCE: Rolf Lüders, "Lessons from the Financial Liberalization of Chile, 1973–1982" (Washington, D.C.: World Bank, 1986), processed.

investment climate for foreigners; the liberalization of the financial markets; the behavior of interest rates relative to operational rates of return on assets; capital gains through 1980; and economic euphoria about the future. In any event, most of the resulting financial groups were created on a relatively small capital base and grew very rapidly on credit. To a large extent, this credit was granted on the basis of a growing capital base derived from capital gains on shares and real estates. When asset prices tumbled in 1980–1982, the capital base of many financial groups (as well as that of thousands of other asset owners) shrank, and financial institutions incurred heavy losses, resulting finally in government intervention. The collapse of ownership networks among these financial institutions and some of the largest privatized enterprises put management of these firms back into public sector hands.

In addition to liquidation and bidding at auction, a third mode was used to privatize SOEs during this stage—direct sales. This mode was usually applied to smaller enterprises, in which the cost of organizing a bidding process was too high in relation to the expected sale price. It was also used in those cases in which the government anticipated that only one bidder might exist or in which the bidding process had not yielded minimum acceptable prices. It was also used to sell assets of enterprises being liquidated and assets in excess of those strictly needed to run the SOEs to be divested by other means.

Divestiture of land in the agricultural sector

As part of the objective of establishing a modern market economy, the military government set out to create a well-functioning agricultural land market. The definition of strong property rights at the Constitutional level and the strict enforcement of the law were perhaps the main instruments to this end, but other regulatory measures, designed to eliminate most obstacles to free trade in land, helped. For example, until the 1980s, rights to the use of water for irrigation were, according to law, to be assigned by the state, but in practice they were a matter of tradition. During the 1980s they became the property of users and could be freely traded. The process was completed with the privatization of most of the land that had been expropriated during the 1960s and early 1970s.

Of total agricultural land taken over by the Agrarian Reform Corporation (CORA), 28 percent that had been expropriated in irregular fashion was the first to be returned to its legitimate owners. Another 52 percent had been divided into 52,603 relatively small plots (*parcelas CORA*) that were large enough to allow a farmer and his family to cover their living expenses, as well as to pay for the land. These plots were sold at subsidized prices and on favorable terms to former workers of the expropriated farms. The selection of workers for this transaction was carried out on the basis of a point system, which included both merits and social factors (such as family size and age). The remaining land was either sold through public auction or turned over to the National Forest Corporation (CONAF).

It has been estimated that the privatization of these CORA plots implied a land transfer worth about US$800 million and represented, of course, significant distribution of land ownership. About 40 percent of the beneficiaries have since sold the land they received: 50 percent back to the old landlords; 10 percent to other beneficiaries; and the rest to others, very often professionals in fields other than agriculture. These new owners, through capital improvements, marketing, and management techniques, have significantly transformed old-fashioned practices in the sector.

Privatization in the social sector

During the late 1970s and early 1980s, the government initiated a number of structural changes, mainly in the social sector, known as "modernizations." These changes involved transferring activities that had previously been carried out by the public sector to the private sector. The most significant of these privatizations, from an economic point of view, and one of the main institutional transformations effected by the military government, took place in social security (pensions and health). Those in education were also important.

Pension funds.   DL 3,500 of 1980 institutionalized a revolutionary social security system. Until then, the pension system was, as in most countries, financed on a pay-as-you-go basis and was largely managed by government-operated institutions. Benefits were indexed to adjusted salary levels of the last five active years, while social security taxes were paid during the whole active life of the employee. As a result, powerful incentives existed to underreport salaries during all but the last five active years, as well as to obtain retirement as early as possible. Fraud and political pressures, while not surprising, eventually forced the government to subsidize the system heavily. At its peak, this subsidy reached 30 percent of system outlays. In addition, the lack of incentives for efficient administration resulted in extremely poor service with relatively high operating costs.

The new pension system, as part of the privatization of social security in Chile, is based on three principles: a minimum pension for all Chileans, benefits based on individual capital accumulation, and private administration. All Chileans are guaranteed a minimum pension, regardless of the payments they have made into the system. Since, as part of the second principle, benefits are directly related to the capital accumulation effort of the beneficiary, this principle implies a system deficit, which is financed by the government. The minimum pension level is, however, very low, so that most employees are expected to finance their retirement with their own capital accumulation. As a consequence, the official subsidy is also minimal.

The system works as follows: employees are required to pay 10 percent of their salaries (up to about US$1,000 annually) into personal accounts within the system. These funds are capitalized with the returns obtained from the investment of the funds and are paid out at the end of the active life of the beneficiary, who, in essence, must then use them to buy life insurance. In this way, benefits are directly related to effort and the previously existing incentive to underreport salaries in a fraudulent way is removed. Discipline is introduced into the pension system, since no one can shift the burden to others.

The real novelty of the pension system lies in the fact that it is privately administered. For this purpose, profit-seeking private pension fund administration companies (AFPs) are allowed to function. These companies compete for the right to manage individual funds on the basis of commissions and quality of service (for example, rates of return on funds, amount of paperwork, speed of service, and information). Each employee can freely choose among these AFPs and can switch from one to the other, if he or she believes the cost is lower or service better elsewhere. Although the initial number of AFPs was relatively low (about ten) and business heavily concentrated in only two, a reasonable level of competition has been generated since then. The number of AFPs has grown and is expected to increase rapidly, as the average value of the individual accounts grows over time.

The AFPs are closely regulated by the Superintendency of AFPs. Among its tasks is the regulation of investment portfolios, fixing investment limits for each type of financial asset. Strict prudential regulation has, to date, circumscribed investment possibilities to government paper, commercial bank deposits, and selected corporate shares and bonds. This latter option is governed by the extremely rigorous share and bond risk classifications of the Risk Classification Commission, especially established to perform that task. The Commission has four private and three public sector members. Most of the investments in shares and bonds permitted to date (up to 5 percent of each AFP's portfolio) have been in prior SOEs. The whole regulatory process is complex and essential for the success of the new pension system. It requires a delicate balance between the need to (1) allow the system enough flexibility to make it competitive; (2) provide enough profitable investment alternatives to satisfy the enormous volume of resources it is accumulating (in 1990, ten years after inception, over 15 percent of GDP; at maturity, around the year 2030, it will be equal to 100 percent of GDP); and (3) avoid excessive risks and major failures, which the system could not support from a political point of view.

The switch from a pay-as-you-go to a "capitalization" pension system presents several problems. Active employees who began to work under the previous system had made a savings effort (paying social security taxes, which allowed the payment of pensions) that had to be recognized by the new system. At the same time, pensions in the passive sector, earned under the pay-as-you-go system, had to be paid, since these people had paid their social security taxes, making the effort to finance their pensions. In Chile, the authorities decided to: (1) finance pensions of the passive sector covered by the old system with general public sector budget resources and (2) to reimburse only at the time of retirement (also from general budget funds) the capitalized value of those social security taxes estimated to have been paid up to 1980. For this latter purpose, a special type of public sector debt (*bono de reconocimiento*) was recognized for each person who was active as of 1980. During 1989, *bono de reconocimiento* payments were estimated at around US$150 million and rising, to over US$300 million in the year 2000.

Financing the switch, as can be gathered from the data, has been a major problem. In the case of Chile, this problem was tackled in different ways at different times, but in general has been based on strong fiscal discipline. The implementation of this new capitalization scheme coincided with the beginning of one of the worst recessions of this century, accompanied by a shift from a central government budget surplus to a deficit. In view of this, the government issued debt to pay the "old" pensions, debt it sold to the same AFPs. During recovery, a significant part of the old pensions was, in fact, financed through the sale of equity in SOEs, about 25 percent of which was purchased by the same AFPs. That is, the government practiced a form of debt-for-equity swap, which proved to be a major form of financing for privatizations in Chile after 1985. During 1988–1989, a growing budget surplus, the result of higher tax revenues due to strongly improved levels of economic activity and repressed government expenditures, must be added to those other sources.

Overall, experience with the new pension system has been very positive. The main problems of the pay-as-you-go system no longer exist, and AFP clients are generally satisfied with the level of services they receive. Rates of return on invested funds have been very high, because of general economic conditions in the country, although it remains to be seen how the system will react during a prolonged business downturn. It is also questionable whether the country will be able to generate enough high-return investment possibilities to feed this rapidly expanding "monster." The alternative, to allow AFPs to invest abroad in times of slower growth of investment in Chile, is gaining acceptance slowly. Major criticisms refer to the system's low degree of income redistribution and the relatively low level of affiliation. In any event, the new system played an important role in the privatization of SOEs during the last stage of that process under the military government.

Health services   Employees in Chile, as in many countries, are covered by the social security system for health purposes. The existing scheme was made more flexible during the early 1980s, making privatization of part of it possible.

Since the 1920s, a portion of social security taxes had been used to finance the National Health Service, which traditionally was run in a centralized fashion and included the most important health facilities in the country. Private hospitals and other services were few and generally served the well-to-do. The official system achieved wide coverage and a relatively good reputation for care, but the service was inefficiently managed, and in the late 1970s it generated an important public sector deficit.

Reform under the military government consisted of (1) decentralization of the official system (in essence, finance was separated from operation of health facilities; operation was decentralized to regional levels, to be financed on the basis of fixed fees for services rendered) and (2) privatization of services in some cases.[2] In that respect, employees were allowed to choose between paying their share of social security taxes designated for health services (in 1990, 7 percent of monthly salaries up to about US$1,000) either into the official system or into a private, profit-seeking Social Security Health Institution (ISAPRE). These latter are specialized health insurance companies that offer a broad range of health insurance plans, financed by the 7 percent of salaries mentioned above and additional voluntary contributions. The more expensive of these plans cover 100 percent of all costs for any contingency in any health facility—even abroad—freely chosen by the beneficiary, while the relatively inexpensive plans cover only a portion of costs, with health services offered only in facilities owned by the ISAPRE.

The new system has been growing rapidly but still covers only a minor percentage of the population. System expansion is limited by the cost of medical services and the income of the labor force. Seven percent of most salaries is not enough to cover minimum expected medical costs, a fact that will not change even in the medium run, no matter how well the economy performs. That is, unless the government decides to transfer the current National Health Service subsidy to the ISAPRE system, for example, by subsidizing health plans for low-income workers, privatization of health services in Chile will continue to affect only a minority of the population.

Housing.   Some aspects of public sector housing programs were also privatized during the 1970s. Before the reforms took place, a considerable proportion of housing for lower-middle- and low-income families (most of the families in the country) was financed and provided (and at times even constructed) by the state. Housing, corrected for size and quality, turned out to be expensive, and choices about location, style, internal space distribution, and other factors were nonexistent for the heavily subsidized "buyer."

Reform consisted mainly of reducing the role of government in this process by providing and managing a housing subsidy for lower-middle- and some low-income families, allowing beneficiaries to buy their houses in the market. In this way, the supply of housing for these income groups became extremely competitive, and construction, efficient.

Subsidies are distributed on the basis of a point system, which favors, among other factors, poorer and larger families, but also rewards those who accumulate higher levels of savings and, therefore, require a lower subsidy. This latter feature not only allows the government to supply a larger number of subsidies, but also permits the families benefited to purchase a better house, if they so wish, since they are able to obtain a larger loan in the financial markets to supplement their savings and the government subsidy. The privatization of this social program has proven to be extremely effective in making the most of necessarily limited resources for public housing purposes.

Education.   The education sector was also partially privatized in Chile during the military regime. At the primary, secondary, and high school levels, the system was decentralized, transferring management of free public schools to the municipailities but leaving policy decisions at the central level. Today government financing of schools is carried out on the basis of school attendance, although the amounts per student-day vary according to the type and level of schooling. This is, in essence, the well-known voucher system. Competition was introduced into the system, offering private schools (which do not charge students tuition or fees) the same financing as that of municipal schools. Yearly tests allow parents to judge the relative quality of education in neighboring schools, both municipal and private. At the university level, public sector financing, which used to be assigned rather arbitrarily among a handful of traditional universities, is now distributed essentially on a competitive basis, and the expansion of the number of private universities has been explosive.

The Second Round

The divestiture process as conceived at the outset of the military government was almost completed by 1981, as were the privatizations related to the social sector. It was then that, as a result of a series of factors explained in Chapter 2, the Chilean economy was rocked by a deep recession and a severe financial crisis. The government intervened in sixteen financial institutions, including those belonging to Chile's two largest financial groups, and thus, as mentioned above, again gained control of about fifty of the nation's largest industries, insurance companies, mutual fund administrators, AFPs, trading companies, and others. The privatization of these companies, the odd sector, in 1984–1985 initiated the Second Round of privatizations in Chile.

Two stages can be distinguished within the Second Round of privatizations: (1) the 1984–1985 divestiture of the enterprises belonging to the odd sector[3] and (2) the privatization of a relatively small number of traditional SOEs, among them the large public service and infrastructure companies[4] (see Appendix A).

Second Round, Stage One: 1984–1985

The modes chosen for the Second Round of privatizations reflected new objectives. Maximizing revenues was no longer a high priority, but distributing ownership was. In addition, the government, having learned that the reversal of privatizations was a distinct possibility, was now willing to incur the cost of reducing that eventuality.

During the Second Round, a variety of modes was used, often even in the divestiture of a single company. During Stage One, the productive companies of the odd sector (such as industrial, commercial, and mining companies) were generally auctioned off. As before, the controlling stock was offered as a package, but unlike the "debt-led" phase of the First Round, no credit was granted and bidders were obliged to prove their solvency. Since local investors were in general still undercapitalized and there was now interest on the part of foreign investors to participate in the Chilean economy, some of the larger reprivatized companies were acquired jointly by local and foreign interests. One outstanding example is the Petroleum Company of Chile (COPEC), a commercial and industrial conglomerate with a high share in the gasoline distribution and forest product businesses, acquired by a large Chilean concern (Angelini), that immediately afterward sold a 50 percent interest to Carter-Holt of New Zealand. Another case is that of the United Breweries Company (CCU), the beer monopoly and a large producer of soft drinks, which was jointly acquired by Luksic, a local conglomerate, and Paulaner, one of the largest German beer producers. There are other examples. The government welcomed these foreign investments, which were perhaps made more attractive by allowing the investors to pay with documents of Chile's foreign debt that could be obtained at about 60 percent of face value. The excessive private enterprise indebtedness that resulted from the First Round of privatizations was thus reduced by inviting foreign investors to participate in the Chilean economy.

"Popular capitalism" was chosen as the means to reprivatize the large financial institutions of the odd sector, especially the stock of the two largest commercial banks of the country (Banco de Chile and Banco de Santiago) and the largest private AFPs (Provida and Santa María). Some other banks were sold directly to "interest groups": for instance, one to a group of miners, another to a group of businessmen from northern Chile, a third to members of the Jewish community. In all cases, care was taken to ensure that, initially at least, control was directly or indirectly distributed among a relatively large number of people.

It must be pointed out that during and immediately after the financial crisis of the early 1980s all financial institutions, except state-managed ones, were allowed to exchange bad financial assets for central bank bonds but were forced to buy back, sometimes over a long period, those bad assets with their profits before being allowed to distribute dividends. Those institutions that had been state-managed and were to be privatized again were allowed to sell their bad loans to the central bank only once they were recapitalized through new stock issues, underwritten by the new owners. In the case of these institutions, the recapitalization was required because the expected period for repayments to the central bank was considered excessive.[5] The new stockholders were to put up 70 percent of the net worth, and the remainder would consist of old shares. In these cases, however, only 30 percent of profits were to be distributed to new stockholders during the period of exchange of assets with the central bank, with the remaining 70 percent to be used to buy back the banks' bad assets from the central bank.

Under popular capitalism, the government offered the new shares of Banco de Chile and Banco de Santiago to the general public, granting an automatic long-term credit at zero interest to pay for them and offering an extremely generous investment tax credit. In fact, the package was so favorable that most income taxpayers expected to receive the shares free, given the foreseeable dividends. There was, however, a limit to the number of shares each person could buy. Both the favorable investment conditions and the quotas of up to about US$5,000 per person were designed to spread ownership of these shares as widely as possible.

In the case of the AFPs, popular capitalism was used to finance 60 percent of the sale of Provida, and about 49 percent of Santa María. This allowed for widespread ownership of shares. To ensure efficient administration of these funds, the control of the remaining stock was offered to two U.S. financial institutions: Bankers Trust and Aetna Insurance Company, respectively. The first bought stock through a foreign debt-equity swap after an international auction, while the second negotiated a price for the small percentage it required to obtain majority control, since it had owned almost 50 percent of the company since its creation.

Second Round, Stage Two: 1986–1989

During the second stage of the Second Round of privatizations in Chile, most of the large SOEs, either created or nationalized by law, were privatized. Total revenues exceeded the equivalent of US$1.2 billion.

These privatizations were politically more sensitive, since it must be recalled that they were not generally favored, so much so that not even the government had originally included them in its divestiture plans. Therefore, as a rule, the government would divest each one of these companies on a step-by-step basis, as a way to gain gradual support for its policy. Accordingly, the government used different privatization modes simultaneously, offering shares to workers, to AFPs, and to other investors. At the same time, it took care to achieve as wide a distribution of the shares as was considered reasonable. This latter measure meant that, usually, the government would first legislate to transform the SOE into a corporation, whose shares could be traded in the stock exchange, and whose accounts and operations would be subject to audits by the Superintendency of Securities and Insurance. It would then announce, for example, the privatization of 30 percent of the equity using one, or at most two, divestiture modes. As soon as that percentage had been successfully divested, the government would announce the privatization of another 19 percent, perhaps making use of a third privatization mode, which meant that the corporation still remained under public sector control. The announcement of the privatization of an additional 2 percent would then complete the transfer of control to the private sector. Privatization of the remaining stock, up to 100 percent, usually by offering small to medium-sized share packages in the Santiago Stock Exchange, followed quite swiftly. Table 3.1 illustrates this process.

The main modes used during this last stage were labor capitalism, institutional capitalism, traditional capitalism, and, in a few instances, popular capitalism. Labor capitalism is the term used for SOE shares sold directly to the workers of the enterprises to be divested, or, in a few cases, notably that of the National Electricity Company (ENDESA), to public servants in general. With relatively few exceptions, workers would acquire between 5 and 10 percent of the stock of the divested corporations. To pay for the stock, workers would receive an advance on their severance pay and, to make the purchase attractive, the stock was offered at a low price, with a repurchase guarantee at the time of retirement. If the value of the stock purchased under this system turned out to be below the forgone severance payment at the time that severance payment should have been received, the workers would have the right to sell their shares back to the corporation at the severance payment value. That is, workers received an offer to buy shares below market price, without having to put up any money and without risking any loss. They could, however, gain substantially if the stock turned out to be a good investment. The main purpose of this generous offer was, of course, to receive worker support for privatizations, but the system also contributed to distribution of stock ownership among the general population. In some cases, workers became so enthusiastic about these investments that they went into debt in order to expand their shareholdings, sometimes becoming, as a group, the largest shareholder. Such was the case with the Steel Company of the Pacific (CAP), Metropolitan Chilectra (CHILMETRO), LAN Chile, and the Chemical and Mining Society of Chile (SOQUIMICH), among others.

Institutional capitalism consisted of the sale of SOE stock to institutional investors in general and to the privately run AFPs in particular. The main purpose of this system has been explained above, and some of its positive effects on the expansion of stock ownership and the development of the capital market are discussed in Chapter 6. Here, it is only necessary to add that the government was extremely cautious about allowing the AFPs to invest in shares, even those of SOEs. It set up the

Risk Classification Commission to classify the risks of these and other investments, with very conservative mandatory guidelines, while AFPs were regulated to limit the risk of their investment portfolios. Investment in shares of privatized SOEs exclusively make up less than 5 percent of the total investment portfolio of the AFPs, amounting to about 25 percent of the stock of the privatized SOEs.

Traditional capitalism refers mainly to other forms of onerous divestiture and during this last phase was heavily concentrated in auctions of small to medium-sized packages of SOE stock in the stock exchange. A significant exception was the divestiture of a controlling interest in the Telephone Company of Chile (CTC), the largest local telephone company, serving Santiago and the central region of the country. In this case, a nearly 51 percent share of the company was offered through an international bidding process, with the requirement that the purchaser invest more than US$200 million in a telephone line expansion program. The stock could be paid for with Chilean foreign debt papers. The bid was won by Alan Bond, an Australian investor. As part of his program to reduce liabilities among his own companies, Bond sold his CTC stock to the Spanish telephone company.

Implementation of Divestiture

Privatization efforts can be organized in very different ways, depending on existing institutional arrangements and the expected scope of the activity.[6] For example, some countries establish specialized ministries, others set up permanent privatization committees, others put the sectoral ministry to which the enterprise is attached in charge of the process, while still others create ad hoc privatization units or have the privatization carried out by a holding company (Vuylsteke 1988). In general, successful efforts, such as that in Chile, have found a way to strike the right balance between decentralized policy decisions and centralized implementation.

Although in Chile the specific institutional setup to implement the privatizations changed over time, its main characteristics did not.[7] On the one hand, the political will to privatize was firmly supported by General Pinochet and the military junta, as can be seen in the yearly ministerial programs prepared for the executive by the National Planning Office. On the other hand, the economic team provided strong support for the process on a day-to-day basis.[8] Several of these bureaucrats, together with high-level CORFO executives also appointed directly by the president, participated in the process of taking the policy decisions required by the privatization process. From a formal point of view, however, decisions were usually made by the CORFO Council of Directors. The CORFO Normalization Unit would then take the necessary steps to implement the privatizations.

During the 1980s, the institutional framework for privatization came to be well established. Policy decisions were formally made by the CORFO Council of Directors, whose chairman was the minister of the economy, while the other members were the finance minister, planning minister, minister vice-chairman of CORFO, and an additional member also appointed by the president of the country. The council authorized the sale of the shares of a company it owned and set the terms for the sales.[9] The decisions of the council were based, after 1984, on recommendations made formally by the normalization manager of CORFO. Informally, however, a Committee for the Sale of Shares was created, formed by the subdirector of the National Planning Office; the cabinet chiefs of the Ministries of Finance[10] and Economy; and the general manager, enterprise manager, normalization manager, and enterprise lawyer of CORFO. The deputy manager of the Normalization Unit of CORFO acted as executive secretary of the informal committee. In a certain sense, this committee was the link between the council and the executive unit.[11] The committee supervised, informally of course, the implementation of the decisions of the council, revised the general privatization plans prepared by the Normalization Unit, and analyzed the particular privatization strategies for each enterprise, defining the modes to be used, the prices to be charged, and the timing subject to council approval. In a way, this committee ensured the coherency of the whole process, internally and with other government policies.[12]

Execution of privatization plans approved by the CORFO Council was overseen by the Normalization Unit. This unit was responsible, directly or indirectly, for the whole privatization process, including preparation of enterprises to be privatized, selection of financial advisory and executing agencies, screening of prospective purchasers, negotiations, and collection of sales proceeds. The final sale of the shares of an enterprise was signed by the minister vice-chairman of CORFO, who had, by statute, the authority to divest.

The staff of the Normalization Unit was quite small, given the scope of the task, becoming an extraordinary example of "the privatization of the privatization process." Its staff consisted of four professionals, three secretaries, and one office assistant, although it obviously made use of CORFO's organizational, legal, and administrative facilities. As far as possible, private subcontractors and the enterprises to be privatized themselves or other official agencies were used to prepare companies for privatization if needed, to prepare valuations, to prepare and print brochures, to sell or auction shares, and to collect sales proceeds. This allowed the staff of the Normalization Unit to concentrate its efforts on establishing privatization strategies, defining contracts for the executing agencies, supervising the progress of these same agencies, and negotiating.

To set the share price of the enterprises to be divested or to establish the minimum offer price in the case of auctions, the Normalization Unit usually received several value estimates together with that of the Enterprise Management Unit. The supplementary estimates were generally prepared by the management of the enterprise to be divested, often on the basis of a contract with a third party (a university or consulting firm), and by the financial agent who had received the contract for the specific divestiture execution process.

During the Second Round, preparation for divestiture was usually not required.[13] During the previous ten years, the government had gradually transformed the economic structure in such a way that all enterprises, public and private, were operating on an almost equal footing, either in a competitive environment (free prices, low tariffs, free entry, antimonopoly legislation) or, if they had characteristics of natural monopolies, subject to special regulations intended to induce them to supply the socially optimum output at the "right" price. Such regulations, legally sanctioned, existed for electricity, telecommunications, air transport, water, and gas supply industries, among others (see Appendix E). In addition, the government had made a special effort to appoint professional management for SOEs and to reduce political interference to the absolute minimum, mandated that SOEs be self-financing and distribute 100 percent of their profits, implemented strict and thorough information systems, and limited their possibilities for contracting foreign debt. As a result, SOEs became relatively efficient and, by 1985, generally had sound balance sheet structures and showed reasonable rates of return.[14]

Divestiture itself was usually carried out by the Normalization Unit with the assistance of a financial agent (investment bank, broker, or other specialist). The role of this agent, in addition to advising on and handling the divestiture, was to reduce political pressures on the unit, while at the same time increasing transparency. The use of an intermediary also proved useful in cases where negotiations took place. Such an agent was normally used in the cases of direct sales, auctions of all kinds, and sales of small packages in the stock exchange. These agents charged fees that fluctuated around 1 percent in the case of enterprises whose shares were sold to relatively few investors and reached about 1.5 percent in cases such as ENDESA, where shares were widely spread.

Overall Accomplishments

By early 1990, when the new civilian government took over, the military government had accomplished its objective of transferring to the private sector the property and management of all but a handful of the nearly 600 enterprises it had controlled in late 1973. It can be argued that the government accomplished significantly more than initially intended, since, at the beginning, it did not aim to privatize traditional public service or infrastructure SOEs created or intervened in through specific laws. These enterprises were divested during the last stage of the privatization process, and their equity exceeded that of all other privatized SOEs.

Perhaps even more important, the privatization process, including that of the traditional SOEs created by law, came to be generally accepted.[15] This acceptance can be attributed largely to (1) the competitiveness of the environment or the types of regulation under which the privatized enterprises were forced to operate, which made them socially efficient, and (2) the privatization modes used to spread stock ownership.

At the end of December 1988, workers directly controlled more than 50 percent of the board of directors in the National Sugar Industry (IANSA) and more than 40 percent in CAP, SOQUIMICH, and Laboratorio Chile (a pharmaceutical company). If directors appointed by the AFPs are added, all the above enterprises become majority-controlled by workers and their representatives. Today, ENDESA must be included in that list, and in most remaining large ex-SOEs worker-appointed directors make up significant proportions of their boards.

In terms of the number of enterprises under public sector control and their value added, changes in the SOE sector during the military government were impressive. Although the government owns and runs fewer companies today than in 1970, the value added by existing SOEs is similar to that of the late 1960s, when, for many citizens, the entrepreneurial activity of the state was already too large. The largest share of this value added comes, of course, from CODELCO, a company the military regime never sought to privatize for strategic reasons and whose large copper mines were foreign-owned until the late 1960s.[16] Without CODELCO, the share of SOEs in total value added would today be about 5 percent of GDP (compared with about 16 percent during the 1960s), a level well below that of most Western nations. That is, leaving aside ''big copper,'' which during the 1960s was in many respects a foreign enclave and today remains so under state ownership, privatization, together with deregulation, has contributed significantly to the transformation of the Chilean economy.

The First Round of privatizations, which did not affect the large traditional SOEs such as the large copper mines nationalized during the late 1960s and early 1970s, left the state still generating almost one quarter of GDP, a high percentage for a market economy. The last stage of privatization was therefore important for the achievement of the government's overall political objectives. During that stage, the entrepreneurial role of the state was drastically reduced, and individual freedom to choose in economic matters increased. Political freedom may also have increased because people were less dependent on a single employer.

In terms of revenue, it is estimated that the public sector received more than US$2.5 billion through the end of 1989 from SOE divestitures (Table 5.2). On an annual basis, revenues varied from 0.1 percent of GDP and 0.3 percent of fiscal revenues, to 3.3 and 10.6 percent of the same variables, respectively. Relative to GDP, these revenues are more significant than privatization revenues in Great Britain during the late 1970s and the 1980s. Given the fiscal discipline of the government, privatization permitted implementation of important expenditure projects it otherwise would have avoided. As a result, during the First Round, it expanded the level of social expenditures, while during the Second Round it increased investment and reduced indebtedness (see Chapter 5).

Another way to put these revenues in perspective is to compare them with the net worth of the remaining SOEs. CODELCO, whose net worth is by far the largest of any of the current SOEs and which therefore can be used as a reasonable underestimation of the net worth of all of them, has an estimated market value of about US$4.0 billion. Therefore, through the divestiture of about 550 enterprises, some of which were relatively large public service and infrastructure companies, the state divested at most about 40 percent of the net worth of the enterprises it had controlled in 1973.

Again, this should not lead to erroneous interpretations. Privatization led the public sector to substantially reduce its participation in all economic sectors except mining (big copper and petroleum—the value added of the latter sector is rapidly shrinking because of the exhaustion of the natural resources), making ample room for the private sector to become the engine of economic growth. This is perhaps the clearest expression of the revolutionary change in economic policy that took place during the military regime, which set the country on a new course that has been sustained by the current democratic government.

FIVE

Effects of Privatization on Government Revenues and Wealth

Privatization of public enterprises implies a transfer of public assets to the private sector, either domestic or foreign. The transfer may be unrequited or onerous. If onerous, the public sector receives cash, which it may use either to carry out current or investment expenditures or to redeem public debt. In other words, privatization can affect both the balance sheet and the income statement of the public sector, as illustrated schematically in Table 5.1.

Researchers have commonly focused on government revenues—even on a fraction of them—under the implicit assumption that stocks (assets and liabilities) do not matter. Although we give relatively detailed attention to revenues or flows in this chapter, we will also consider the impact of privatization on public sector net worth. Since privatization also has some bearing on deficit financing, another fiscal impact area of privatization, we also analyze that issue here. Our empirical observations are mainly for the period 1985–1989, for which more information was available; whenever possible, we also cover the period 1974–1981.

Government Revenues

Maximizing government revenues was perhaps the single most important economic objective of privatization during the second stage of the

TABLE 5.1

Public Sector Balance Sheet and Income Statement

Balance sheet			

Assets		Liabilities	
$p^g \cdot K^g$	Shares in public enterprises	B^H	Net domestic credit (in
$e \cdot R$	Net foreign reserves		indexed pesos)
T	Present value of future taxes	eB^F	Net foreign debt
L	Other (social capital, natural	H	Currency
	resources, and imputed value for	G	Present value of future
	monopoly on money issuing)		government expenditures
		A	Other (social security, trans-
			fers to the private sector)
		W^g	Net worth

Income statement			

Credits		Debits	
Current account			
C^g	Consumption	τ	Taxes
D^g	Imputed consumption of capital	$r^g p^g K^g$	Profits
N	Transfers	P	Other (interest on foreign
i^g	Interest paid (on domestic and		reserves, imputed income
	foreign debt)		from social capital)
Capital account			
Z^g	Gross investment	S^g	Surplus current account
F^g	Financial investment	D^g	Depreciation
		$p^p \cdot \alpha \dot{K}^g$	Assets sale
		$\dot{B}$	Indebtedness

NOTE: In this balance sheet, the symbol g is used for government; $p^g K^g$ represents public assets valued from the point of view of the public sector (p^g); the same assets could have a different value for the private sector at the moment of divestiture, so in the expression $\alpha p^p K^g$, p^p stands for the price paid by the latter for each unit of the public assets being divested, and α represents the share of total assets being sold. The dot is used to indicate absolute changes; e represents the exchange rate so that foreign reserves and foreign debt are valued in domestic currency; the average rate of return net of taxes on public assets is indicated by r^g. Finally, it should be pointed out that the net worth includes the public sector surplus and reserves for depreciation. The income statement presented here differs also from the actual one prepared by budgetary offices around the world: at least, imputed accounts are usually not included.

SOURCE: Authors.

First Round (1975–1979). Former Chilean Minister of Finance, Jorge Cauas recommended "the sale of enterprises belonging to the State . . . and that are administered by CORFO. This permits the reduction of expenditures and provides a source of greater income" (Cauas in Méndez 1979).

Divestiture, therefore, was defended as a means of raising revenues and reducing the size of future central government transfers to inefficient firms. Revenues obtained from divestiture are detailed in Table 5.2. Because the impact of privatization on public revenues is greater than that indicated by the direct receipts arising from divestitures, we must also analyze certain indirect effects. This issue is discussed in full below, especially in light of the fact that by 1988 and 1989, property distribution and the reduction of the size of the public sector clearly became prime divestiture objectives.

A distinction between the immediate or short-term effects and the longer-term impact of privatization will be useful. "Short term" refers to the year of the transfer of public firm equity to the private sector, and "longer term," to an indefinite time horizon.

TABLE 5.2
Government Revenues from Divestitures, 1974–1989

Year	Revenues from divestitures (millions of US$)	Percentage of total government revenues	Percentage of GDP
1974	15.7	0.9	0.1
1975	224.1	10.4	2.0
1976	106.8	4.6	0.9
1977	124.2	4.4	1.0
1978	114.8	3.3	0.8
1979	164.6	3.2	1.1
1980	69.7	1.0	0.4
1981	112.0	1.4	0.6
1982	20.0	0.3	0.1
1983	n.a.	n.a.	n.a.
1984	n.a.	n.a.	n.a.
1985	10.3	0.02	0.1
1986	231.7	4.9	1.4
1987	312.6	5.8	1.7
1988	560.0	10.1	2.9
1989	234.4	n.a.	n.a.

n.a. = not available.
SOURCE: D. Hachette and R. Lüders, "Aspects of Privatization: The Case of Chile, 1974–1985" (Santiago: Institute of Economics, Pontifical Catholic University of Chile, 1988), processed; Budget Office, Ministry of Finance.

In theory, when the public sector transfers a firm to the private sector, it will receive (1) the value of the stock at the time of divestiture plus (2) a flow of expected taxes on the actual income generated by the divested firm minus (3) the expected forgone gross earnings that would have accrued had the firm remained public, consisting of profits and depreciation charges less anticipated gross investment. Flows can be expressed in terms of present value at the time of divestiture. When the transfer is unrequited, factor 1 will be zero, but the present value of the difference between expected taxes and forgone income will affect fiscal revenues. And a difference can be discerned between the impact of divestiture during the year of the transfer and the total impact. The first will include factor 1 minus 3 for the year of divestiture and will be called the short term, while the latter will include 1, 2, and 3 over an indefinite period of time and will be considered the longer term.

The short term

Gross revenues obtained by the public sector will depend on the sale price of the divested firm's equity, the share of that equity transferred to the private sector, and its share paid in cash.[1] The sale price may differ from the "social" price of the enterprise because of subsidies, risks inherent to the privatization of that particular activity, and different discount rates and degrees of efficiency between the public and the private sectors. This issue will be discussed below.

In the short term, the net revenues from divestitures expressed in terms of items from public sector balance sheet (Table 5.1) will be:

$$R_0 = \alpha_0 \, K^g \, p_0^p - \alpha_0 \, r^g \, p^g \, K^g \qquad (1)$$

where R_0 represents the proceeds obtained from the share α_0 of public capital sold to the private sector in year zero, net of forgone income during that same year as a consequence of the divested portion; p_0^p, the price paid by the private sector; $r^g \, p^g \, K^g$, the return of the firm divested if it had remained in the public sector; and $p^g \, K^g$, the book value of public firm shares in the public sector's hands.

Public sector revenues from state-owned enterprise (SOE) divestitures totaled US$2.3 billion. Of this total, the equivalent of more than US$1.4 billion in gross proceeds—the first term on the right-hand side of equation 1—was obtained from the divestiture of only 27 SOEs, more than four-fifths of which accrued during the last three years of the process (Table 5.2). For the onerous privatization of 223 enterprises, however, the public sector received the equivalent of less than US$1 billion between 1974 and 1982. On a yearly basis, revenues varied from a minimum of US$10 million in 1985 to a maximum of US$560 million in 1988, represent ing up to 10 percent of current government revenues in 1988 and up to 39 percent of income taxes in 1987 and 1988, a sizable proportion. Income of the State Development Corporation (CORFO) doubled in 1986 and 1987 and more than tripled thereafter as a consequence of divestitures. It is also interesting to note that the proceeds from privatization did finance a high proportion of deficits during the period covered and even increased surpluses in the last years of the same period. The issue is discussed in the last section of this chapter.

Although it obtained additional revenues from the private sector by privatizing public firms, the government lost tax revenues and dividends on the divested shares. Consequently, on a yearly basis, the net income obtained—R_0—was less than that shown in fiscal accounts, and gross revenues should be corrected accordingly. Forgone earnings have been calculated based on the prior rules of earnings distribution and in proportion to the public enterprise share sold to the private sector during the relevant year. The net proceeds obtained in each year from the divestiture carried out that same year are presented in Table 5.3, line 3. Because the relevant information was not available for all firms sold during the period 1985–1989, Table 5.3 is built on a sample of ten firms, which cover about 80 percent of total proceeds during that period. Values obtained for net proceeds do not show major differences from values for gross proceeds, since forgone income represented at most 10 percent of gross proceeds between 1985 and 1989.

TABLE 5.3
Fiscal Impact of Privatization, 1985–1989 (millions of 1988 pesos)

	1985	1986	1987	1988	1989
1. Gross proceeds from privatization	4,947	58,503	83,383	141,111	71,271
2. Forgone income	324	4,625	5,400	19,595	5,868
3. Net proceeds (1 − ?)	4,623	53,878	77,713	121,516	65,403
4. Present value of taxes	3,325	43,167	58,010	89,418	27,764
5. Present value of forgone income	10,906	143,630	180,332	238,150	71,766
6. Net government revenues (1 + 4 − 5)	−2,634	−41,960	−39,209	−7,621	27,269
7. Net goverment revenues as share of budget deficit (%)[a]	23.0	380.9	610.4	−81.1[b]	n.a.

NOTE: This table includes only ten firms of the twenty-seven privatized during the period, covering 80 percent of sales proceeds. The sample was used because of information availability.
a. Corrected deficit.
b. Negative number indicates a budget surplus.
SOURCE: Authors' estimates.

The longer term

In the longer term, the impact of privatization on government revenues in a given year will include the difference between the present value of the flow of revenues *with* privatization and the flow *without*. The government will obtain the proceeds from the sale of firms plus a flow of tax revenues from the divested firms over an indefinite period of time, while it will lose another flow of taxes—if public firms are required to pay them—and dividends in the form of transfers of profits to the Treasury had the firms remained in the public sector.

The present value of net revenues obtained from the divestiture of a package of shares in year zero will be, in terms of items in Table 5.1 where t is the relevant tax rate paid by the private sector on persons and firms and r_i^p is the rate of return of the divested firm once in private hands:

$$R_0^t = \alpha_0 K^g p_0^p + \sum_i^t \frac{t_i r_i^p \alpha_0 p_0^p K^g}{(1 + r^{dg})^i} - \sum_i^t \frac{r_i^g \alpha_0 p_0^g K^g}{(1 + r^{dg})^i} \qquad (2)$$

The first term on the right-hand side of the equation represents the proceeds from the sale to the private sector; the second, the present value of taxes paid by that sector on benefits obtained from divested firms; and the third, the present value of income that would have accrued to the public sector had divestiture not occurred—the forgone income.[2] To the extent that receipts from the sale price plus the present value of additional taxes paid by the private sector is different from the present value of profit flows from the firms remaining public, total government revenues would be altered.

The results will be influenced by the difference in rates of return (r^p and r^g), in pricing (p^p and p^g), rates of discount (r^{dp} and r^{dg}), and between rates of return and rates of discount. If risks, discount rates, and efficiency do not differ between public and private sectors, and to the extent that the transfer has not been subsidized (fully or partially), the net impact of divestiture on government revenues would be zero in the long run. That is, the level of public revenue would not be altered; only its composition would change: a higher proportion of public revenues would come from taxes paid by the private sector firms, even without changes in their rates, and a lower proportion, from public assets profits and taxes. In this particular instance, as far as government revenues are concerned the rate of tax imposed on the profits of privatized firms is to some extent immaterial as long as the price paid by the private sector included a correctly estimated discount of that event at the moment of divestiture.

Differences in efficiency between the private and the public sector will make the first two terms of the equation different from that related to forgone income. Higher expected efficiency in the private sector compared with the public sector will induce a higher price paid for the divested share $(\alpha_0 p_0^p K^s)$ over its public counterpart $(\alpha_0 p_0^g K^s)$ at a given rate of return on equity (r_i^p). However, the more similar the rules of the game applied to the two sectors before privatization, the smaller the difference between sector efficiencies. This consideration is particularly relevant when the firm to be privatized had been subject to a process of deregulation before its divestiture, as was the case in Chile after the mid-1970s.

Fiscal impact was estimated on the basis of the following assumptions:

1. The private rate of return on net worth (net of taxes) does not change with privatization (an extreme assumption).

2. The public rate of return is the average observed in public firms before divestiture, with the exception of the National Electricity Company (ENDESA), which had shown a negative rate of return in the years before privatization.

3. The share of dividends (on returns net of taxes) was 50 percent for the public sector and 30 percent for a private firm.[3]

4. The rate of discount used to obtain the present values for different flows derives from the application of the capital assets pricing model (CAPM), to be explained later.

Flows at constant 1988 prices were obtained by deflating the relevant data by the Chilean consumer price index. The period of analysis relevant to each divested firm begins when the first share of equity is divested and ends in 2008.

The net fiscal impact of privatization, given the assumptions made, was negative until 1988 and positive in 1989 (Table 5.3). The present value of taxes, even if high, is obviously lower than the present value of forgone income, given the assumption of no change in efficiency after privatization. In this framework, net proceeds are necessarily negative if a subsidy was involved in the divestiture, such as those granted to workers and taxpayers to achieve widespread ownership. When compared with the sum of gross proceeds in the period 1985–1989, net government revenues lost, under the extreme assumptions made, as a consequence of the subsidy of sale prices at the time of divestiture would represent 18 percent (this issue is analyzed below). For the net government revenue impact to be nil, the average rates of return, over book value above, would have to increase by less than 2.5 percentage points over what they obtained before their privatization in five out of the ten divested firms.[4] This is a modest requirement, one amply surpassed by most firms since their full privatization. In fact, net government revenue is positive for ENDESA, the Telephone Company of Chile (CTC), the Chemical and

Mining Society of Chile (SOQUIMICH), and the National Telecommunications Company (ENTEL), even without changing the rates of return existing at the moment of privatization. At any rate, in the worst year, 1986, the estimated "loss" of net government revenues, under the extreme assumptions made, did not represent more than 2.6 percent of total government revenues.

Public Sector Net Worth

Although the objectives of Chilean privatizations did not explicitly include net worth maximization or wealth redistribution of a specific type, it may be interesting to look into these issues on two grounds: First, since public sector net worth is a way of representing the sector's capacity to generate net revenues, if public enterprise divestiture affects public net worth, it will also alter the flow of fiscal revenues. Second, it is likely that undesirable wealth redistribution will generate political reactions that will eventually affect the stability and continuity of the privatization process.

Both topics have been a matter of considerable public debate in Chile. On the one hand, critics took the view, especially after 1984, that the modes of privatization used led to a significant reduction of the public sector's capacity to generate revenues and, hence, to finance programs or activities considered essential by the critics. The implicit assumptions underlying those views are that divestiture implied an actual loss to the public sector and that the public sector was a more efficient provider of these services than the private sector and, consequently, should continue to provide them. On the other hand, the divestitures of the First Round had left the impression of a significant transfer of wealth, even if unintended, from the public to the private sector (see Chapter 4). Furthermore, apparent private sector gains were concentrated in relatively few hands, increasing the already very uneven distribution of wealth in the country (Lüders 1990). It is no surprise, then, that the wealth redistribution arising from public firm divestitures should be hotly debated and that the authorities should take advantage, after 1984, of their prior experience to avoid further undesirable results. For these reasons, it is important to look into the actual impact of privatization on government net worth and on its distribution.

Public sector net worth in the First Round

Although it is impossible to apply the methodology used to estimate the impact of privatization on net government wealth during the Second Round to the First Round, mainly because of lack of information, some tentative inferences can be made. These suggest that the public perception described above is probably partially wrong and that the second stage of the First Round of privatizations turned out to be, in essence, an unintended form of public borrowing, at interest rates that were extremely high in real terms. Some apparent big winners in the private sector went bankrupt during the 1981–1983 recession and lost any gains they might have made on their initial capital (admittedly relatively insignificant). The government used these "loans" (divestiture proceeds) to invest in social programs, which, seen in retrospect, probably never achieved social rates of return even close to the "interest rate" paid (implicit once the government assumed, during the early 1980s, the debt of the holding companies of the divested SOEs). In turn, in the final analysis, government losses were matched by financial asset holders' gains.

In general, it is possible to assert that government wealth and overall wealth distribution will not be affected by privatizations, if (1) divestitures take place at market values, (2) financial and capital markets are relatively well developed, and (3) operating efficiency is not altered by the transfer of ownership.[5] Although it is impossible to argue that, strictly speaking, these conditions were ever met in the case of Chile, the economic environment was moving in that direction. During the Second Round of privatizations, existing conditions were close enough to those described to justify the expectation that those privatizations would have little effect on public sector wealth or overall wealth distribution, with the exception of the price paid by the government to distribute stock ownership among workers and middle-class taxpayers (more on this later).

Comparing alternatives at the moment of sale, however, it is almost impossible to judge the probable level of the prices of stock divested during the first stage of the First Round of privatizations. Economic conditions in Chile were still extremely unstable and uncertain, and past SOE performance had little meaning for the future. Hachette and Lüders (1988) compared the present value, as of the divestiture date, of the stock of different privatized SOEs at the end of each year, from divestiture to 1982, with the prices paid for that stock, corrected for dividends received and new investments financed. Stock prices, dividends, and new investments were discounted at the rate paid on the most common form of deposit, thirty-day deposits.[6] The results provide a comparison of the return on investments in privatized SOE stock with that on short-term deposits in local currency.

Although at the end of 1979 and 1980, stock investments in divested SOEs fared much better than deposits, toward the end of 1981 and 1982 the process was reversed. In late 1980, those who had purchased SOE stock on credit (some of the large new conglomerates) appeared to have benefited enormously from the privatizations. It was argued that the SOE stock had been sold at very "low" prices. Journalists and some scholars criticized privatization because of the potential capital gains made by purchasers.[7] Less than two years later, the holding companies of most of these conglomerates went broke, their debts significantly exceeding the value of their assets. For the government, since it was then impossible to obtain foreign financing, the cost of borrowing was directly related to the high rate of interest used to calculate the present values above. That is, divestiture of SOEs at low prices reflecting the high interest rate might still have been the best alternative for the government to finance some of its expenditures. Then the question became one of determining if the prices obtained for the stock of the privatized enterprises were really too low. Now, it is of course possible to argue that the opposite was true, since some entrepreneurs grossly misjudged the speed at which interest rates would fall, together with the prospects for stable economic growth in the country, and in so doing, they offered prices for the SOE stock that were too high to pay, over time, out of profits at the going interest rates in Chile.

In spite of this, the government did not profit from the high prices it received during the First Round of privatizations (this topic is analyzed later in this chapter). Our conclusion, then, is that the so-called direct impact of privatization on government net worth, if negative, was unimportant. As will be seen below, however, privatization had a genuinely indirect effect on public net worth.

Public sector net worth in the Second Round

If the government did not lose significant net worth during the First Round, has it incurred such a loss in the privatization process since 1984? The answer can be divided into two parts: the direct effect of privatization and the indirect effect. The direct effect is the impact on government income of transferring a public asset to the private sector. The indirect effect refers to the use made of those proceeds. The answer will give new insights, even if essentially qualitative in nature, into assets and liabilities, an often forgotten but nevertheless important aspect of public accounting and management (Table 5.1). This section will address the direct effect; the indirect one will be discussed later in the chapter. As shall be seen, the answer is negative again: no significant loss of public sector net worth was detected as a result of the privatizations.

To the extent that the revenue obtained by divesting the firm, including the sale price and the present value of taxes to be paid by the privatized firm, is equal to its public sector valuation corrected for transaction costs, the public sector net worth will remain unaltered until the government decides to finance consumption expenditures with such revenues. Of course, the structure of public assets could change in the process: for example, fixed assets could be reduced while cash (ΔO) or foreign reserves (ΔeR) could be increased proportionally, or liabilities could be curtailed, either foreign debt (ΔeB^F) or domestic debt (ΔB^H).

$$\Delta W^g = 0 = \Delta(p^g K^g) + \Delta (eR + T + L)$$
$$- \Delta (B^H + eB^F + G + H + A) \tag{3}$$

For public revenues to remain unchanged, public sector net worth must remain unchanged, but that condition alone is not sufficient. In equilibrium and in a frictionless world, risk-adjusted returns on one additional peso invested in any asset would be identical to the reduction in payments arising from a decrease of one additional peso in any liability. In those extreme conditions, the change in the composition of assets or liabilities as a consequence of divestiture would affect public net revenues to the extent that there is a change in the risk level of the investment portfolio. Returns differ at the margin among assets (shares in public enterprises compared with cash or foreign reserves, likely means of payment for divestitures), and the flow costs to the government of various public liabilities (such as bonds in the hands of foreigners) also differ. The allocation of divestiture proceeds can also be influenced by mistakes and political pressures. Thus, changes in composition of public assets and liabilities would affect government revenues, given a certain level of net worth. However, the main changes in net government revenues derived from privatization are likely to be caused by other forces, described below.

Changes in public sector net worth

The principal causes of reductions in public sector net worth as a result of privatization are outright gifts, underpricing, transaction costs (related to promotion, professional fees, underwriting, etc.), and financing of current expenditures with the divestiture proceeds. The first two factors—especially underpricing—affect the selling price and are at the heart of the privatization debate; the fourth factor points to another issue: deficit financing or the use of cash accruing to the public sector as a consequence of the divestiture. Underpricing may be the consequence of transferring public equity to the private sector at a price below market value or below what the private sector would have been willing to pay. Also, the price offered for an SOE by the private sector, even if it reflects full market value, may be lower than the relevant price from the public sector point of view, and the difference would affect public sector net worth. This will be the case if legitimate differences exist between public and private sector risks and, therefore, in discounting parameters. On the other hand, the private valuation could be higher than the public valuation if cash flows are expected to increase when the firm is divested, because of monopoly income, greater efficiency, or possibilities of diversification.

Relevant private sector risks concern the possibility of expropriation. Other risks arise when the private sector expects monopoly or price controls, imposition of maximum tariffs, or cross-subsidization arising from distributive considerations.[8] These risks affect the expected cash flow of the enterprise and could therefore cause the private sector to offer lower prices for the SOEs. These risks tend to be particularly high for public utilities such as electricity, telephone, and water service. They should, however, affect the valuation of SOEs from a private and public sector point of view symmetrically, since redistributive goals can be implemented just as easily whether the enterprise is run by the government or the private sector. Consequently, the transfer of property should not affect comparisons in this respect. But the risk of reverse privatization, irrelevant for the public sector, will influence the private sector valuation, because that possibility implies a reduction in expected cash flows. Insofar as this factor is taken into account, the price the private sector is willing to pay will be below the public sector valuation of the same firm.[9]

Higher discounting parameters for the private sector than for the public sector, for reasons other than the risk of reverse privatization, may be another reason for lower private sector valuations. The question is whether the two sectors should use two different discounting parameters as is usually recommended for projects, because financial and capital markets suffer from shortcomings and distortions may affect the relative price of funds. A case can be made that such a distinction was irrelevant in Chile in the late 1980s, since the structural reforms introduced during the 1970s and early 1980s and described in Chapter 2 eliminated significant differences between private and social prices.[10]

Moreover, given the known rates of return, it appears that the most reasonable choice for both sectors is to reinvest in the same firm. If so, both public and private sectors should use the same discounting parameter, which would include a premium for nondiversifiable sector-related risks. This conclusion may seem rather strange in the light of traditional public sector evaluation theories, but it follows logically from the fact that, in the SOEs analyzed, rates of return systematically exceeded discount rates, and from the observation that even if this were not the case, SOEs tend to reinvest their surplus in themselves (including in Chile) to keep up with service "needs."

In conclusion, prices paid for SOEs by the private sector might be lower than public sector valuations owing to several factors. Most of these differences reflect evaluation errors. For example, public net worth may apparently be negatively affected by expropriation risk differences between private and public sectors, since the former naturally estimates that risk in expected cash flows, whereas the latter does not. In practice, however, private and public evaluations should not differ, since redistributive pressure must be assumed to be equal and, if anything, easier to implement if the enterprise belongs to the public sector. Some might also be tempted to evaluate SOEs by using a sectoral risk-adjusted discount rate for private sector valuations, and the often lower straight social discount rate for the valuation of the enterprise if it remains in the public sector. There might also, however, be other reasons for the phenomenon analyzed here, such as the subsidizing or underpricing of shares sold to the private sector or straightforward imperfections in the divestiture process. The two risk factors mentioned do not imply any public sector net worth loss, while subsidies and underpricing, desired or not, legitimate or not, do.

Divestiture of public enterprises could also bring about increases rather than decreases in public net worth. Such increases, which are usually considered the most likely result, could stem from either an increase in efficiency induced by privatization, expanded exploitation of market power by the privatized firm, or greater flexibility to widen the firm's sphere of action and thus obtain income from other activities. Increased efficiency would induce the private sector to expect larger cash flows, other things being equal, than those perceived in the public sector. The former would then be inclined, in competitive bidding or any other efficient divestiture process, to offer a price that would reflect such a gain. In addition, the privatized enterprise would yield higher income taxes.

Underpricing. Were there differences in valuations of SOEs that led to gaps between market and actual prices during the 1985–1989 period, and if so, why?[11] Most opponents of privatization postulated that the public sector had lost net worth and revenues, but only one serious analysis was carried out to demonstrate that point. It reached the conclusion that "although divestitures have had a significant impact on public revenues, if the longer term is taken into account, the result for public finances will probably be negative. This will be the consequence of, on the one hand, a net worth loss from selling public concerns at a price below their economic value. . . ." (Marcel 1989b). It also concluded that "the sale of equity from public enterprises to the private sector between 1986 and 1987 had caused a loss to the state equivalent to 40 percent of their value" (Marcel 1989b).

We will first consider the issue of price gaps as part of the larger issue of underpricing, and then we will compare public valuation and revenues obtained from divestiture. We will show that the government divested SOEs during the 1980s without any significant loss of wealth, while at the same time achieving some of its other policy objectives, such as spreading ownership and capital market development. In fact, the estimates presented suggest that the loss of public sector wealth was probably limited to that judged necessary by the government itself in order to achieve its objective of spreading ownership of stock among workers and middle-class taxpayers.

Models of estimation.   The objective of the following exercise is to estimate, from the private sector point of view, the ex ante value of the net worth of SOEs. This value corresponds to the present value of expected dividend flows, which were projected on the basis of the information that can reasonably be assumed to have been available at the moment of divestiture of each stock package. In the projection of all the variables involved, we used optimistic criteria so our estimates may be considered maximum values. Thus, errors in our estimations should result in overestimations of the price gaps favoring purchasers of stock of privatized SOEs unless significant increases in efficiency were expected by the private sector.[12]

Estimated SOE stock values, as described above, must then be compared with the prices paid for the stock, in order to determine the existence of a difference or price gap in the sale. However, this price gap, if relevant, is not equivalent to a public sector net worth gain or loss in the transaction; it implies only that the government is obtaining less from the divestiture than it could have obtained otherwise. Since we assume that during the second stage of the Second Round of privatizations, differences in discount rates between private and public sectors, apart from cases of reverse privatization, can be ignored for all practical purposes, the estimated price gap—positive or negative—must reflect efficiency gains in the privately run enterprise (which would reduce the subsidy), a policy of divestiture subsidization, or imperfections in the divestiture process.

The general method used to estimate the value of SOE stock at any given moment is an adaptation of basic financial theory. The novelty consists in the estimation procedures for some of the variables. According to the method employed, the price of a package of shares at any given moment is equal to the expected dividend during the next period, plus the price of the share at the end of that time, all discounted by one plus the pertinent discount rate. This is then expanded to n periods, and the price of the package becomes equal to the present value of the expected dividend flows.[13]

$$p_0 = \sum_{t=1}^{\infty} \left[\frac{DV_t}{\prod_{t=1}^{n} (1 + r_t^d)} \right] \tag{4}$$

where p_t = the price of the share at t; DV_t = the dividend obtained by the end of t; and r_t^d = the discount rate at t.

Expected dividends, in turn, are a function of (1) the expected rate of return on capital, (2) the amount of capital (net worth), and (3) the profit retention rate.

$$DV_t = r_t \bullet PA_{t-1} \bullet (1 - \Omega_t) \tag{5}$$

where r_t = the expected return rate on capital at t (after corporate taxes); PA_t = net worth at t; and Ω_t = the profit retention rate at t.

On the other hand, net worth at t (assuming no new capital contributions) is:

$$PA_t = PA_{t-1} \bullet (1 + g_t) \tag{6}$$

where $g_t = \Omega_t \bullet r_t$.

The discount rate corresponds to the opportunity cost of the company's capital and is obtained by the risk-free rate of return, plus a premium for nondiversifiable risk.

$$r_t^d = r_t^{rf} + PR_t \tag{7}$$

where r_t^{rf} = the rate of return free of market risk at t, and PR_t = the premium for nondiversifiable company risk at t.

The nondiversifiable company risk corresponds to the stock market risk premium (MRP) adjusted by the return variability of the enterprise in question (r_t) in relation to the variability of the average rate of return of the stock market (r_t^m).

$$PR_t = b_t \bullet MRP_t \tag{8}$$

where $b_t = r_t/r_t^m$.

In the estimates, the following data were used:

1. The risk-free rate of return until 1989 was represented by the annual real interest rate paid on 90- to 365-day bank deposits as reported by the central bank, and, from then on, as projected by the Institute of Economics at the Pontifical Catholic University of Chile. Rates used started at slightly more than 4 percent per year in 1986 (after monetary correction) and approached 5 percent during the later 1980s and early 1990s.

2. We tried several methods of estimating the MRP for Chile. Reliable values could not be estimated directly from the Santiago Stock Exchange data because of their extreme instability.

   In a first attempt to obtain the MRP, we followed the method developed by Ibbotson and Sinquefield (1982). They estimated the annual real rate of return for a representative U.S. stock portfolio and compared it with the rate of return of U.S. Treasury bonds. In this way they obtained the premium for stock market risk for the 1926–1982 period, calculated the arithmetic mean of the series, and projected the MRP on the basis of this mean. The application of this method required, first of all, an estimate of an ex post annual rate of return of the stock market. To this end, an estimate made by Coloma (1988), based on a portfolio made up of the thirty most important shares, shown in Table 5.4, was used. However, the high variability (measured by the standard deviation) shown by the mean MRP suggests that this method is not appropriate for the Chilean case.

TABLE 5.4
Profitability of a Stock Portfolio, 1977–1985 (percentage)

	1977	1978	1979	1980	1981	1982	1983	1984	1985
r^m	322.7	70.0	127.0	38.1	−44.2	−35.8	−35.7	0.9	99.4
MRP	307.2	52.5	112.6	29.7	−57.3	−47.8	−43.4	−7.6	91.3

Average MRP, 1977–1985 = 48.6; s = 114.7
Average MRP, 1978–1985 = 16.3; s = 74.1

NOTE: r^m = annual rate of return on the stock market; MRP = market risk premium; s = standard deviation.
SOURCE: Authors' estimates.

The alternative we finally used is an extension of interest rate parity theory. The basic concept behind this method is that Chile's MRP should correspond to the United States' MRP, adjusted by the degree of variation of the Chilean economy with respect to that of the United States, under the assumption that the variation rates in the gross domestic product (GDP) of each country are related to the degree of variability of the respective stock markets.[14] That is,

$$\text{MRP}_C = \partial \cdot \text{MRP}_{USA} \qquad (9)$$

The interpretation of the adjustment factor ∂ is similar to the one of the financial b defined above and was estimated based on the following regression:

$$\dot{\text{GDP}}_C = a + \partial \cdot \dot{\text{GDP}}_{USA} \qquad (10)$$

Using the information for the 1974–1987 period, we obtained the following result: $\bar{\partial} = 1.84$; $s_d = 0.56$; and $t = 3.31$.

The key assumption behind this estimate is that international capital markets work well enough so that rates of return reflect the relationship between the U.S. and Chilean MRPs described above. If not, profits could be obtained by arbitrage. Given an MRP for the United States of 8.3 percent (Ibbotson and Sinquefield 1982), the average MRP for Chile has been estimated to be 15.3 percent. This average MRP appears conservative in light of the data obtained by the alternative method explained above. In line with our deliberate choice of relatively optimistic assumptions, however, this risk premium will be reduced linearly starting in 1986 to reach 10 percent in 1996, a rate only slightly higher than the MRP for the United States. This downward trend assumes reduced Chilean economic sensitivity to international fluctuations.[15]

3. We obtained risk premiums for each enterprise from estimates made by Brealey and Myers (1988) of the sectoral risk premiums for the U.S. economy, adjusted to each company's leverage.[16] Less reliable estimates based on Chilean data for broader sectors correspond roughly to those of the United States, so we preferred to use the Brealey and Myers estimates.

4. We estimated rates of return on the basis of balance sheet information at the end of each year. To obtain monthly rates of return, we assumed that they varied linearly over the year, implicitly assuming that the information was known progressively during the year and that there were no information differentials among the agents involved. We further assumed that agents acted as if rates of return would converge toward the discount rate in 1996, lower in all evaluated cases than the rates of return. This assumption is probably very optimistic, because it means that the enterprises offer reinvestment opportunities with returns that are higher than the opportunity cost of capital during more than ten years.

5. We assumed that the historic profit retention rates were constant at their historic level until 1990, when they became 75 percent.[17] The military government sought to make participation attractive to the private sector, especially in those cases in which nontraditional investors, such as workers, were involved. It therefore required privatized SOEs to distribute 100 percent of profits as a rule. Given expected rates of return higher than discount rates, such a policy was expected to be drastically changed once enterprises were privatized and became firmly established in the private sector.

Based on the method and data presented above and on information provided by CORFO's Normalization Unit and the stock exchange, we estimated the ex ante value of the stock packages of ten of the larger CORFO subsidiaries, divested between 1986 and 1989. We then compared this value with the prices received for the stock. The results are shown in Table 5.5.

The results show that (1) on average, the prices paid for the stock have been about 15 percent below the valuations estimated here; (2) workers have, on average, received a relatively higher share of this difference than have the capitalists (other investors); and (3) a sustained increase in the volume of transactions is accompanied by a systematic drop in the gap between prices and valuations, with the exception of 1989. The increase of the percentage gap in 1989 is puzzling. Packages of stock of only three firms were divested: ENDESA, ENTEL, and CTC. The difference was

TABLE 5.5

Estimated and Actual Prices of Ten CORFO Subsidiaries, 1986–1989 (annual summary)

	1986	1987[a]	1988[b]	1989[c]	Total
Estimated price (millions of UF)[d]	12.838	20.226	40.279	11.816	85.159
Actual sale price (millions of UF)	7.454	18.611	38.132	9.901	74.098
Price gap					
Millions of UF	5.385	1.616	2.147	1.915	11.062
%	41.94	7.98	5.33	16.20	12.99
Interest subsidy[e] (%)	0.00	4.78	2.47	0.90	2.42
Total price gap[f] (%)	41.94	12.76	7.80	17.10	15.41
Price gap in favor of workers (%)	44.79	23.33	8.90	0.00	18.65
Price gap in favor of capitalists[g] (%)	41.67	9.92	7.63	17.10	14.96

NOTE: The ten firms are ENTEL, CTC, CAP, ENDESA, SOQUIMICH, CHILGENER, CHILMETRO, CHILQUINTA, IANSA, and Laboratorio Chile.
a. This includes one sale, with subsidized credit, of a package of shares of ENDESA approved by Law 18,681 to public employees in December 1987.
b. This includes the sale of two packages of shares of ENDESA, with subsidized credit, approved by Law 18,747, in March and December 1988; the sales were made directly to public employees and indirectly through popular capitalism.
c. In 1989, CORFO sold stocks only of ENDESA, CTC, and ENTEL among the ten firms considered here. This includes the sale, with subsidized credit, of two packages of shares of CTC in March and April 1989.
d. The *unidad de fomento* (UF) is a constant value unit of account that is adjusted daily according to the change in the consumer price index and is widely used in many kinds of transactions. Therefore, the values expressed are in real terms. As of April 15, 1989, the UF was equivalent to US$18.50.
e. This line indicates the subsidy secured by purchasers of stocks when using subsidized credit from CORFO to buy those shares.
f. This line represents the sum of the difference between estimated and actual prices and the interest subsidy.
g. This includes sales to public employees.
SOURCE: Authors' estimates.

positive in the case of ENDESA and negative in the other two. The price gap in the sale of ENTEL stocks was high in absolute terms but nevertheless lower than in previous years, according to the consistent trend mentioned above. The price gap involved in the transfer of CTC stock is related to a sale to public employers that was subsidized both on the credit side and on the price side.

Sales of ENDESA stock through popular capitalism and of both ENDESA and CTC stock to public employees were made on a term basis (between four and six years) at lower-than-market interest rates (between 2.5 percent and 6 percent). Consequently, a price gap is involved in that share of total stocks of both firms sold in the manner described. It was assumed that an average interest differential existed between the market and the subsidized rates of 5 percentage points and that amortization of those credits was linear over a period of five years. Thus, the total price gap for the sale of the ten firms amounted to about 15 percent.

The gaps found between prices and valuations are important but smaller than generally assumed, and they are significantly smaller than those estimated by Marcel (1989b).[18] Furthermore, it would be a mistake to automatically classify these gaps as subsidies, since, strictly speaking, they might reflect many factors not considered in the valuation estimates, including the conscious bias introduced in the calculations, transactions carried out under imperfect or frankly uncompetitive conditions, factors such as reverse privatization risks, and the existence of personal income taxes, and efficiency changes. Consequently, we use the term "price gap" here rather than "subsidy," which may not be fully appropriate to describe the results obtained.

As Table 5.6 shows, the gaps between the estimated price and the price actually paid vary a great deal from enterprise to enterprise, ranging from almost 32 percent in the case of the Metropolitan CHILECTRA (CHILMETRO) to a negative subsidy ("tax") of about 7 percent in the case of CTC. The range of gaps favoring capitalists appears to be even broader, because gaps involved in the sales to workers vary greatly among firms (Appendix B). Price gaps favoring workers varied between 60.9 percent (1986) in a particular sale of National Sugar Industry (IANSA) shares and –8.7 percent (1986) in a Laboratorio Chile transaction. Thus, price gaps favoring capitalists went from 56.2 percent in the same sale of IANSA shares noted above to –28.6 percent in transfers of CTC shares carried out in 1987. We have made no effort to explain these gaps, for this would require a case-by-case analysis, but the general arguments presented below to account for the observed average price gap are applicable.

Causes and effects of price gaps. The results shown above raise several questions. Is this gap merely the result of the bias in estimates? How

TABLE 5.6
Estimated Price Gaps for Ten Firms, 1986–1989 (percentage)

Firm	1986	1987	1988	1989	Total
ENTEL	45.67	19.65	31.44	22.86	29.55
CTC	25.90	−8.92	−19.30	13.07	−7.00
				14.20[a]	−6.90[a]
CAP	18.04	29.22			28.76
ENDESA		−11.46	9.94	−6.90	5.00
		0.49[a]	18.90[a]		14.20[a]
SOQUIMICH	42.25	11.59	−0.99		24.25
CHILGENER	34.98	17.41	9.80		21.73
CHILMETRO	40.51	23.76			31.81
CHILQUINTA	44.11	7.62			25.45
IANSA	58.66	36.62	−3.17		12.51
Laboratorio Chile	45.30	7.63	10.10		15.69
TOTAL	41.94	7.98	5.33	16.20	12.99
		11.62[a]	6.58[a]	16.64[a]	14.51[a]

NOTE: Blank cell indicates no sale.
a. Includes the implicit interest rate subsidy on stock divestitures on credit.
SOURCE: Authors' estimates.

significant was the decision to subsidize sales to workers and taxpayers? Could part of the gap have originated in the existence of asymmetric information? If so, was this asymmetry intentional and a result of lack of transparency in the privatization process? Could the relatively small estimated price gap be the result of significant expected gains from increased efficiency, offset by other important effects, such as those mentioned here? These different forces have not been measured, but merit comment. Finally, what is the relationship between these price gaps and any gains or losses in public sector net worth?

Imperfections could, as many argue, have come from sales procedures that may have limited competition, restricting participation unnecessarily in bids or offering discriminatory conditions in favor of a specific group. As explained, in some cases the latter measure was adopted intentionally to spread ownership of stock and to offer special terms to workers (labor capitalism) and to the middle class (popular capitalism). Earlier we estimated the first of these two types of subsidies, the stock price reduction to workers. The cost to the state of popular capitalism has been only partially identified,[19] but it has not been significant in comparison with total revenues received from all privatizations, except perhaps during 1989.

Factors that could properly be called defects in sales procedures may have had a significant impact on divestiture revenues. The decline over time of the relative importance of the estimated gap between the price actually paid for shares of divested SOEs and the one calculated in this chapter on the basis of projected dividend flows, corrected for the implicit subsidy to popular capitalists, is consistent with this hypothesis. Evaluating these defects is, however, complex. The phenomenon is perhaps best described as one in which privatization generated capital market improvements that allowed authorities to use competitive sales techniques at an increasing rate, such as in auctions of small packages of shares in the stock exchange. Using the same technique in 1985 might not have produced the positive results of 1988, while changes in external factors, produced by successful privatizations together with improving economic conditions, could help to explain the volume of transactions at the stock exchange, which was ten times greater in 1988 than in 1985. If so, little could have been done to avoid this cost, and it must then be seen as a legitimate transaction cost, even though it affects public sector net worth.

Imperfections could also have resulted from asymmetric information. This would have been the case, for example, if any group had had inside information that allowed it to foresee increases in profitability better than the rest of the bidders. This would probably have reduced both the number of bidders and the price actually paid, and would have widened the gap between the true market price and the price eventually paid. The absence of clear evidence on the importance of these factors does not mean they did not exist. It is difficult to believe that the new owners of privatized firms who had recently been administrators of those same firms did not possess privileged information at the moment of sale, even if the divesting authorities were doing their best to disseminate basic information adequately. The problem is studied in greater depth in Chapter 8 for the cases of ENDESA and the Steel Company of the Pacific (CAP).

Furthermore, after the experience of the First Round of divestitures, which ended in a significant reverse privatization in 1982–1983 for financial reasons, the authorities made a more careful selection of potential SOE buyers. In so doing, they were certainly discriminating among buyers, at least in terms of capacity to pay cash, perhaps reducing the transaction price, but also enhancing the likelihood of cash payment and therefore of fiscal revenues and lowering the probability of future reversals arising from financial weaknesses. On the whole, while the cash payment condition may have lowered the price actually obtained, discrimination among buyers may have improved the likelihood of payment.

Errors exist in the valuation estimates, not only as a consequence of our intentional bias toward an overestimation of stock values, but also because we ignored personal income taxes. We excluded them because there was no way of estimating their influence with any reliability. Such an estimate would require knowledge of shareholders' income distribution and alternative investment opportunities. However, members of the economic study departments of several conglomerates that presented bids for SOE stock after 1985 used total income tax rates of 30 percent on profits before taxes in their calculations of present values—a significantly higher rate than the actual corporate rates. This factor alone might explain a 20 percent gap between estimated and true values, more than the estimated gap. Expected tax increases could also have reduced the price paid below valuations estimated without taking tax increases into account, although little weight should be given to that consideration until late in the period, particularly in 1989 when the tax reform issue started to crop up.[20]

As mentioned, we did not include a reverse privatization risk factor, because we found no way to estimate it. Chile has had a long history of erratic rules of the game. Although during its seventeen years of rule, the military regime had done everything possible to reassure private agents about its respect for private property, government interventions in 1982–1983 and discontent among the likely successors to that regime with respect to privatization triggered some valid fears of reversals of the privatization process, especially during the mid-1980s. Critiques were particularly strong against divestiture of public services, and less strong against other activities recognized as being outside of the accepted sphere of influence of the public sector. This factor can probably partially explain the discrepancies in the gaps among the various privatized SOEs presented in Table 5.6. Since the SOEs belong to different sectors, they are subject to different reverse privatization risks. Another aspect of these gaps is, no doubt, related to the time of divestiture. Early divestitures, during which the perceived reverse privatization risk must have been much higher, were more affected by this factor.[21]

On the other hand, expectations of improved efficiency in the divested SOEs could have had some impact on the actual price paid by the private sector. Foreseeing potential areas for improvements in those firms, private bidders would have been induced to offer a better price than otherwise. The effective selling price would then include a premium, and, since our valuation did not take that factor into account, the gap between the two would be reduced as the premium would compensate partly or fully for the effect of the upward biases introduced into the estimate of the market value of the stock transferred.

It is also interesting to note that increases in efficiency derived from privatization raise national net worth if sold to nationals. This increase can be fully or partially internalized by either the public or the private sector. In the first case, either sector would increase its net worth as a consequence of the transfer. However, public sector net worth is not necessarily reduced if the price obtained in the divestiture does not include the positive impact of the expected increase in efficiency. This result may simply reflect the fact that as long as the enterprise remains in public hands its efficiency will be lower than if in private hands and, consequently, will be the relevant factor for public valuation. Employment and wage policies, among other considerations, may help to explain this asymmetry. If the capital market is efficient, however, this result will not occur, because the government will be able to capture the relevant difference.

At this stage, it is difficult to obtain a precise picture of the importance of efficiency increases. Dispersed information suggests, in retrospect, significant changes in rates of return in several of the twenty-seven divested firms between 1985 and 1989 (Table 5.7). Most of these changes are probably related to the high rate of output growth in Chile during that period. Some of these changes resulted from unusually high output prices and from nonoperational considerations, such as foreign debt management, blurring the evidence in favor of efficiency modifications. Furthermore, it has been noted in previous chapters that authorities decided, soon after the military takeover, to use similar rules of the game for both sectors. As a consequence, these firms improved their efficiency (Hachette and Lüders 1988). Evidence for the cases of CAP and ENDESA can likewise be found in Chapter 8. Consequently, significant efficiency gains by divestiture could not be reasonably expected on these grounds.

TABLE 5.7

Evolution of Rates of Return, 1980–1989
(percentage of net profits over net worth)

Firm	1980	1981	1982	1983	1984	1985	1986	1987	1988	1989
CHILGENER[a]	n.a.	n.a.	4.9	6.0	3.5	3.2	7.1	3.1[b]	7.6	8.0
CHILMETRO[a]	n.a.	n.a.	14.9	3.1	4.7	10.3	11.4[b]	10.0	14.7	21.7
CHILQUINTA[a]	n.a.	n.a.	12.3	7.7	5.1	5.1	8.5[b]	8.7	12.2	18.4
ENDESA	4.5	3.0	−10.4	6.4	2.4	−19.0	−19.0	9.2	12.9[b]	7.3
CTC	4.5	2.6	−15.1	11.9	9.2	15.5	15.0	12.1	19.0[b]	17.2
CAP	3.8	−6.6	−9.6	0.7	0.8	1.5	2.1[b]	4.5	8.3	12.0
IANSA	−5.7	−36.4	−21.7	−30.2	−4.2	−9.0	5.8	7.3	42.6[b]	57.2
SOQUIMICH	−0.3	n.a.	−17.1	10.1	10.8	28.2	29.5[b]	34.9	43.4	21.1
ENTEL	12.1	11.2	11.5	13.0	16.8	21.3	42.4	42.9	49.5[b]	40.0
Laboratorio Chile[c]	n.a.	n.a.	n.a.	n.a.	n.a.	n.a.	n.a.	14.7	30.8[b]	23.8

n.a. = not available.
a. Before 1982 these companies were not independent; with others, they formed CHILECTRA.
b. Indicates the year of transfer of 51 percent of net worth to the private sector.
c. No information is available until 1987, when it became an open stock company.
SOURCE: Balance sheets of firms.

Our perception is that the bias introduced by not considering the efficiency factor in the estimate of the market price could not have compensated for the reverse biases introduced by all the other considerations discussed above, which induced underpricing of the divested shares. On all these grounds, it is doubtful that public net worth was reduced.[22]

It is also now clear that several divested firms enlarged their sphere of action by investing in areas related to and different from their own.[23] Public firms were not allowed to do this, with the exception of CAP. The success story of this firm, told in Chapter 8, is clearly a case in point, but not the only one. CAP, CHILMETRO, CTC, ENTEL, and SOQUIMICH became new holding companies, although most of them invested in related fields. It is therefore likely that some of the potential buyers of divested firms had precise ideas about expansion possibilities and consequently offered a higher price than they would have without those possibilities.

All the factors mentioned are relevant if they influence cash flows and discount rates and bias the estimated price gap. Some of them reflect divestiture procedure imperfections and true transaction costs that do affect wealth distribution between the public and private sector. Others simply reflect estimation defects, which can be overcome only at a high cost and which have biased the result in favor of a positive price gap. Considering the average estimated gap of 14.5 percent, in practice, no significant transfer of wealth might have existed at all between the state and the private sector if the cost of spreading ownership among workers and middle-class taxpayers is taken into account. Moreover, the data and analysis suggest that the state may have captured some part of any expected efficiency gains (such as in the case of CTC). That is, divestiture mode imperfections, transaction costs, intentional subsidies for middle-class investors and workers, the lower than "true" discount rate used especially during 1985–1986, and the effect of expected efficiency gains lead to the conclusion that divestitures could hardly have produced, as a direct effect, a negative change in government wealth, beyond that explicitly anticipated from the implementation of labor and popular capitalism.

The divestiture of the so-called natural monopolies during the period 1985–1989 (basically, electricity transmission and distribution[24]) was accompanied by the imposition of a complex set of strict rules that prevented private firms from acting as de facto monopolies[25] and affected tariffs to be charged in the future by the divested firms. Any monopoly profit was thereby eliminated beforehand and could not produce a gap between the relevant valuations discussed here. Other monopolies, such as steel and nitrate production, had lost their monopoly power with the opening of the economy.

The data, taken without adjustment, appear to suggest that the net worth and long-term financial position of the public sector were reduced during the Second Round. In the first place, however, the measured reduction represents at most 4.6 percent of 1988 government revenues and no more than 12 percent of the net worth of CODELCO (the copper mine still in the hands of the public sector).[26] In the second place, given the extreme set of assumptions made, in particular, in the choice of parameters, to obtain estimates of market prices of divested stock, this reduction clearly represents a gross overvaluation of the actual loss, if any. Only the presence of transaction costs and expected increases in efficiency once the firm was privatized, factors not taken into account[27] in the estimate of the so-called price gap, would represent biases in the opposite direction.[28] Significant gains in efficiency, however, are unlikely, as has been postulated in various chapters and will be demonstrated in Chapter 7. Also, to the extent that actual efficiency increases in the divested firms, the present value of taxes will also be higher than otherwise, a factor that would reduce any public sector net worth loss, although this would not fully compensate for direct impact of that increase in efficiency. Furthermore, transaction costs, although difficult to estimate precisely, should not represent a large proportion of divestitures.

Finally, as long as the public and private sectors use the same discount rate, its level is immaterial for the estimation of the present value of net revenues obtained from divestiture, given the price paid by the private sector, and for the estimation of the gap between market and actual prices paid for stocks divested.

The Indirect Effect: Deficit Financing

The First Round

Two points can be made on the issue of deficit financing. On the one hand, in the final analysis and in spite of all intentions to the contrary, the debt-led phase of the First Round of the Chilean privatizations turned out to be a way for the government to raise money at high local interest rates in order to finance social expenditure projects that in all likelihood had a much lower rate of return (Hachette and Lüders 1988). These ''excess'' expenditures contributed to the generation of extremely high interest rates in a market still relatively closed to foreign capital inflow. Our assumption, based on the behavioral pattern of the military government, is that it would have reduced expenditure levels had it not had the revenue from the divestitures, and aggregate demand would have been reduced, together with interest rates.

SOE divestitures might also have contributed in other ways to the high prevailing interest rates in Chile during 1975–1982.[29] Until 1981 the privatization process probably increased the perceived existing wealth of the private sector and therefore induced capital expenditures that probably would not have occurred otherwise, at a time when the openness of the Chilean financial market to international capital flows was still very limited. Moreover, firms indebted from the purchase of stock from divestiture preferred to postpone the amortization of their debt, despite the high interest rates, and accumulated larger debts and interest payments to finance additional investments expected to yield returns higher than interest rates. The debt levels generated during this debt-led phase therefore contributed to occasional distress borrowing, especially during the crisis periods of 1975 and late 1981 to 1982.

This analysis leads to the view that net depositors (financial asset holders) were the likely winners and taxpayers the likely losers of the First Round of the Chilean privatization process. Depositors received significantly higher interest rates than those that would have prevailed otherwise, and once the government assumed private debt as a result of the bank intervention, taxpayers paid a portion of those interest costs as it became obvious that the private sector was in no position to pay that debt.[30] Net depositors were, with few exceptions, not among those who acquired the divested SOEs during the debt-led phase of privatization.

Net depositors are defined here as those persons or corporations that on a net and consolidated basis had a higher volume of financial assets than liabilities. Into this category fall the relatively few traditional Chilean private sector conglomerates and corporations that survived the Allende period and that later did not succumb to the temptation to grow fast on the basis of debt, along with professionals with significant savings capacity and the not-insignificant number of private investors who "monetized" their assets. The expression monetization is used here to denote the process whereby investors in real estate or stock sold those assets to invest the proceeds in bank deposits, with the banks using the resulting increase in deposits to finance loans to the purchasers of those assets. This process normally takes place on a limited scale as people adjust their portfolios, but it reached extraordinary proportions in Chile during the last part of the boom phase, which ended with the crash of the early 1980s. These monetizers were probably the most important winners of this first privatization episode, and present and future generations of taxpayers were the corresponding losers.

As a result of the insolvency of the new and highly indebted conglomerates, the government intervened in the largest financial institutions of the private sector, as already described. Most of them were restructured and reprivatized later on. In the process, the government guaranteed 100 percent of the value of deposits (and foreign loans granted to the financial institutions) in all financial institutions, except those to be liquidated. Although the owners of the failed conglomerates, as well as the stockholders of the intervened financial institutions, lost their investments, these losses were minor compared with those sustained by the government.[31]

Consequently, unlike in the Second Round, the public sector suffered a loss in net worth during the First Round. This occurred because most proceeds from the divestitures financed current expenditures. However, the loss was larger. When, at the end of this round, the government took over management of several large conglomerates with negative net worth, the public sector took over the accumulated debt—related to, among other things, the purchase of stock at the time of divestiture—of the state-managed firms. Its net worth was correspondingly reduced by approximately the amount of interest accumulated on that debt between 1974 and 1980.

The Second Round

While proceeds from privatization, defined in the crude terms used in this study so far, were growing in absolute value between 1985 and 1988, the government budget deficit (defined conventionally or corrected to include, among other factors, the sale of public assets) was reduced and even became a surplus in 1987 or 1988, depending on the definition used (Table 5.8).[32] Proceeds from divestitures did finance budget deficits, but only in 1985 and 1986; in fact, they financed more than 80 percent of it in the latter year. In 1987 and 1988, the proceeds were used to reduce domestic public debt with the central bank.[33]

TABLE 5.8

Allocation of Public Expenditures, 1984–1988 (millions of 1977 pesos)

	1984	1985	1986	1987	1988
Divestiture proceeds	0	231	5,187	6,569	12,360
Deficit (corrected)[a]	18,718	11,477	11,016	6,424	−9,398
Current revenues	82,667	82,553	87,900	94,478	101,965
Current expenditures	117,077	117,093	115,253	113,555	104,728
Capital formation	20,876	25,201	28,368	27,667	25,385
Domestic financing	5,741	−5,026	−2,244	−527	−29,722

a. Traditional deficit minus sale of assets, plus financial investment, minus loan recovery.
SOURCE: Budget Office, Ministry of Finance.

The question is whether public sector expenditure policy has generated a loss of net worth resulting from privatization by using divestiture proceeds for current expenditures or whether the proceeds were invested in alternatives that have a higher rate of return than the discount rates used for the valuation of the divested enterprises. To the extent that the government divests onerously, it receives additional gross revenues. These revenues may be earmarked either for current or capital expenditures or for debt redemption (or interest payments). However, the revenues from divestitures cannot be considered current income or even income from capital and consequently cannot be considered an ipso facto reduction of public deficit. On the contrary, an asset reduction or liability increase finances a deficit in any firm.[34] These revenues replace the sale of bonds in the capital market and, as such, finance any expenditure or reduction in current revenues. Furthermore, the use of the proceeds from public enterprise divestiture is not part of the privatization process itself but part of the overall fiscal policy.

Consequently, the indirect impact of divestiture on public net worth will be no different from the impact of any other source of deficit financing, which, given the fungibility of money, will cover current expenditures, asset accumulation, or liability reduction. Privatization in itself represents merely a change in assets or liabilities without affecting public sector net worth, under the assumptions already discussed. Two noneconomic issues—the size of the public sector and the responsibilities assigned to it—are the crucial issues for net worth. That is, if the government wants to reduce the size of the public sector or transfer functions to the private sector, privatizations will be accompanied by additional current expenditures and public sector net worth will diminish. Previous conclusions are valid if the public sector faces a perfectly elastic source of funds. However, it is likely that since Chile's public sector was facing a rising supply curve of funds, at least during the first part of the period analyzed, the revenues from privatization were tied to specific expenditures.

It may, nonetheless, be worthwhile to consider briefly some qualitative factors involved in privatization to bring to light the probable uses of divestiture funds, since critics insist that the revenue obtained from privatization has been badly used. For example, Marcel (1989b) suggests, ''On the other hand, only half the funds obtained from divestitures had a compensatory impact (real investment, credits and public debt reduction), a situation that worsened in 1988. So, the privatization of public firms in Chile led to structural reduction of the public sector, which will be reflected in reduced future incomes.''

An important consideration is that the choice of deficit financing, if made on economic grounds only, will be indicated by comparing the cost of divesting with the cost of additional indebtedness since ''privatization is simply the sale by government of equities in place of bonds" (Vickers and Yarrow 1988:187).[35] The cost of obtaining an additional peso by divesting a public enterprise will be equal to the difference between the present value of the flow of interest payments on public debt (bonds) and the present value of forgone public revenues as a consequence of the privatization. The public sector does not necessarily incur higher or lower costs by selling a public enterprise than by selling bonds, as many critics who do not appreciate the relevant alternative imply. When both the public and private sectors face a rising supply curve of funds in relation to the interest rate, revenues obtained through divestitures may put upward pressure on the interest rate similar to that created by a sale of bonds. But, to the extent that the selling of a firm is a cheaper source of funds than alternatives, the public sector may have to divest to finance its expenditures or to redeem debt.

So, whether divestiture funds financed more current expenditures than capital expenditures—or debt service—in Chile is difficult to ascertain. Furthermore, even if the funds were used to finance additional capital expenditures, their profitability could be either higher or lower than those of the divested firms. These two issues merit additional comments on the basis of the Chilean experience between 1985 and 1989.

The need for additional revenue was justified by Chile's budget director:

> With regard to public expenditure, reallocation and growth should be centered on those areas that have been most neglected. Once again, our analysis of the Chilean situation reveals that the distribution function and the provision of public goods have been neglected for forty years in favor of public entrepreneurial activity and the state's regulatory (the word should really be controlling) function. It is obvious that growth in budget outlays should be centered essentially on the distribution function, accompanied by significant efforts to achieve more efficient production (Méndez 1979:19).

Indeed, this approach was followed as social expenditures increased as a percentage of total public expenditures in the late 1970s. However, informal estimates of defense expenditures suggest an even more pronounced upward trend (Hachette and Lüders 1988).

It might be assumed that one monetary unit obtained from any source of revenue, unless earmarked or unless fungibility is absent, would be allocated to a given type of expenditure in the same way as any other unit. The 1985–1988 period, however, presents characteristics that lead to more interesting conclusions. In the first place, an overall budget deficit prevailed until 1987, becoming a surplus in 1988 (Table 5.8). In the second place, 1985 is not a relevant year because divestiture proceeds were almost nonexistent. Third, three different trends can be observed: current expenditures decreased throughout the period, while the reverse occurred with current revenues, and capital formation grew until 1986, decreasing slightly thereafter—all measured at constant prices. While revenues grew at an average annual rate of 5.4 percent between 1985 and 1988, capital expenditures were 21.5 percent over the 1984 level in 1988, at constant 1977 prices, and current expenditures decreased throughout the period at an annual average rate of –2.2 percent. This is hardly evidence of consumption financing by divestiture funds, although it is not clear that deficit financing covered capital expenditures exclusively.

In that regard, further comment is in order. The public sector reduced its domestic debt systematically between 1985 and 1988 (Table 5.8). In other words, deficit financing also covered liability reduction, which, all things being equal, increased public sector net worth. So, during the 1985–1988 period, divestiture funds, through deficit financing, were allocated to asset creation and liability reduction, given the fungibility assumption. Unfortunately, exact allocation is impossible to estimate. Nevertheless, our view is that a high percentage was dedicated to these objectives, given the opposite trends in current and capital expenditures and given the reduction of domestic debt.[36] Thus, when the deficit existed, revenues from the privatization of state enterprises replaced revenues from other sources, thereby financing government expenditures in capital accumulation, domestic debt reduction, and, to some extent, current expenditures as well in 1986 and 1987.[37]

In 1988, the problem of financing the deficit disappeared, as a large surplus developed in the consolidated public sector, while both current and capital expenditures were lower in real terms than in 1987 and domestic debt was significantly reduced (Table 5.8). The surplus and the proceeds from divestiture clearly financed the reduction in domestic debt, while external funds covered the difference. Divestiture proceeds financed 42 percent of total liability reductions.[38] As such, this operation is symmetrical to an asset accumulation, since public net worth is not affected and it generates a reduction in a flow of future payments instead of producing a flow of receipts.

Even if all proceeds from privatization had been reinvested, however, the relevant consideration for estimating the indirect impact of privatization on public net worth is the present value of gross benefits on additional public investment and not its original cost equivalent to the value of additional investment. As suggested above, returns to the public sector from investments that constitute an alternative to the divested enterprises could be higher or lower than the return those enterprises would probably have generated. If higher, net worth would be enhanced, and if lower, it would be reduced. It has not been possible to find an empirical counterpart to actual returns from new public investments. A theoretical consideration suggests that the return should be at least equal to the capital shadow price for the investment. It will be assumed here that additional investment would obtain at least that return. Therefore, the present value of gross benefits of additional investment should be equal to the cost of investment.

A final comment may be justified. In general, if a unit of deficit financing has the same social value, whatever its application, the question of allocation becomes irrelevant. An additional unit of current expenditure has the same value to society as one spent on capital formation. The distinction between current and capital expenditures is relevant only when distortions may hamper either the savings or the consumption process. Consequently, the analysis carried out in this section is made in the worst possible framework of widespread distortions, an assumption of limited validity in the context of the Chilean economy at that time.

SIX

Effects of Privatization on the Capital Market, Savings and Investment, and Employment

Both supporters and opponents of privatization often make assumptions about the effects of privatization on the capital market and ownership distribution, savings and investment, and employment. In this chapter, we will attempt to determine the actual effects of privatization in these areas in Chile. We will also analyze differences in the performance of private, privatized, and public firms. Some of these topics are obviously related to one another, but because of their importance we will analyze them separately here, with some slight overlapping.

The Capital Market

Privatization processes and the capital market are interconnected in two ways, apart from the obvious fact that the divestiture of assets is a capital transaction. On the one hand, privatization and the mode of divestiture employed may be instrumental in strengthening the capital market. On the other hand, specific characteristics of the capital market may support or hinder the divestiture process. Both factors are relevant to the Chilean experience.

The impact of privatization on the capital market

Domestic financial liberalization was an integral part of the general economic liberalization that took place in Chile after 1973. The reforms aimed to limit government intervention, redefine the jurisdiction of monetary authorities, dictate uniform norms for financial intermediaries, and restructure the nonbanking financial intermediary market (Lüders 1986:45).

One of the first actions taken for the purpose of limiting government intervention, consistent with the desire to strengthen the private sector, was to transfer all publicly controlled commercial banks, with the exception of the Banco del Estado, to the private sector by way of auction. Delayed payments were accepted over a period of two years, although that time horizon was shortened to one year after the first round of bidding took place between the end of 1975 and February 1976. Meanwhile, the public sector was forbidden to buy shares in the banking industry. These transactions affected thirteen banks, in ten of which the State Development Corporation (CORFO) had held majority shares. This process of financial institution divestiture was completed toward the end of 1978 with the sale of remaining stock packages on the stock exchange.

The government, while privatizing banks, also divested other commercial, industrial, and financial institutions in a way similar to that employed for banks (see Chapter 4). In all, 223 institutions were transferred onerously to the private sector, while another 325 were returned to their prior owners. The whole process certainly had an effect on the development and characteristics of the capital market, although it is difficult to separate this effect from other forces influencing that market.[1]

In the first place, the privatization of banks and industrial concerns was concomitant with a significant deepening and broadening of the capital market. Financial liabilities increased from 5.9 percent of gross domestic product (GDP) in 1973 to 54.4 percent in 1981 (Table 6.1). Stock transactions related to the privatization of financial and nonfinancial enterprises increased tenfold during the same period. This result, however, should be interpreted with care. New equity capital was growing extremely slowly during that period, and a significant part of this increase was due to the high rate of monetization of existing financial assets. Nevertheless, monetization was strictly related to increases in the real price of assets, a phenomenon itself related to the economic boom after 1977 (the General Index of Share Prices rose about sixfold between 1977 and 1980) and to the development of the capital market, supported, indirectly, by the privatization efforts of the 1974–1980 period.

On the other hand, privatization may have had a twofold negative effect on the development of the capital market during the 1970s. These negative effects, however, are the result of the mode of privatization and not of the divestiture per se. First, privatization indirectly helped push up the interest rate. Purchasers of public enterprise shares often financed those acquisitions with bank credit, which they tended to capitalize and

TABLE 6.1

Financial Liabilities, 1961–1989 (billions of 1980 pesos, end of each year)

	1961	1973	1981	1984	1989
Total financial liabilities	103.3	157.6	1,927.4	1,841.5	4,383.7
Public sector	16.9	45.2	113.5	407.8	817.6
Central bank	n.a.	n.a.	80.9	158.6	746.7
Treasury	n.a.	n.a.	32.6	249.2	70.9
Banks and financial institutions	16.5	1.3	1,008.2	983.8	1,715.9
Corporate sector	69.6	77.5	792.0	443.5	1,850.2
Stock	69.6	77.5	745.8	400.6	1,696.5
Other	0.0	0.0	46.2	42.9	153.7
Other	0.3	33.6	13.6	6.4	0.0
Financial liabilities as % of GDP	5.7	5.9	54.4	57.3	108.0
Stock as % of GDP	3.8	2.9	21.1	12.5	41.8
Balance of AFPs as % of GDP	0.0	0.0	0.3	5.0	19.8

n.a. = not available.
SOURCE: Central Bank of Chile, *Boletín Mensual*; F. Pérez, "Necesidades de Inversión para los Fondos de Pensiones," Documento de Trabajo no. 92 (Santiago: Centro de Estudios, 1987).

eventually were unable to repay. This debt capitalization was possible and seemed desirable to shareholders and financial institutions, in spite of the high interest rates, because of the rapid increase in both the price of shares and the level of financial assets. The special ownership relationship that existed between the owners of the banks and the privatized enterprises may have helped during 1975 and after 1980 (Chapter 2 and Lüders 1986). The government, however, used part of the divestiture proceeds to finance expenditures, whether or not it realized that any additional expenditures not financed with new taxes implied upward pressure on the interest rate unless the private sector were to reduce its expenditures at the same rate, which was not the case.

Second, privatization may have affected the stability of the system. Although this issue has been analyzed in Chapter 4, the matter merits attention here. The lack of capital in the private sector stimulated the government to privatize on an installment basis, with down payments varying from 10 to 20 percent. A medium-term loan to purchase shares of the financial institutions being divested would usually be granted by the government, with those same shares serving to guarantee the transaction. By using credits from the recently privatized bank, the same persons or corporations that had managed to acquire shares financed with government credit would buy additional packages of shares and, in this way, be able to control that bank (Chapter 4). The results were a high concentration of bank equity and the formation of highly leveraged conglomerates, built around one or more financial institutions, which tended to capitalize a high proportion of their interest burden. Finally, "the owners of the banks tended to channel a high proportion of 'low-cost' foreign loans to their own enterprises, thereby aggravating the concentration effect on the existing market segmentation" (Lüders 1986:98).

In any event, most of the new financial groups were created with a relatively small capital base and grew rapidly on credit. When asset prices tumbled in 1980–1982, the capital base of many financial groups (as well as that of thousands of other asset owners) suddenly shrank and financial institutions incurred heavy losses. The ensuing crash started in November 1981 with the government takeover of eight financial institutions (four of them banks). It was followed by the takeover of eight additional private financial institutions (among the largest in the country), as the authorities, with some difficulty, discovered their state of insolvency. This measure implied a major reversal of the privatization process of the 1970s, since all concerns involved in the conglomerates suffered the same fate as their holding company. Although the mode of privatization employed was far from being the only cause of the 1981–1983 crisis, it was clearly instrumental in setting the stage for it, insofar as it accentuated the factors of instability present in the Chilean capital market.[2]

Since 1984, the effects of the divestiture, first of the odd sector and later of the traditional state-owned enterprises (SOEs), have been positive for the development of the capital market. The authorities learned from prior experience. They avoided concentration of equity, especially in banks, and installment payments. They perfected controls, mainly based on regulation changes approved during the early 1980s, and made them operational. Further strengthening of the private sector and of the capital market surfaced again as privatization objectives. The main preoccupation of the government, however, was the distribution of ownership, both to avoid the weaknesses inherent in concentration and for ideological reasons. Consequently, privatization after 1984 favored the development of a deeper and broader capital market, without the inconveniences described above.

Again, it is difficult to define the precise role of privatization in capital market development. However, it is interesting to note the following: first, while financial liabilities were increasing two and a half times as a percentage of GDP, stocks increased fourfold. Financial liabilities surpassed GDP in 1989, while stocks, which had fallen by half a percentage point of GDP during the crisis, doubled their relative weight compared with 1981 and were fifteen times higher during 1989 than before privatization (Table 2.1). Second, stock transactions increased more than twenty times between 1984 and 1989 (Table 6.2), and since 1985 privatized SOE

TABLE 6.2

Privatization, Shares, and Shareholders, 1984–1989

	1984	1985	1986	1987	1988	1989
Transactions of shares (millions of Dec. 1988 US$)	41.9	59.7	337.1	542.8	654.4	917.6
Transactions of shares of privatized firms (millions of Dec. 1988 US$)	2.6	18.7	187.2	368.7	448.2	578.8
Transactions of shares of privatized firms as % of total transactions	6.2	31.2	55.5	67.9	68.5	65.5
Shares and debentures in AFPs (millions of Dec. 1988 US$)	n.a.	19.0	19.0	260.0	527.0	899.0
Number of shareholders (thousands)	371.8	435.4	478.6	497.0	571.7	629.3
Shareholders of privatized equity (thousands)	n.a.	26.6	50.2	92.2	151.7	151.7[a]
General index of share prices	77.9	100.0	201.6	357.5	449.4	666.6
Index of shares of divested firms	n.a.	100.0	145.4	245.8	261.6	392.0

n.a. = not available.
a. Includes only 19 out of 27 privatized SOEs.
Source: CORFO and Santiago Stock Exchange.

stock transactions have represented almost two-thirds of all such operations, a clear indication of the effect of privatization on financial deepening. By March 1990, more than a third of equity registered at the stock exchange was that of privatized firms,[3] most of which had been registered during the previous five years. Third, as a result, the Santiago Stock Exchange has become one of the most active in South America, with ratios of total value traded to GDP, market capitalization to GDP, and turnover reaching values similar to those of Brazil, which has large markets and relatively well-developed capital markets among developing countries (Lüders 1990). Fourth, by the end of 1988, 169,733 persons had become direct shareholders of privatized enterprises and potential users of the capital market, through labor and popular capitalism and through direct sales and bidding at auction.[4] About 3 million persons out of a labor force of 4.8 million (that is, 62.5 percent) became shareholders indirectly through their stake in the AFPs (institutional capitalism).

Before 1985, participants in institutional capitalism, especially the privately owned pension fund administration companies (AFPs), had invested mainly in paper from the public sector and the central bank. Significant diversification of financial assets was necessary to improve profitability, to move the system toward becoming a clearly privately run capitalization system, and to avoid financing government deficits automatically or becoming the sole private sector counterpart of central bank open market operations. However, the number of available financial assets, particularly instruments issued by the private sector, was limited. On the one hand, immediately after the 1982–1983 crisis, private instruments were considered highly risky. On the other hand, the private sector did not offer numerous alternatives, because many owners would not relinquish control of their firms. The privatization of SOEs appeared, then, to be an efficient means of strengthening the recently established AFPs, which were to be subject to strict rules concerning risk and property distribution. In this way, divestitures gave a boost to the stock market, where AFPs now trade actively as part of their portfolio management function. By the end of 1989, 10 percent of AFP assets represented shares of private—and privatized—firms, compared with 6 percent two years before, but in the meantime total AFP assets had doubled. However, the divestiture of the social security system itself, the single most important privatization effort of the military government, constituted perhaps the most significant advance in the development of the Chilean capital market in this century.

The impact of the capital market on privatization

It appears, in retrospect, that the overall condition and absorptive capacity of the capital market were of some concern to authorities during both rounds of privatization. Fortunately, the capital market did not present a significant constraint to the privatization process. Although the desire to liberalize and develop the capital market was explicit, it was not directly or uniquely related to the process of privatization, which was, from the beginning, a coherent measure in its own right. Some characteristics of the Chilean capital market, however, may have influenced the sequencing, modes, and prices obtained in divestitures.

In both rounds, the privatization process began with the divestiture of financial institutions immediately after a major recession and in conditions of extremely low national savings. During the First Round, the capital market was initially depressed, and, despite the gradual opening of the capital account and the enactment of DL 600, which established liberal and nondiscriminatory conditions for foreign investment, foreign investors showed no interest in buying Chilean SOEs.[5] These conditions were not supportive of high prices. It is not strange then that the public sector should provide credit to support sales of its own equity. The "high" prices obtained for bank shares, however, throw doubts on this pessimistic view.

The minimum price was fixed at the book value of the banks, prices far superior to their stock exchange value before the privatization process, since they were all virtually broke despite a process of financial strengthening—albeit very brief (1974 and part of 1975)—before divestiture. Furthermore, Law 818 of December 1974 had established limits on the size of share packages that any one person could buy, in order to avoid concentration of property. In those conditions, it seems amazing that CORFO could obtain what it considered to be relatively high prices in the divestiture of the eleven banks (Valdés 1988). Several factors shed light on this apparent contradiction. First, potential buyers were interested in one specific asset: the name of the institution. By acquiring an existing bank, buyers retained the bank's traditional clients and avoided the cost of having to create a reputation. Second, these buyers expected a profit from their new asset with the liberalization of the financial market. Third, the use of subsidized credit to buy packages of stock enhanced the price in the bidding process. Fourth, the regulation of property concentration was poorly worded and, although properly enforced, could not hinder concentration. Fifth, the fact that the same law permitted foreign investment in Chilean banks may have boosted prices somewhat in the auctions, even though no foreign banks actually participated in the bidding.[6] Sixth, the first signs of the authorities' willingness to insure deposits 100 percent in early 1977, that is, before the process of transferring financial institutions to the private sector was complete, gave an additional boost to share prices.[7]

The Second Round of privatizations began much like the First Round, after a major recession, with low total savings (same share of GDP as in 1976) and the banking industry almost fully controlled by the public sector. The capital market, however, or at least its institutional framework, was far more developed than during the First Round, as a consequence of the financial liberalization of the late 1970s and early 1980s. Foreigners were showing great interest in investing in Chile in order to take advantage of both the boom that followed the recession and the generous conditions offered by the new debt-equity swap policy. Authorities made good use of these developments, offering new modes of privatization that corrected the shortcomings of the First Round. These new modes were institutional, labor, and popular capitalism and sale of equity to foreigners within the framework of Chapter XIX of the Foreign Exchange Law.

The impact of these developments on prices could not have been negative. No hard evidence, however, is available to demonstrate this claim. Greater competition, both internal and international, and greater availability of information within a more sophisticated capital market could not depress prices. In fact, the capital market showed great absorption capacity. Transactions of shares of privatized firms accounted for more than 60 percent of total transactions during the period (Table 6.2) and more than a third of private savings, which represented a more significant share of GDP than during the First Round (Table 6.3). Never-theless, the price of these shares did not rise as much as that of other components of the General Index of Share Prices (Table 6.2). Several factors help to explain this trend: (1) the relatively brief period since privatization took effect; (2) the high weight of nontradables among the privatized SOEs, in a period of rapidly increasing prices and real exchange rates worldwide; and (3) the sale of a large volume of divested SOE shares at a fixed price to workers, public employees, and "popular capitalists."

During the Second Round of privatization, the authorities intended to combine divestiture with a reduction of the external debt, largely through debt-equity swaps. This mechanism considerably increased the potential demand for SOE equity. Foreigners "invested" US$260 million through Chapter XIX in nine of the twenty-seven divested concerns, an amount representing 17.4 percent of the equity sold to the private sector. They also spent US$217 million in 1985 and 1986 through the same channel to buy large packages—mostly controlling interests—of five firms of the odd sector. However, some of the major debt-equity swap operations cannot be tied directly to privatizations since they became effective after the firms had returned to the private sector. For example, the Petroleum Company of Chile (COPEC) and the United Breweries Company (CCU) were transferred from the public sector to Chilean private groups, which later invited foreigners to share equity in those firms through Chapter XIX operations.

Savings and Investment

Any theoretical or empirical analysis of savings and investment deter-minants will encounter many hurdles. The task is even more difficult when the intention is to analyze the relationship among the privatiza-tion process, savings, and investment. Too many factors influenced savings and investment during the two rounds of privatization to permit precise definition of those relationships. Recessions; high rates of growth; significant institutional changes, such as the liberalization of the current account and the financial sector; and changes in the conditions for foreign investment are a few factors that could have had some effect on those variables, along with privatization.

Acknowledging these limitations, we will first present the facts related to privatization and savings and investment in the 1974–1989 period, which reveal the concomitant trends of the three variables. Second, we will investigate the possible relationships among them, based on the perceptions of relevant authors, which appear to be consistent with

TABLE 6.3
Investment and Savings, 1973–1989

	1973	1974	1975	1976	1977	1978	1979	1980	1981	1982	1983	1984	1985	1986	1987	1988	1989
Investment (% of GDP)	7.9	21.2	13.1	12.8	14.4	17.8	17.8	21.0	22.7	11.3	9.8	13.6	13.7	14.6	16.9	17.0	20.4
Private	-0.5	8.7	4.0	6.7	7.5	11.1	12.7	15.8	17.6	6.6	5.0	7.6	6.6	7.1	10.0	11.0	n.a.
Public	8.4	12.5	9.1	6.1	6.9	6.7	5.1	5.2	5.1	4.7	4.8	6.0	7.1	7.5	6.9	6.0	n.a.
Savings (% of GDP)																	
National	5.2	20.7	7.9	14.5	10.7	12.6	12.4	13.9	8.2	2.1	4.4	2.9	5.4	7.7	12.6	16.3	16.9
External	2.7	0.4	5.2	-1.7	3.7	5.2	5.4	7.1	14.5	9.2	5.4	10.7	8.3	6.8	4.3	0.7	3.5
Domestic	6.3	22.3	11.1	17.1	12.6	14.5	15.0	16.8	12.4	9.4	12.5	12.5	17.3	18.9	21.6	25.0	24.6
Private (national)	25.0	14.1	0.0	4.6	2.2	3.9	3.4	3.3	2.9	3.4	4.5	2.3	1.5	3.1	7.3	8.1	n.a.
Public	-19.8	6.6	7.9	9.9	8.5	8.7	9.0	10.6	5.3	-1.3	-0.1	0.6	3.9	4.6	5.3	8.2	n.a.
Proceeds from privatization																	
As % of GDP	0.0	0.1	2.0	0.9	1.0	0.8	1.1	0.4	0.6	0.1	n.a.	n.a.	0.1	1.4	1.8	3.3	0.0
As % of private savings	0.0	0.7	0.0	19.6	45.5	20.5	32.4	12.1	20.7	2.9	n.a.	n.a.	6.7	45.2	24.7	40.7	n.a.
As % of public savings	0.0	1.5	25.3	9.1	11.5	9.2	12.6	3.8	11.3	0.0	0.0	0.0	2.6	30.4	34.0	40.2	n.a.
Private sector "investment"[a] (% of GDP)	-0.5	8.8	6.0	7.6	8.5	11.9	13.8	15.9	18.2	6.7	n.a.	n.a.	6.7	8.5	11.8	14.3	n.a.

n.a. = not available.
a. Private investment plus proceeds from privatization.
SOURCE: Central Bank of Chile, *Indicadores Económicos y Sociales, 1960–1988*, and *Boletín Mensual*, 1989.

the facts, but are not proven either right or wrong by the qualitative analysis used.

We perceive a number of stylized facts describing the behavior of the three variables:[8]

- Both rounds of privatization coincided with rising levels of domestic investment relative to GDP (Table 6.3). This is particularly true for private investment, which reached 17.6 percent in 1981. This figure is even higher when the transfer of SOEs to the private sector is calculated as private sector investment (it has clearly been perceived as such), although, from the point of view of the national economy, it is nothing more than a transfer.

- Public investment, on the contrary, followed a declining trend during the First Round of divestitures, whereas it first increased and then decreased during the Second Round.

- Domestic and national savings remained at a relatively constant level during the First Round. They increased notably during the Second Round, starting from a low level. By 1989, however, domestic savings attained levels never reached before.

- External savings were significant during the First Round of divestitures, but only after 1978 when most divestitures had occurred. Foreign savings financed more than half of domestic investments in 1981, another historical record. The reverse occurred during the Second Round of divestiture, as the share of external savings fell from 10.7 percent in 1984 to 0.7 in 1988 and 3.5 percent in 1989.

- Private savings remained low during most of the period covered. They were relatively stable during most of the First Round and grew substantially during the Second Round, reaching record levels in 1988 (8.2 percent). It is likely that this figure was even surpassed in 1989, the last year of the Second Round of privatization, given that private consumption was reduced as a percentage of GDP in relation to 1988.[9]

- During both rounds, the proceeds from privatizations represented substantial shares of private savings, ranging from 2.9 percent in 1982 to 45.5 percent in 1977. Added to other private savings, they represent the private sector surplus. Proceeds from divestiture did reach 100 percent of the private sector surplus in 1975 when, according to the traditional definition, private savings were nonexistent.

For the private sector, the purchase of any SOE represents an investment. The actual transfer may be financed by private, public, or external savings. The first question is whether this investment (savings) is "additional" or "substitute" investment from the point of view of the private sector. The second question is whether the aggregates of savings and investment will be affected by the privatization. This will also depend on the reaction of the public sector. The net effect on aggregate savings and investment thus depends on the probable indirect impact of divestiture on private sector savings and investment decisions and on the spending reaction of the public sector.

Thus, divestiture could either stimulate or hinder aggregate savings and investment. Analysis of this issue requires plausible hypotheses about the behavior of economic units relating divestiture to saving-investment decisions.

The indirect impact on private savings and investment

The Chilean privatization process could have had an effect on private savings and investment on three counts: investment opportunities, the mode of divestiture, and the consequent increased wealth of that sector.

Investment opportunities.   Private saving is contingent on investment opportunities, among other variables.[10] This hypothesis is based on the argument that an intertemporal maximization of consumption will not depend on an exogenously obtained flow of income, as is usually assumed, but rather on an intertemporal income flow, subject to alterable savings decisions and affected by the rate of time preference related to utility, as well as by resource availability and investment opportunities. Under such conditions a vector of profitable investment opportunities, all else being equal, would stimulate savings (investment).

Therefore, the question is whether divestiture of public firms increased opportunities for private sector investment after 1974. The answer is obviously affirmative.[11] Of course, the profitability of the opportunity depended on the price paid during divestiture, but that is only one facet of a larger opportunity. The divested firms were equipped with better and more information than usual—that is, information accumulated from past experience, which was not available to new firms. This is not the equivalent of eliminating all risks, since future market conditions are uncertain, especially during a period of such extensive structural changes as during the First Round of privatization, but it probably helped.

During the First Round, these opportunities appeared at a time of low rates of private savings and, moreover, coincided with the hard-hitting recession of 1975 (Table 6.3). Despite the lower than usual overall investment rates, however, private investment was already higher than historical averages (Hachette 1988) and grew steadily until the end of the round. To say the least, this is not an indication of significant substitution among alternative investment projects by the private sector,[12] although divestitures may seem to displace other investment projects to be funded by available private savings, which remained relatively constant until 1981. In fact, the private sector used relatively more external savings to finance additional investment during the First Round of privatization, while during the Second Round, new private investment was financed mainly by private domestic savings, which far surpassed historical levels after 1986, while investment increased less rapidly than during the First Round despite higher rates of GDP growth. The analysis of this combination of factors suggests that opportunities created by the privatization of SOEs may have been relatively more competitive vis-á-vis other projects during this Second Round while they tended to stimulate private savings more than during the First Round.

Within the context of investment opportunities, we should mention an interesting development during the Second Round. Several of the privatized firms, apart from making decisions related to their particular sphere of action (that is, production lines, personnel, and technological changes), began investing in previously unrelated fields (see Chapter 5). This had previously not been possible for them as public concerns, because rules forbade such diversification. To what extent the privatization process, by creating this possibility, has stimulated investments that otherwise would not have been made is an interesting question, although it remains a matter of mere speculation.[13]

A related question is whether divestiture attracted foreign savings and, if so, whether these savings complemented private domestic savings. Available evidence suggests that foreign savings, through direct foreign investment and foreign debt, had no impact on divestiture and helped with the financing of installments during the First Round only marginally. However, foreign investment, though not foreign savings, was relatively significant in the divestiture process of the Second Round.

Fewer than ten firms were bought by foreign concerns during the First Round. In addition, this first transfer of public firms occurred during a period of either negative or no foreign investment (1974–1978), which reflected a lack of enthusiasm on the part of foreign investors, in contrast to that of Chilean businessmen (Table 6.3).[14] No direct evidence is available on the possible use of foreign credit by Chilean nationals in the privatizations, but spotty evidence suggests that if there was any such activity it was quite limited. Even if foreign credit was used, decisions about the purchase of most public firms were made when the domestic capital market was still relatively closed to foreign capital markets.

The situation changed somewhat during the Second Round. About 20 percent of divestitures between 1985 and 1989 were financed through Chapter XIX. However, operations carried out through Chapter XIX, although called "foreign investment," are not equivalent to foreign savings since they result from a change in the composition of external liabilities: a conversion of debt into equity. Consequently, given the mode of divestiture employed, it is unlikely that the privatization process attracted foreign savings during the Second Round.

However, even if generous use of foreign savings had been made to finance divestitures, how much would that have added to domestic savings? The best evidence available for Chile to date suggests that, on average, foreign savings have been a good substitute for domestic savings in that they displace each other (Foxley 1985). At best, they may have been mutually complementary during part of the first period (1975–1977), but, as discussed in Chapter 2 and by other authors,[15] between 1978 and 1981, foreign savings financed domestic consumption, foreign reserves, and, to a modest extent, investment. A clear substitution of domestic for foreign savings became possible again after 1984 (Table 6.3). On the whole, then, divestiture was not conducive to increasing private domestic savings.

The mode of divestiture. Divestiture has different facets. Information on divestiture can be made known widely or selectively. Similarly, the type of ownership of divested firms can vary in response to privatization goals, the mode of divestiture (sales of small or big lots), or the natural dynamics of the capital market (selling shares on the stock exchange). In addition, the transfer of public assets can be either legally onerous or unrequited. In sum, the methods used to effect divestiture can influence private savings. Our contention is that the mode of privatization used in Chile probably hindered private savings to a limited extent during the First Round. This contention is based on the fact that the system (described fully in Chapter 4) was biased, between 1974 and 1981, in favor of a small group with preferential access to credit and that it functioned within the framework of a relatively inefficient, segmented capital market. While the reverse occurred after 1985, the divestiture modes chosen may have even stimulated private savings, although not investment.

On the one hand, since divestitures during the First Round favored previous owners and large conglomerates in a shallow capital market, information on firms to be privatized was not widely disseminated, a factor that hampered greater savings. On the other hand, easier access to the financial market could have stimulated wider use of credit by buyers rather than increased savings. This argument is weak, however, since credit was extremely expensive and sooner or later credit users would have had to amortize their loans.[16] It can be also argued that greater use of credit to buy divested firms would have sent encouraging signals to other potential savers. Still, the impact of divestiture may not have been significant, since divestiture payments were only important as a percentage of private savings (more than 20 percent) in 1975, a recession year, and in 1977, while remaining below 5 percent after 1979 (Table 6.3).

Private savings showed greater dynamism during the Second Round than during the First, while the reverse is true for private investment. Opportunities, in addition to cyclical factors, help to explain this result. The diversification of modes of privatization may have helped raise private savings to some degree as well, for this set of modes did cater to a cross section of savers, in terms of income. But too much ought not be made of this argument. A significant part of payments for divestitures—about 30 percent—came from forced savings (funds accumulated for severance payments and social security), mostly from labor capitalism and institutional capitalism. Moreover, operations carried out through Chapter XIX did not involve new savings, as explained above. The greater diversity of modes of privatization could be characterized as an improvement in efficiency of the capital market: more information and a greater number of instruments available for savings. Greater market efficiency in the stimulation of savings, however, has not been demonstrated to date, even though market composition may have changed and reduced the effort necessary to achieve a given amount of savings, with a consequent positive effect on general welfare (Valdés 1988:100). In short, the effect of the diversity of privatization modes on private savings was limited. Moreover, it is difficult to see any relationship between the modes of privatization and the volume of investment.

The transfer of wealth.   Capital is a source of income and consequently of savings (investment). The mere act of buying SOEs would not enlarge private sector wealth; it would only alter the composition of its assets. This is true even if the efficiency of those firms rose in step with the transfer, unless market imperfections or deceit were to allow the private sector to internalize part of the present value of the efficiency gains. Moreover, it is well known that an increase in wealth is not necessarily concomitant with an increase in savings. However, to illustrate the order of magnitude involved and the resulting conclusions, saving will be assumed to occur in proportion to the full increase in returns of divested firms. If the increase in efficiency is supposed to increase returns by 2.5 percentage points (net of taxes)[17] on divested capital of about US$1 billion during the First Round and US$1.5 billion during the Second, then, all things being equal, private sector savings should have increased by about US$13 million per year during the First Round, only 0.9 percent of actual effective private gross savings, and by an average of US$44 million between 1985 and 1989 and US$63 million thereafter, which would represent about 3.0 percent of private savings. These estimates are clearly biased toward high figures, as returns of SOEs, when privatized, are assumed here to increase on average by 2.5 percentage points, which may appear to be relatively high on the basis of available, though scanty information, especially for those firms privatized during the First Round. In addition, the effect on total savings will depend also on the behavior of the state. And last but not least, increases in wealth may have negative effects on private savings. The empirical evidence concerning the effects of wealth on private savings is certainly not unequivocal and, if positive, is thin.

Public and total savings and investment

Did public savings and investment increase as a result of the revenue-raising privatization of state corporations? Divestiture funds are unrelated to public savings as measured in the national accounts. As shown in Chapter 5, the proceeds from SOE privatization represent deficit financing and not revenues. As such, they cannot, at the same time, be public savings (or dissavings). Consequently, only if private savings increase with privatization will aggregate savings also increase. Gains in efficiency internalized by the public sector in smoothly working markets do lead to increases in public wealth but not in public savings. Since we have already concluded that the privatization process affected private savings only marginally, its impact on aggregate savings, though positive, must also have been marginal.

From the point of view of investment, however, the government can use the proceeds of divestitures to finance either current or capital expenditures or debt reduction. The issue of assignment was discussed at length in Chapter 5 and the conclusion was somewhat complex.

The fiscal accounts of the central government show that between 1974 and 1978,[18] when most public assets were transferred, total current revenues increased from 21.9 percent to 23.0 percent of GDP, while current expenditures and capital expenditures decreased from 20.7 percent to 18.2 percent and from 11.7 percent to 5.6 percent of GDP, respectively. Finally, the deficit was reduced from 10.5 percent to 0.8 percent of GDP. This accounting suggests that the revenues obtained from divestiture did not stimulate public investment and that investment reduction (in terms of GDP) financed about two-thirds of the deficit.[19] On the other hand, during the Second Round (1984–1988), while current revenues were increasing at an average annual rate of 5.4 percent and current expenditures were falling at a rate of 2.8 percent, capital expenditures were rising at a rate of 5.0 percent (the rate was higher before 1987) and the deficit was systematically shrinking, to become a surplus at the end of the period.[20] This combination of trends suggests that proceeds from SOE divestitures probably financed part of the increase in public investment. Consequently, it appears that a higher level of aggregate investment was not made possible during the First Round of privatization but it was stimulated by the Second.

Thus, it is likely that during the First Round neither savings nor investment was stimulated by the privatization process. The new investment opportunities created by privatization did not attract private savings, much less external savings, and their influence on investment appears to have been neutral. The impact of the mode of divestiture on investment was similar, while it was somewhat negative for savings. Even if the transfer of wealth resulting from First Round of privatizations had initially been positive for the private sector, it was almost fully reversed before 1981, since privatized firms belonging to the main new conglomerates had lost their entire net worth. The effect of divestiture on public savings was nil; the effect on investment was probably neutral, or perhaps slightly positive, as a consequence of new investment opportunities. The results were different during the Second Round insofar as the combination of effects was positive on both savings and investment. Foreign savings were not affected by the privatization process after 1985, because many debt-equity swaps took place.

Employment

Privatization as a means of divestiture does not seem to have had negative effects on the number of persons employed during the period analyzed. On the contrary, although the adaptation of all firms—private and public—to the rules of the market in the 1970s created unemployment, the sale of public firms to the private sector per se was not a contributing cause. In the 1980s, that is, during the Second Round of divestitures, while relatively stable rules applied to all sorts of enterprises—private and public—employment in privatized firms actually increased with divestitures. In this section, employment is defined as the number of people employed. Because of a lack of information, we do not consider changes in composition—such as skills, age, and sex—or in hours worked.

During the First Round, it was feared that unemployment would increase as a direct result of the process, although the reason was never clear. Since this argument was raised again during the Second Round, though less forcefully, the logic and empirical ground of this position must be examined. One possibility is that, all else being equal, factor proportions are different in private and public sectors for similar activities.

This could be the case if public management took the social value of labor as the relevant criterion for choosing production technology, and the private sector took its market value, which is usually higher. The result would be a higher proportion of labor in public enterprises than in private firms and, consequently, a decline in employment when divestiture occurs. Another possibility is that firms owned or controlled by the public sector employ a higher than necessary proportion of workers under pressure from authorities to reduce unemployment or as political favors. Thus, public firms would participate in public programs of disguised unemployment, which are more difficult to impose on private firms. Then again, privatization would reduce employment, if the private sector were free to hire and fire as needed.

Under the first argument proposed above, comparable public and privatized firms would act differently with respect to employment, even within the same environment. In general, both types of firms experienced the sweeping changes that affected the entire economy. Trade and financial liberalizations called for significant changes in productivity. Also, privatized firms were generally expected to reduce employment relatively more than enterprises which, by remaining public, were not subject to the same market rules.[21] But, since public firms were also obliged to operate according to those rules during the period analyzed, it follows that they would have had to make adjustments similar to those of privatized firms. Thus, there should be no significant differences in employment behavior in the two types of firms during the process of privatization. However, these two types of firms should show a relatively higher reduction of employment than private enterprises, for public and privatized firms would have had initially a greater proportion of labor per unit of output than comparable private enterprises.

The Chilean experience suggests that privatized firms actually began with an overload of employment because of the disguised unemployment imposed by the government, at least between 1970 and 1973. Thus, it was expected that divestitures would be accompanied by a reduction in employment and, consequently, that comparable privatized and private firms would have different employment patterns after 1974 and during an adjustment period of a few years. The reduction was not expected to be significant compared with similar public firms, since disguised unemployment programs were discontinued after 1974.

The First Round

The employment behavior of all three types of firms was compared for the 1970–1983 period to test these hypotheses. The period chosen corresponds roughly to the First Round.

Methodology.   The analysis was based on a sample for each type of firm: privatized, public, and private. The relevant employment information was available only for the years 1970, 1974, 1976, 1979, and 1983. Although far from satisfactory, this information at least covered the pre- and post-privatization periods of the First Round.

Firms were classified according to the Standard International Industrial Classification (SIIC), but the results were given for aggregates, which are less reliable. Unfortunately, missing information for the SIIC subsectoral two-digit categories precluded potentially interesting conclusions on differential behavior between tradables and nontradables, and between exportables and importables. Consequently, a clear link between privatization and trade liberalization could not be established.

Employment after 1974 was affected by the elimination of disguised unemployment. The latter is assumed here to have arisen during the presidential period of Allende and so is here christened the "Allende effect." The first step in our empirical analysis was to estimate that effect and eliminate it from the relevant information on employment between 1974 and 1983. Thus, we obtained an estimate of what employment would have been had firms not been obliged to hire unnecessary labor between 1970 and 1973. These figures were obtained by applying subsectoral employment-production elasticities, calculated from the 1960–1970 time series, to changes in production observed in each subsector between 1970 and 1973.[22]

Normal employment for 1974, minus the actual employment in that year, represented the Allende effect. The estimate was made first at the level of individual firms, then aggregated at the two-digit SIIC subsectoral level, and then aggregated to obtain the total for each sample of privatized and public firms.

In order to test the first hypothesis (the adjustment of divested firms to changes in labor prices, that is from the shadow price of labor to market value), we eliminated the Allende effect or disguised unemployment from total employment figures of the firms belonging to the sample. We assumed that firms eliminated the Allende effect on a linear basis between 1974 and 1979.[23] Thus, 1976 employment at the firm level— the only figure available between 1974 and 1979—was reduced by 60 percent of the excess employment generated at that level, since it was assumed that about 60 percent of the initial disguised unemployment remained in the relevant firms. By the same token, corrections were made on employment figures for 1979 and 1983, since disguised unemployment related to the Allende effect had been fully eliminated by then, or, at least, it was so assumed.

Results and conclusions.   As expected, disguised unemployment was much greater in privatized firms than in private firms. Disguised unemployment represented 24.4 percent of 1970 employment for privatized firms and less than 6 percent for private firms (Hachette and Lüders 1988: Appendix III–2, Table III–1). However, this last figure may be an underestimate, since the calculation of the relevant Allende effect was based partly on employment figures for 1972 instead of 1970 because of a lack of information; it is possible that by then some private firms already had been subjected to pressure to hire more workers than they needed. Nevertheless, the error is small since the pressure was not particularly strong before mid–1972. The bias in the results is likely to be reversed when it is observed that this sample of privatized firms includes none liquidated after 1974. Obviously one of the reasons others failed was that they carried an unbearable overload of labor when transferred to the private sector.

Unexpectedly, the Allende effect was weaker for public enterprises (17.1 percent) than for privatized firms (24.4 percent), which were controlled by the public sector during only part of the 1971–1973 period. This result is consistent with the hypothesis that the relatively stronger management of public enterprises was better able to avoid pressure from the authorities; by contrast, the management of privatized firms was in disarray when transferred to the public sector, and consequently could have been easily compelled to hire nonessential labor.

When the Allende effect was eliminated between 1974 and 1976, privatized firms did behave like public enterprises in reducing employment, although to a lesser degree (Table 6.4). After 1976, significant differences in employment levels do appear: the privatized firms increased employment between 1976 and 1979 while the opposite was true for public firms. Both reduced their labor force between 1979 and 1983, but privatized

TABLE 6.4

Employment Changes by Type of Firm, 1970–1983
(percentage, net of Allende effect)

Type of firm	1970–1974	1974–1976	1976–1979	1979–1983
All sectors				
Public	1.6	−9.7	−6.1	−23.2
Privatized	3.1	−4.0	21.2	−6.4
Private	2.0	−8.7	1.5	−19.4
Manufacturing sector				
Public	2.2	−6.7	−7.1	−34.7
Privatized	2.1	−14.3	55.4	−9.8
Private	2.2	−10.6	−2.2	−20.2

SOURCE: D. Hachette and R. Lüders, "Aspects of Privatization: The Case of Chile, 1974–1985" (Santiago: Institute of Economics, Pontifical Catholic University of Chile, 1988), mimeo, Appendix III–2.

firms to a lesser degree. At first glance, all the results run counter to the first hypothesis, which postulated that privatized firms would generally hire less labor when operating by the rules of the market, since their relevant price for hiring would be the market price and not the shadow price that eventually could have been used by public firms.

To be consistent with this hypothesis, results should show a greater reduction in employment in privatized firms than in public and private firms up to 1976. From 1976 to 1983, when market rules were applied to public firms as well, public and privatized enterprises should show a greater reduction (and a lower increase) of employment relative to private firms. The results, however, do not support the hypothesis. When employment is reduced in privatized firms (1974–1976 and 1979–1983), it declines much more in public enterprises at the same time, which is the expected result. When employment increases in privatized firms (1976–1979), it continues to decline in the public firms, which is not the expected result. In addition, the rate of employment in private firms, rather than rising less than the rate of the other two groups or remaining higher when the rate falls, is actually in between the rates of the other two groups.

The first contradiction, the large difference in behavior between privatized and public firms, may be more apparent than real. Employment reduction, greater in public than privatized firms, reflects public enterprises' structural adjustments to the market rules imposed on them. This meant reducing labor more than required by the Allende effect. The result achieved, then, is consistent with the first hypothesis, although the adjustment seems unexpectedly high. However, this may be the reasonable consequence of the laying off of a significant quantity of excess labor, hired over a period of decades, in order to begin to play a completely new game in which market rules require firms to adopt new technologies to keep pace with changing market conditions. The difference in the composition of samples also helps explain the second contradiction observed in the results.

The sample of firms suffered from the fact that the two-digit SIIC subsectors were unevenly represented. Consequently, the results observed on employment variations are strongly influenced by changes unrelated to privatization, such as commercial and financial liberalization and recession, each of which affects subsectors differently.[24]

An interesting question is whether privatized firms would have acted differently had they remained in the public sector. This can be studied by comparing similar firms in the privatized and public sectors at the two-digit level. It was shown previously that first, the public firms of the sample generated less employment and more unemployment, net of the Allende effect, than did the privatized firms. This conclusion, qualified by certain differences in the sample composition, still suggests that privatized firms could not have caused less employment (or more unemployment) by remaining in the public sector. Second, the main reasons for the differences in behavior of similar privatized and public firms at the two-digit level were differences in the sample composition, plus the likely nonoptimal labor employment of public firms before the Allende effect made its impact felt, as explained above.

Our conclusions from this analysis are first, that changes in employment were unrelated to the privatization process per se. What did affect employment was the fact that all firms were exposed to the rules of the market. In other words, had divested firms remained in the public sector and been subjected to the rules of the market, the employment outcome would not have been very different. Another question is whether public firms should play by the same rules as private firms, a largely philosophical and ideological question. Second, the differences in the samples make comparisons difficult; thus, the conclusions presented above are only tentative, although they seem reasonable.

The Second Round

The scanty evidence available suggests that, if privatization had some impact on employment during the Second Round, it was positive, although not very significant (Table 6.5). Total employment of the ten divested SOEs increased systematically after 1985. Part of this trend is explained by the recovery from the 1982–1983 recession, the sustained growth of demand after recovery, favorable conditions in international markets (for the Chemical and Mining Society of Chile, SOQUIMICH), and supportive policies (for the National Sugar Industry, IANSA). In addition, the privatization strategy of CAP, for example, by permitting rapid new investments directly related to steel production that otherwise might not have been made, certainly stimulated a fraction of the 50 percent increase in employment since its divestiture.

These results are consistent with those obtained for the First Round in the sense that privatization per se—as defined in this research—does not seem to have been a significant factor in employment and unemployment trends. Furthermore, the data presented in Table 6.5 for the period before divestitures underline the importance of the Allende effect (compare 1973 with 1970) and show its gradual elimination by 1981; they are consistent with the hypothesis that even public firms, when exposed to market rules, can reduce excess labor just as well as any private enterprise. Of course, the observed result may appear related to privatization, if this process is defined as including the application of market rules to public firms. But this is neither the definition used here nor the one referred to when critics (unions, in particular) have voiced their disagreement with privatization and its likely negative impact on employment.

TABLE 6.5
Employment in Ten Firms Privatized after 1984, 1970–1989

Firm	1970	1973	1974	1975	1976	1977	1978	1979	1980	1981	1982	1983	1984	1985	1986	1987	1988	1989
CHILGENER	n.a.	n.a.	n.a.	n.a.	n.a.	n.a.	n.a.	n.a.	n.a.	n.a.	n.a.	n.a.	748	779	819	852[a]	869	845
CHILQUINTA	n.a.	n.a.	n.a.	n.a.	n.a.	n.a.	n.a.	n.a.	n.a.	n.a.	n.a.	n.a.	948	968	983[a]	956	770	746
CHILMETRO	n.a.	n.a.	n.a.	n.a.	n.a.	n.a.	n.a.	n.a.	n.a.	n.a.	n.a.	n.a.	2,283	2,421	2,631[a]	2,746	2,828	2,962
ENDESA[b]	n.a.	8,504	8,460	5,776	5,629	5,530	4,763	4,270	4,018	2,828	2,728	2,705	2,813	2,950	2,905	2,928	2,925[a]	2,980
CTC	n.a.	n.a.	n.a.	n.a.	n.a.	n.a.	n.a.	n.a.	n.a.	n.a.	n.a.	n.a.	6,635	6,850	7,185	7,374	7,518[a]	7,366
CAP	7,045	12,493	11,637	11,363	11,065	10,822	9,886	9,321	9,049	7,944	6,961	n.a.	4,062	6,656	6,767[a]	6,923	9,329	9,785
IANSA	2,214	2,825	2,881	3,143	3,423	3,524	2,386	1,598	852	642	673	1,079	1,434	1,702	2,029	2,102	2,022[a]	2,144
SOQUIMICH	10,504[c]	10,900	10,684	10,246	9,247	8,264	8,024	7,109	6,534	5,005	4,421	4,053	4,402	4,442	4,704[a]	5,024	6,001	5,453
ENTEL	1,151	1,312	1,421	1,475	1,459	1,173	1,192	1,236	1,261	1,311	1,336	1,336	1,366	1,386	1,402	1,456	1,460[a]	1,546
Laboratorio Chile	567	987	844	810	687	735	778	660	669	545	517	527	559	586	592	618[a]	681	749
Total	21,581	37,021	35,927	32,813	31,510	30,048	27,029	24,194	22,383	18,275	16,636	9,700	25,250	28,740	30,017	30,979	34,403	34,576

n.a. = not available.
a. Year in which the private sector share reached 51 percent.
b. Corresponds to ENDESA Matriz.
c. 1971.
SOURCE: CHILGENER, CHILQUINTA, CHILMETRO, ENDESA, CTC, CAP, IANSA, SOQUIMICH, ENTEL, and Laboratorio Chile.

SEVEN

Are Private and Public Enterprises Different?

Are asset ownership and efficiency related? If so, how? To what extent? Does the Chilean privatization experience suggest interesting and significant conclusions in this area? Does that experience indicate a change in the behavior of the firms once privatized? Apart from efficiency and employment, what other facets may be influenced by divestiture? These questions are at the heart of the privatization issue. They are, however, complicated matters, where the theory is still developing in the almost total absence of empirical evidence. In these circumstances, the aims of this chapter will necessarily be modest.

We look at the issue of differences between private and public firms from several perspectives. We begin by focusing on the relationship among competition, regulations, and efficiency, drawing on specific cases of privatization of traditional public enterprises. The approach followed is essentially theoretical. More detailed descriptions of competitive conditions and regulations in the productive sectors where privatization was significant are left for Appendix E. We then present the main conclusions of our comparative study of several groups of firms, in an effort to discover behavioral differences between private and public firms and the likely effects of divestiture. Although we consider efficiency, given measurement limitations we necessarily treat it as a by-product of the research. We base our analysis on the assumption that differences among groups go beyond efficiency considerations. The approach is essentially descriptive. Two different methodologies based on ratio analysis are applied to different time periods with partial overlapping; each case covers distinct groups of firms.

Privatization, Competitive Forces, and Regulation

Efficiency and privatization are two different concepts. Public ownership had been considered, in Chile, to be a solution to problems related to allocative efficiency derived from market failures, such as externalities or impossibility of competition. Even if optimal allocative efficiency had been reached, however, which was not the case, internal efficiency was neglected. The efficient control of public enterprises, which could have been a partial substitute for competition, became ever more difficult as a result of continuous demand and technology changes (for example, in telecommunications). It became clear, then, that competitive conditions, even if imperfect, and improved regulations would be required to increase efficiency—allocative and internal—for both public and privatized enterprises. The question was therefore whether the potential competitive conditions at the moment of divestiture were sufficient to ensure a reasonable degree of both types of efficiency. If not, the task was to discover how to regulate the different industries being privatized to create competitive conditions. The answer was clear for only a few traditional state-owned enterprises (SOEs), such as the Steel Company of the Pacific (CAP), for which competition was ensured long before its actual divestiture by the relatively low tariff on imports and the absence of quantitative trade restrictions established during the First Round. It was not at all clear for the other enterprises to be divested.

The disciplining effect of competition and opportunities for innovation were considered important conditions for efficiency, both static and dynamic. Creating these conditions in Chile, however, would not be easy. For example, if a divested firm had a preponderant share of the market (which would be the case for most of the traditional public firms in the areas of electricity, telecommunications, air transport, steel, sugar production, and nitrates), only the entry and growth of new rivals could provide competitive discipline. In their absence, regulation to make entry threats effective would be required. Would the forces of potential competition operate with such efficiency as to remove or diminish the need for regulation? And then, would the liberalization policies applied to public enterprises require regulation to ensure effective competition?

In the Chilean context, the contestability theory may not be relevant to describe likely competitive conditions or threats in the divested sectors. To the extent that sunk costs[1] (not fixed) were important and given the dominant position of the divested enterprises, entry threats, on their own, may have been insufficient to ensure competitive conditions in the relevant industry. The government then had to adopt effective competition policies to prevent anticompetitive behavior against potential entrants in various markets and submarkets (for instance, telecommunications and airline transport).

Strategic entry deterrence or predatory behavior can limit effective competition by making the threat of responding to entry credible. Firms can take several actions to prevent or retard entry by competitors. On the cost side these include overcapacity (undercapacity, in some circumstances), cost-reducing research and development expenditures, high salaries to raise rivals' costs, and preemptive patenting (with resulting sleeping patents). On the demand side they include advertising, brand proliferation or product differentiation, low prices as a signal of high efficiency or of low demand, and aggressive pricing. The individual circumstances of each divested industry would influence the choice of either entry deterrence or accommodation and, consequently, make a simple presentation of the matter difficult in this chapter. Nevertheless, it is a fascinating and important topic for further research.

Another issue that liberalization policies raised at the time of divestiture was how to promote and maintain effective competition in activities where there existed a monopoly in related activities. The Telephone Company of Chile (CTC), for example, was a natural monopoly in its local network but subject to competition in long-distance calls. In the electricity subsector, transmission and distribution have the characteristics of a natural monopoly, while generation activity is competitive. The satellite connection held by the National Telecommunications Company (ENTEL) makes it a natural monopoly, while its other activities are competitive. Actually, there is a wide range of circumstances in which the monopolist could profitably refuse to supply at reasonable prices inputs required by its competitors in related activities. Two measures can safeguard competition: vertical separation and interconnection. Both measures were adopted in the case of electricity and later in telecommunications (CTC and ENTEL).

Vertical separation in the case of electricity (separating generation from transmission and distribution) allows competition but may have drawbacks for social welfare under specific assumptions, such as fixed proportions (the double-wedge problem; Vickers and Yarrow 1988). Interconnection, or the regulation of the price at which the potentially competitive subsector is to obtain the input from the natural monopoly, is another policy measure to combat the natural monopoly desire to exclude potential subsector competitors. Interconnection is also required to ensure competitive conditions when network externalities are present (for example, in telecommunications). Appendix E explains how both processes were carried out in Chile.

One way to regulate a potential monopoly is through franchising or competitive auction of the monopoly. If successful, this approach stimulates competition and efficiency and destroys undesirable information monopolies. This approach commonly faces difficulties, such as uncompetitive bidding resulting from collusion between bidders, from strategic advantages on the part of the holder of the franchise to be renewed, or from information asymmetries that would deter competition with the knowledgeable firm. There is, however, no hard evidence of such behavior in Chile. Other problems can arise from the asset handover, especially in bilateral monopolies,[2] and from difficulties of specification and administration of franchises due to technological and market uncertainty. In the latter case, incomplete contracts occur more frequently than costly complete contracts, but the former require monitoring. Incomplete contracts do not consider all possible outcomes and therefore require discretionary decisions during the contract period. If significant uncertainties exist, the advantages of franchising are limited. Nevertheless this option was taken in several cases (ENTEL, CTC, and LAN Chile).

To encourage competition in the electricity sector, a virtual public monopoly before its divestiture, authorities applied the principle of what Vickers and Yarrow (1988) have called yardstick competition. This option illustrates the proposition that, given asymmetric information, when a principal has many agents under control the optimal incentive scheme involves the creation of circumstances in which the rewards of each agent are contingent upon the performance of other agents, as well as his own (this arrangement was used for CHILMETRO and CHILQUINTA). Thus, the price that one agent can charge depends on costs incurred by others. Incentives for allocative and internal efficiency exist, provided agents face similar circumstances (in the absence of collusion). Internal efficiency exists because each retains the benefits of its cost-reducing activities, and allocative efficiency is obtained because industry prices are kept in line with industry costs. However, environmental characteristics may differ among firms. In those cases, some reduced form of regulation could be used, based on diverse observable characteristics among firms (this is the system used for ENDESA, CHILGENER, Pilmaiquén, and Pehuenche).

Regulation to provide for freedom of entry is also required to maintain effective competition. Apart from the specific caveats in the legislation governing privatization (Appendix E), the body of antimonopoly legislation and related institutions existing at the time of divestiture constituted the basic framework for competitive entry. Was it effective? Was it adequate for privatized public utilities? Who is to apply the regulations, and does it make sense to legislate before privatization (with uncertainty)? These are important questions to be answered.

Another important issue is the relevance of regulations in the face of asymmetric information. Firms make monopoly profits, thanks to their monopoly on information, while the price usually exceeds marginal costs and generates allocative inefficiency. How does the regulator obtain information about costs in order to fix the price of electricity? (Appendix E). Setting the price equal to unit cost does not stimulate internal efficiency through cost-reducing efforts, but it does promote allocative efficiency. Setting a maximum price may stimulate cost-reducing efforts and internal efficiency but not allocative efficiency. A compromise implies lower output and higher prices than desirable (or attainable with symmetric information), together with inefficiency and rents from the monopoly of information. This is another significant problem intimately related to the divestiture of some public enterprises that must be studied in theoretical and empirical terms. In any case, adjusted marginal cost pricing, if feasible, is the optimum solution.

Comparative Analysis

One of the hypotheses that supported the process of divestiture between 1974 and 1989 is that private enterprises are better managed than public concerns. If that is true, the efficiency of divested enterprises should come to resemble that of private more than public firms, all other things being equal. On the other hand, it is to be expected that firm behavior would differ according to rules and regulations that affect dimensions other than internal and allocative efficiency. Investment and indebtedness are two cases in point. Consequently, in this section, we will draw conclusions about the behavior of several groups of firms within the process of privatization. These conclusions, even if clear-cut, are drawn from the Chilean experience and therefore must be generalized with caution.

The availability of information about different groups of firms, particularly traditional public firms, imposes unavoidable limits on this analysis. Furthermore, all comparisons will be based on a vector of ratios obtained from available balance sheets and income statements. These ratios will then be used as proxies for different factors: investment, indebtedness, relations with other firms, and efficiency. Although this approach may help to contrast behavior among groups of firms, it may be insufficient to cover such a complicated facet as efficiency in a precise fashion. By using ratios taken from balances, the analysis of both internal and allocative efficiency is implicitly left aside, although it is not completely absent. It also should be clear that a significant difference in efficiency-related ratios, for example, between private and public firms, may only reflect the pursuance of objectives other than benefit maximization and not differences in "economic" efficiency. So conclusions drawn from a comparative analysis based on ratios should be interpreted with care. However, the answers to the following questions may suggest discrepancies or similarities in behavior which, if added to a priori judgments based on experience or on theoretical analysis, carry considerable weight: Did the investment behavior of privatized and intervened firms differ from that of those that remained private? Did they become more or less indebted? How did their results compare with those of other private and state-owned firms? What are the reasons for differences?

Methodology

The effects of privatization in Chile will be analyzed through ratios based on balance sheets and income statements. We chose two different approaches based on comparisons of specific ratios among different groups of firms. The first approach seeks to reveal differences among private, privatized, and public firms in terms of investment, indebtedness, relations with other enterprises, and efficiency, using combinations of nine or ten different ratios. The financial ratios are as follows:

R1: inventories/total assets

R2: investment in related companies/total assets

R3: operational results/total assets

R4: financial expenditures/debt

R5: total benefits/total assets

R6: distributed dividends/total assets

R7: current liabilities/total liabilities

R8: long-term liabilities/total liabilities

R9: debt/total assets

R10: investment/total assets

This method relies on information gathered between 1980 and 1987—that is, overlapping both rounds of privatization but including slightly more of the Second Round. The firms included in the sample are assembled into six groups:

1. eighty-two private enterprises that have always been in the private sector

2. sixteen firms that belonged to the odd sector after 1982 until their reprivatization in 1984 and after

3. twelve firms, originally private, that became legally public before 1974 and were privatized after that year

4. fourteen firms, originally private, in which the state intervened in the period 1971–1973; management control was returned to the legitimate owners after 1973

5. twelve traditional public firms privatized after 1985

6. eight traditional public firms that are still public

We then used discriminant and canonical variate analysis to determine which ratio variables best explain the differences among the six groups.

The second approach makes a simple comparison among groups of firms based on the historical evolution of chosen ratios beginning in 1965 and ending in 1985. This approach, although insufficient in itself, throws some light on particular insititutional and policy changes that occurred during that period. In this case groups of firms are distinguished on the basis of one ratio rather than combinations of nine or ten ratios.

The main difference between the two approaches, besides the period covered and the set of firms selected, is the use of econometric criteria in the first approach to determine the statistical significance of differences found. Neither of the two approaches is really Round specific, with the above-mentioned caveats. Methodological details on the first approach can be found in Appendix C, while the full empirical justification for the basic conclusions presented here is given in Hachette and Lüders 1991.

Basic conclusions

First, on the whole, firms classified in any of the six groups chosen are adequately classified when a vector of nine or ten weighted financial ratios permits discrimination among those groups. This means that when these ratios are used to differentiate one firm from another, the latter can be meaningfully put together in differentiated groups called private, public, etc. One example is presented in Table 7.1, where the extreme cases of never-divested traditional private firms (group 1) and never-divested traditional public firms (group 6) are compared.

Second, no significant differences of behavior have been found among public, private, and privatized enterprises under similar sets of rules and regulations. This was found to be true even when such diverse criteria as those related to efficiency, investment, indebtedness, and relations with other firms were lumped together. Although statistical differences could

TABLE 7.1

Discriminant Analysis of Groups 1 and 6

A priori classification	Classification based on R1–R9		
	Group 1	Group 6	Total
Group 1			
Number of firms	499	132	631
Percentage	79.1	20.9	100.0
Group 6			
Number of firms	25	39	64
Percentage	39.1	60.9	100.0
Total			
Number of firms	524	171	695
Percentage	75.4	24.7	100.0

A priori classification	Classification based on R1–R10		
	Group 1	Group 6	Total
Group 1			
Number of firms	334	61	395
Percentage	84.6	15.4	100.0
Group 6			
Number of firms	20	20	40
Percentage	50.0	50.0	100.0
Total			
Number of firms	354	81	435
Percentage	81.4	18.6	100.0

Source: Authors' estimates.

be found among different groups and every group could be distinguished from the others, the differences observed were so small in absolute values that, for all practical purposes, the results obtained do not demonstrate any important dissimilarity between public and private firms when they are playing by similar rules of the game.

Third, public firms adapted rapidly to changes in regulations, becoming more similar to private enterprises. One of the most striking results of the analysis from 1965 to 1985 is the difference, after the military takeover, between the behavior of SOEs and other groups of enterprises. The SOEs reduced their already low indebtedness level relatively little, they were more conservative with respect to new investments, and they managed to improve their results relative to those of the private sector (Figures 7.1, 7.2, and 7.3 illustrate some of these characteristics).

FIGURE 7.1
Ratio of Debt to Total Assets in Selected Years, 1965–1985

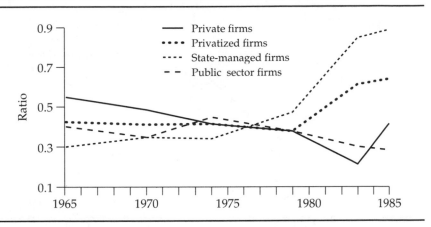

SOURCE: Authors' estimates.

FIGURE 7.2
Ratio of Operational Income to Total Assets in Selected Years, 1965–1985

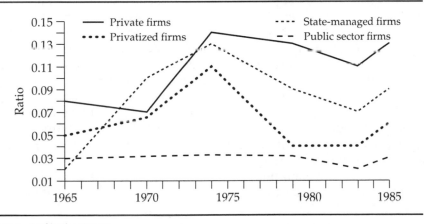

SOURCE: Authors' estimates.

Information obtained from the stock exchange reinforces the impression of marked improvement in the behavior of public enterprises, reflected in significant gains in market value compared with the privately managed companies. The available information also suggests a slightly better performance for the 1976–1982 period for the private firms compared with

FIGURE 7.3

Ratio of Total Investment to Total Assets in Selected Years, 1965–1985

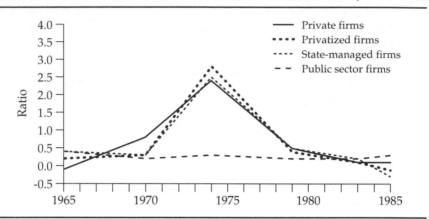

SOURCE: Authors' estimates.

the privatized and state-managed firms. This result probably reflects the higher excess indebtedness level of the latter categories.

These exceptionally good results for state enterprises can be attributed to many factors. Most important, the government evaluated management on the basis of profit maximization, the same basis used for enterprises in the private sector. Similarly, state enterprises had to finance themselves, which limited their investment possibilities. Moreover, public enterprises did not receive any state guarantees to assume new indebtedness during most of the period 1974–1987. As a logical counterpart to the previous set of policies, the government fixed profitable tariffs (to allow SOEs, if efficiently managed, to achieve a return of 10 percent on assets) for most public utilities, and in general refrained from interfering in the management of corporations. At the same time, government control over eventual results was increased through the creation of a centralized information system and the demand that state enterprises provide a set of monthly data similar to that required from private corporations with publicly traded shares. Finally, in an effort to allow the private sector to expand and to reduce public entrepreneurial activities, the government forbade some state enterprises from undertaking profitable investment projects if it believed the private sector could conduct them as well. This policy probably prevented new indebtedness and further losses once interest rates rose again during 1981.

Of course, the fact that SOEs behaved more like private firms does not imply that both are internally efficient today. It only means that the SOEs reduced their level of inefficiency, while their other objectives—mainly redistributive—faded. It could be argued that the entire effort to improve the economic performance of traditional SOEs in the 1970s was in preparation for a new round of divestitures. But this view is contradicted by government officials' belief in the late 1970s that the public enterprises remaining after the First Round of privatizations had strategic importance. There is no doubt, however, that the satisfactory results achieved by the state enterprises during the late 1970s and early 1980s facilitated the last round of divestitures, especially the sales to pension funds and workers.

Fourth, it is interesting to note that the ratios that best discriminate among different groups of firms concern indebtedness (R7, current liabilities/total liabilities; R8, long-term liabilities/total liabilities; and R9, debt/total assets) and relations with other enterprises (R2, investment in related companies). In a few cases, ratios related to efficiency explain behavioral differences (R3, operational results/total assets; R5, total benefits/total assets; and R6, dividends/total assets) (Table 7.2). This outcome is consistent with the fact that, if, on the one hand, rules were made more competitive for the public firms, they were still ties attached to specific facets of their management such as indebtedness and investment, and on the other hand, the levels and ratios of indebtedness were significantly lower for them than for the other firms at the beginning of the period used to make the relevant comparisons.

TABLE 7.2
Best Discriminant Variables

Groups	R1–R9		R1–R10	
	Can_1	Can_2	Can_1	Can_2
1, 6	R7		R10	
1-2-3-4, 5-6	R2		R2	
1-2-3-4, 5,6	R2	R6	R2	R1
1, 2-3-4-5, 6	R8	R2	R8	R2
1-3-4, 2, 5-6	R8	R6	R8,R9	R10
2, 3, 4, 5	R2	R5	R2	R8
1, 2, 3, 4, 5, 6	R8	R3	R8	R3

Blank cell indicates that no variable discriminates among these groups.
NOTE: Can_1 and Can_2 refer to the canonic axes 1 and 2. Can_1 gives the combination of financial ratios that best discriminates among groups. Can_2 gives the combinaiton that discriminates second best.
SOURCES: D. Hachette and R. Lüders, "Privatizing the Economy" (Santiago: Institute of Economics, Pontifical Catholic University of Chile, 1991, processed); Tables D.7 and D.8 in Appendix D.

Finally, we must stress that the empirical conclusions refer to an exceptional period in Chile's history in which the rules applied to SOEs were similar to those that governed the private sector. Public choice theory, however, suggests that such a case may be unstable. It says that in the medium and long term political pressures are likely to produce a change in the rules, which would allow SOEs to be used for patronage and for supplying merit goods at "low" prices—that is, to become inefficient.

EIGHT

Two Polemic Cases of Privatization: CAP and ENDESA

Not all public enterprises were divested by the straightforward methods described in previous chapters, such as popular capitalism, labor capitalism, institutional capitalism, direct sale, or open bidding. For example, the government transferred the Investment Steel Company of the Pacific (CAP) to the private sector partially in an indirect way through a repurchase of shares, which reduced its net worth. In other cases, preparation for divestiture involved major surgery. Before privatizing the airline LAN Chile and the National Electricity Company (ENDESA), the government transferred a significant share of their liabilities to the State Development Corporation (CORFO). These operations were strongly criticized from different quarters and at this writing still raise numerous strong objections. Consequently, we want to tackle these issues in depth and to give a detailed view of some specific divestiture operations, to improve understanding of the actual process of privatization. Here we present a detailed account of two polemic cases, CAP and ENDESA, in the hope of putting these delicate issues in proper perspective.

The Reprivatization of CAP: A Gift from CORFO to Former Shareholders?

The reprivatization of CAP triggered more criticism than almost any other privatization. One author describes the repurchase operation that produced a substantive part of the privatization of CAP as the privatization of enterprises by means of equity operations without any share transactions with the private sector. The best-known case is CAP's privatization, in which the company bought a considerable part of its shares from CORFO and later annulled them. Thanks to this operation, private shareholders increased their participation in the company from 16 percent to 49 percent, without a significant disbursement. [They lost assets (cash) in proportion to their share in the capital of CAP.] This has been one of the most criticized operations of the privatization program, not only with respect to the procedure employed, but also with respect to the prices at which the CAP shares were valued, both in the previous sale to the private sector and in the sale of the shares to CORFO (Marcel 1989a).

This section will study the causes and consequences of this share repurchase operation and analyze other interesting aspects of the privatization of the enterprise, including the preparation for the operation, the policy and management changes it generated in the company, and the role of labor capitalism.

Historical background

The historical evolution of CAP ownership is directly related to the prevailing economic and political trends of each period. The Steel Company of the Pacific was constituted as a private enterprise in April 1946 and organized as a stock company, with capital contributions from CORFO (33 percent), the Bank for the Amortization of the Public Debt (14 percent), and private shareholders (53 percent). In July 1968, a state takeover of the company was initiated. CORFO signed an agreement to increase the state share in the company to 41 percent and then to 54 percent. In November 1970 CORFO acquired a package of shares that made the state 98.8 percent owner, of which 82.2 percent belonged to CORFO. By the end of 1972, the private sector share of stock ownership had decreased to 0.98 percent, and the following year, to 0.4 percent. Significant investments were made after 1973, financed mainly through debt.[1] In 1974, there was a radical change in the rules of the game for public enterprises, which were subsequently obliged to finance themselves: personnel cuts and investment program reviews ensued. This, together with a worldwide fall in demand for steel after 1975, called for extensive transformations in the operational and administrative structure of the company.

By the end of 1989, CAP was constituted as a holding company, whose main source of income was steel. It had annual consolidated sales of approximately US$200 million, of which 87 percent came from the domestic market and 13 percent from sales abroad.

The reprivatization of CAP was one of the slowest within the whole restructuring process, not so much because of the indifference of authorities with respect to its divestiture as because of a lack of private investor interest in acquiring CAP shares at stock market prices.

Preparations for privatization

As mentioned, after the military government took over in 1973, there was a radical change in the treatment of public enterprises (see in particular Chapter 2 and Appendix E). In essence, self-financing and a strict control on investments were imposed on state-owned enterprises (SOEs), while their prices and tariffs (on services) were allowed to be fixed by market forces. One of the main objectives of the new policy orientation was to curb the strong inflationary pressures inherited from the previous government by reducing fiscal support for SOEs. Although that policy shift was not for the explicit purpose of privatizing public enterprises, it contributed to their subsequent divestiture by improving their financial performance.

Moreover, the military government added new policies with respect to SOEs and modified others between its takeover in 1973 and the beginning of the Second Round of privatization in 1985. Among these were policies leading to the privatization of many SOEs, including CAP. For instance, the ministerial programs of 1975 established that public enterprises and the public sector in general were not allowed to hire additional labor, fixing a maximum number of staff for each enterprise and public service, to be made effective within a short period.[2] In order to finance themselves, they were obliged to sell dispensable assets and gather resources in the domestic and foreign capital markets. In 1979, the ministerial programs established that public enterprises would no longer be entitled to special benefits, while receiving, in exchange, greater management flexibility, although not in investment decisions. In addition, it was established that they should not broaden their scope of action, but rather should concentrate on those specific activities for which they had been created. Thus, public firms transferred all those activities not directly related to their main line of business to the private sector. Public enterprises therefore faced the same restrictions as private enterprises, while losing one of the main benefits enjoyed by the latter: free allocation of investment funds and the possibility of diversifying. That same year, the government instructed CAP not to contract additional debt.[3]

These governmental policy reforms were reflected in the CAP implementation of an administrative and financial rationalization process that continued until 1985, which improved its performance substantially and implied personnel cuts carried out mainly by not filling vacant positions (Table 8.1).

In 1980, CAP was instructed by the ministerial programs to divest its unexploited mining concessions. In addition, the company was requested

TABLE 8.1
Evolution of CAP Performance, 1979–1989

	1979	1980	1981	1982	1983	1984	1985	1986	1987	1988	1989
Investment/equity (%)	3.7	2.2	1.9	1.1	0.6	1.8	1.4	1.4	1.4	18.6	29.6
Ratio of indebtedness to investment	11.9	3.8	17.8	6.7	6.1	9.3	18.3	0.0	0.0	0.3	0.9
Ratio of total debt to equity	0.9	0.8	0.9	0.9	0.9	0.9	0.9	0.9	0.7	0.5	0.7
Ratio of long-term debt to equity	0.7	0.6	0.7	0.7	0.6	0.6	0.7	0.7	0.6	0.2	0.4
Ratio of current liabilities to current assets	0.8	0.6	0.6	0.8	0.9	0.6	0.3	0.5	0.6	1.0	0.9
Profits/equity (%)	0.2	3.8	−6.5	−9.6	0.7	0.9	1.3	2.3	4.6	8.8	10.6
Operational profits/equity (%)	4.2	5.4	0.0	−1.8	6.1	7.5	7.4	8.5	8.5	17.0	17.0
Taxes paid/gross profits (%)	0.0	3.7	0.0	0.0	0.0	14.3	44.1	21.9	9.3	13.2	5.2
Personnel	9,321	9,049	7,944	6,961	n.a.	6,630	6,656	6,767	6,923	9,403	n.a.

n.a. = not available.
SOURCE: CAP annual reports.

to submit a program of stock issues to reduce indebtedness and increase private sector participation in ownership. In April of that year, CAP's Extraordinary General Assembly of Stockholders agreed to increase capital by around US$65 million, distributed in about 260 million shares with a nominal unit value of US$0.25, equivalent to 40.4 percent of total shares issued. Nevertheless, during 1980, no one was interested in taking out an option on them at that price.

In 1981, CAP's administrative structure changed as a result of ministerial programs that stipulated that it should operate as a holding company. The reform sought an effective division of activities through the creation of subsidiary enterprises, making administration by objectives possible, with independent profit centers. As a consequence, the company's name and purpose were changed: its name became the Investment Steel Company of the Pacific, and its purpose, the investment of capital for any kind of objective in order to obtain maximum profitability.[4] That year, to implement the new organization, the following subsidiaries were created: the Huachipato Steel Company, the Mining Company of the Pacific, Commercial Steel, Atacama Manganese, the Steel Company of Rengo, Pacific Ores & Trading N.V., and CAP Supplies.

In July 1981, the first potential buyer, William A. Wilson, appeared. He withdrew his offer in February 1982, having lost interest in the investment at the price demanded by CORFO (US$0.25 per share). In May 1983, the legal deadline for the increase of capital agreed upon in 1980 was reached with a subscription and payment of only 0.4 percent of the issued shares. The initial attempts to reprivatize CAP were, therefore, unsuccessful.

The sale of CAP

In 1984, the previous agreement, authorizing the floating of shares for approximately US$82 million, was revalidated. This arrangement would leave CORFO with 51 percent of the stock of CAP and private parties with 49 percent. The deadline for the sale of shares of this preferential issue was November 16, 1987. To attain this objective, CAP distributed ten thousand copies of a prospectus containing information on the company's history and projections for the 1985–1990 period. Based on these projections, a price of US$0.25 per share was maintained, identical to the offer price for the 1980 issue. At that moment, the relevant price in the stock exchange was US$0.12.

As of September 1985, only 10 percent of the total issue had been sold, of which CAP workers and executives had acquired 90 percent with the help of special loans. This lack of interest in the purchase of shares on the part of the private sector within the country and abroad was due to three factors:

1. An investment in CAP shares had a high level of risk. Historically CAP had shown low profitability, and in 1981 and 1982 the company even showed negative net results (losses of US$46 and US$65 million).[5] These losses can be explained by the drop in gross operational margins and rises in financial expenses during those two years, which did affect the price of CAP shares, although in theory the price should have been determined exclusively by expected profits. In practice, however, the Superintendency of pension fund administration companies (AFPs) and most other investors consider prior results in the risk classification of investment instruments. Given its losses, CAP's possibilities of selling a significant package of stock to AFPs, by far the most important institutional investors in the country, were clearly circumscribed. It is clear, then, that investors considered CAP shares a high-risk investment at that time, because of the company's high leverage.

2. The macroeconomic situation was unfavorable and other investment alternatives were available. In 1985, the economy was still recovering from the dramatic recession of 1982–1983. National savings were extremely low (5.4 percent of gross domestic product), as was domestic investment (13.7 percent of GDP). It is no wonder that tight conditions prevailed in the capital market. Furthermore, the reprivatization of several financial institutions was offering less risky, more advantageous investment alternatives through popular capitalism.

3. There was a world surplus in iron production at that time owing to large investments in that sector provoked by strong demand for steel until 1973. This situation meant that CAP had to face strong foreign competition—even dumping—which implied increased steel imports. It should be recalled that trade rules were already very liberal at that time, based on a reasonably low, nondiscriminatory tariff.

Consequently, the price of the new issue of shares was too high to elicit large purchases of share packages. However, CAP could not offer shares at a price below US$0.25, since the Shareholders' Assembly of November 16, 1984, had decided that shares could not be sold at a lower price than that already established until thirty days after the deadline of the "preferential" offer (November 16, 1987). However, since 1986, CORFO's goal had been to privatize several public enterprises for two fundamental reasons: on the one hand, it would allow the state to acquire funds to finance its macroeconomic program, and on the other hand, the government's political goal was to limit state intervention to only those areas in which the private sector was not socially efficient.

Given that the offer of new shares at the fixed price was not successful, some other method of divestiture had to be found. This is when the idea of reducing the firm's net worth emerged.

The operation consisted of a CAP purchase of CORFO-owned shares at US$0.25 per share, the same price as that of the "preferential" offer described above, thus increasing the amount of stock in private shareholders' hands—the existing shareholders—to 49 percent and reducing CORFO's share to 51 percent. CORFO collected US$72 million in this operation, approved and announced in March 1986 and executed on June 20, 1986.[6] As a result, the ownership of capital, as of June 30, 1986, was distributed as follows: CORFO held 51 percent; workers, 22 percent; and the general public, the remaining 27 percent.

Later, in October 1986, a reduction of CORFO's share in CAP equity to 35 percent was authorized—this time, however, by divesting shares in CORFO's hands. In November, the goal was changed to 20 percent. In December of the same year, 4,500,235 shares (3 percent of equity) were sold to 1,842 workers (27 percent of CAP workers) at a price of US$0.408 per share.

In January 1987, CORFO started to sell CAP shares in the Santiago Stock Exchange. The price per share of the first sale was US$0.489. In June 1987, CORFO decided to privatize the company fully, which meant selling the 20 percent remaining in CORFO's hands. It met this goal in July of that year. Thus, privatizing about 49 percent of CAP took three years, while privatizing the remaining 51 percent took only one year. Table 8.2 summarizes changes in shareholder composition.

Labor capitalism in CAP

In December 1988, CAP workers owned 36 percent of the company's capital and were represented on the Board of Directors by three directors of a total of seven. As already stated, the reprivatization of CAP had begun with the sale of shares to workers and executives, who eventually became the majority shareholders as a group.[7] Initially, this had been a slow

TABLE 8.2
Sales of CAP Shares, 1985–1989

	1985	1986	1987	1988	1989[a]
Number of shareholders	5,654	7,030	8,896	9,961	9,909
Percentage controlled by the 10 largest shareholders	92	62	33	46	47
Percentage of shares held by the private sector	11	52	100	100	100

a. June.
SOURCE: CAP.

process, given the low returns of shares acquired between 1960 and 1965 and their subsequent loss of value in 1970. Moreover, unions were, in general, strongly opposed to the national privatization scheme of the military government. Nevertheless, personal gains to be obtained from investments induced some workers to subscribe to CAP shares, which, in turn, attracted growing numbers of CAP workers to this alternative (Table 8.3). Although the number of CAP worker-shareholders fell by over 300 to 4,743 during 1989, during 1990 their numbers increased to 6,079.

Worker-shareholders have benefited greatly from high capital gains and dividends obtained on CAP shares since 1986, which are among the highest of all privatized enterprises (Table 8.4). They also began to act like average shareholders, becoming sensitive to share price behavior.[8] In fact, between August and October 1987, the number of worker-shareholders decreased by about 200—6 percent of the worker-shareholders in June of the same year—probably because of the significant drop in price that occurred at that time.

Consequences of the privatization of CAP

The evolution of CAP share prices (Table 8.4) and the increase of capital returns since 1986 (Table 8.1) seem to suggest that privatization has had a positive impact on CAP. Before reaching that conclusion, however, we must analyze the reasons for these results and determine whether they would have occurred had CAP remained a state-owned enterprise.

Macroeconomic situation.   After recovery from the 1982–1983 recession, the capital market in Chile recovered and boomed. CAP share prices rose rapidly in line with the general trend of share prices until mid-1987, when the capital reduction took place (Table 8.4). So, at least until then, and despite prior privatization efforts, the process does not appear to explain much of the performance of share prices. The macroeconomic situation

TABLE 8.3
Number of CAP Worker-Shareholders, 1985–1988

Month	1985	1986	1987	1988
February	0	2,516	2,845	4,039
April	0	2,419	3,238	4,737
June	0	2,419	3,238	4,920
August	1,462	2,295	3,459	4,880
October	2,121	2,295	3,055	4,700
December	2,336	2,395	3,061	5,121

SOURCE: CAP.

TABLE 8.4
Share Price Indexes, 1985–1989 (March 1985 = 100)

Month	1985		1986		1987		1988		1989	
	GISP	CAP	GISP	CAP	GISP	CAP	GISP	CAP	GISP	CAP
January			162.4	149.3	408.7	380.6	515.7	768.7	673.0	2,026.1
February			174.8	153.0	401.0	359.3	518.4	895.5	725.7	2,238.8
March	100.0	100.0	204.0	179.1	403.5	348.9	541.5	858.2	766.6	2,238.8
April	114.2	110.1	213.2	178.4	388.7	324.6	495.6	742.5	808.0	2,500.0
May	117.6	108.2	222.5	238.8	373.7	306.0	472.4	772.4	860.7	2,574.6
June	125.4	123.1	235.7	289.2	381.2	358.2	514.5	1,037.3	823.0	2,276.1
July	134.0	145.5	260.6	298.5	428.1	552.2	551.8	1,082.1	796.4	2,119.4
August	130.0	164.2	264.0	261.2	489.3	653.0	569.0	1,399.3	819.6	2,014.9
September	130.7	162.3	271.8	328.4	562.6	783.6	588.6	1,455.2	744.9	1,981.3
October	144.3	130.6	274.0	303.4	529.2	570.9	561.9	1,343.3	857.3	2,283.6
November	146.7	149.3	287.6	309.7	455.7	488.8	569.4	1,492.5		
December	151.0	156.7	336.1	376.9	454.9	641.8	612.6	1,634.3		

NOTE: The GISP corresponds to monthly averages of the General Index of Share Prices; the CAP index, to prices at month's end.
Source: Santiago Stock Exchange.

seems to be responsible for the trend. However, after mid-1987, CAP share prices increased rapidly relative to the General Index of Share Prices, reaching a ratio of 3 in January 1989. Macroeconomic considerations cannot explain such an extraordinary performance.

Change in financing decisions. In 1985, when the government made its second attempt to privatize CAP, it set a price of US$0.25 per share. This price reflected the current value of CAP based on a projection of its results, at a 16 percent discount rate. The unfavorable results of this attempt seem to indicate that either these projections were too optimistic or the discount rate was too low. On the one hand, when CAP tried to encourage its creditors to buy shares in 1985, the International Finance Corporation of the World Bank indicated that the minimum rate of return required from a risky investment like that of CAP was 18 percent. This suggests that the discount rate was perhaps somewhat low, but does not explain the difference between market and share offer prices. On the other hand, a comparison of current data with projected performance shows that the operational projections were quite accurate, while financial expenses were notoriously lower than those projected. Why were these lower financial expenses not generally anticipated?

To answer this question, it is necessary to understand that in December 1985 CAP's long-term debt was US$519.6 million, while CAP was, at the same time, cash rich. In 1983, CAP's debt had been rescheduled, together with the country's debt, taking advantage of the fact that it was a state-owned enterprise. But in the 1984–1985 period, because of the overall cash flow generated by the company, national debt rescheduling was not necessary for CAP, although the government still included its debt in the national debt reschedulings that took place at the time.[9]

In 1986, at about the same time that CAP's share repurchase took place, the central bank created mechanisms to enable companies to reduce their debt by means of debt-equity swaps and, in particular, the so-called Chapter XVIII device, which allowed Chilean companies to repurchase their debt documents with significant discounts in the international capital markets. Making use of this and other similar mechanisms created later, CAP reduced its debt to US$117.6 million during the next two years, obtaining, on average, a 25 percent discount on its foreign debt repurchase.

At the time of the repurchase operation in early 1986, however, these debt-repurchasing mechanisms were just beginning to be implemented. And, although the initial intention was to exclude SOEs from using them, the government changed its mind in the case of some SOEs that were in the process of privatization and had government-guaranteed debts. One of these was CAP. In those cases, the government was interested in granting the debt repurchase privilege in order to reduce the guarantee as much and as fast as possible. To the extent that these operations were not generally anticipated by investors during 1986, they must have produced important capital gains to CAP shareholders, as the data suggest.

Changes in the company's objectives.   Contrary to the general rule governing public enterprises, CAP was allowed to diversify as an SOE. In 1981, according to CAP's statutes, its social objective had changed from "producing iron ingots and laminated steel from national mines" to "investing capital in shares, bonds, debentures, savings and capitalization plans, quotas or rights in mutual funds and any kind of instruments or unregistered securities, and administrating these investments."

CAP further diversified its activities after the privatization process had begun, acquiring an AFP in September 1986,[10] forming a real estate and construction company in 1987, and participating in the forestry business beginning in 1988 (essentially an export concern).

A diversification strategy may be profitable because return differentials almost always exist among sectors, as do deficiencies in the domestic capital market. To the extent that these differentials and deficiencies can be exploited, profits can be made. This strategy, on which most large holding companies are based, is of course especially profitable in countries that, like Chile, have relatively undeveloped capital markets.

At any rate, the CAP diversification strategy as implemented after mid-1987 was profitable, since most new activities undertaken by the holding company boomed during the 1986–1989 period. Therefore, it appears that diversification had some impact on corporate results and rapidly rising share prices.

Changes in investment decisions.   As mentioned, during the 1980s in Chile, all new public investment projects had to be screened before implementation. Their economic suitability was analyzed and only those with a rate of return in excess of the minimum established by the National Planning Office (ODEPLAN) could be carried out, subject to the availability of investment resources. Even if the result was a relatively sound resource allocation, this system suffered from rigidities and some political pressure that might have affected the rates of return of CAP and other SOEs despite the best intentions of the relevant authorities.

In addition, public enterprise investment financing—such as CAP's—posed two problems in the 1980s: on the one hand, the government limited indebtedness of public enterprises, and the major shareholder of such companies, CORFO, rarely made capital contributions to its subsidiaries. Consequently, public enterprises such as CAP operated under severe restrictions on investment project financing. On the other hand, although they were not forbidden to issue preferential shares, such shares could not be issued at a convenient price because of the crisis affecting the national capital market in the early 1980s.

Privatization of CAP began just as the crisis of the early 1980s was ending, when, in addition, debt prepayment facilities were granted. Debt prepayment made room for new indebtedness in a rapidly expanding capital market, allowing CAP to engage in a wide diversification policy. In this sense, the greater availability of investment funds for CAP was partly due to privatization and the debt repurchases, but also partly to the recovery of the capital market.[11] Available funds and investment flexibility allowed the privatized CAP to take advantage of new, highly profitable areas of investment.

Changes in efficiency. Privatization affected operational efficiency of CAP through the mentioned instruments in new ventures, either within the steel business, where they produced a 20 percent increase in sales, or in unrelated sectors, such as forestry, real estate, and finance. However, the spectacular increase in operational profits as a proportion of equity during 1988 and 1989 (Table 8.1) was also influenced by price increases. Employment reductions, which must have increased technical efficiency significantly, took place mainly during the early 1980s, mainly as a consequence of the government's economic policies forcing SOEs to be more efficient.

The capital reduction operation

As mentioned, the main criticism of the CAP reprivatization refers to the capital reduction carried out in 1986. This section will analyze that operation in order to discover problems in that process, to study their causes, and to determine who benefited and who was harmed.

Description of the operation. The law forbids stock companies to acquire or own their own shares, with one exception: when the acquisition complies with the capital reduction statute (Law 18,046, Article 27, Number 3).

On March 20, 1986, CORFO informed CAP of its resolution to reduce the company's equity capital, allowing it to purchase some of its own shares. CORFO would then sell its CAP shares at a price of US$0.25 each and reduce its share in CAP's equity to 51 percent. On March 21, the Superintendency of Securities and Insurance and the stock exchange were notified of this decision.

Between March 21 and April 30, CORFO widely publicized its objective of reducing CAP's net worth so that a maximum number of investors could participate in the process by purchasing shares of issues previously approved. Sales rose, but only 20 million additional shares were sold (approximately 6 percent of the new issue). On April 30, CAP itself agreed to reduce capital by US$80 million through the purchase of 320 million shares at a price of US$0.25 per share.[12] The option would be offered to all shareholders. On May 22, CORFO made use of its option, selling 266 million shares. No other shareholder participated (the price in the stock exchange on May 22 was US$0.32 per share).

On June 16, CORFO expressed its determination to sell 22 million additional shares at US$0.25 each. This sale would bring CORFO's share in CAP to 51 percent.

Analysis of the operation.   Some observers have criticized this operation with respect to the procedure employed and the transaction price of shares (Marcel 1989b). The procedure was legal, however, as confirmed by the state controller, and the necessary formalities, such as providing information to the Superintendency of Securities and Insurance and the stock exchange, were respected.[13] Moreover, the measure was publicized so that private investors could buy shares, knowing that when CORFO had made use of its option, private shareholders would hold 49 percent of CAP's capital, and perhaps expecting, on the basis of known government objectives, that additional steps would be taken later to privatize the company. It could be argued that the two months between the moment CORFO decided to carry out the operation and the moment of the actual repurchase transaction were too short, or perhaps the operation was not widely enough publicized. Although more time and wider publicity might have informed more people about the operation and would have been preferable, the small size of the Chilean capital market and the almost daily contact among those who operate in it suggest that all relevant participants had the opportunity to buy shares if they so wished.

Given the information available at the time of the repurchase operation, the price at which CORFO sold its shares was, if anything, high. This judgment is based on market conditions at the time CAP shareholders made the decision to repurchase a proportion of their own shares. Shares had been offered to the public at US$0.25 over a long period of time, right up to the moment the decision was made to execute the repurchase operation. Moreover, this decision was made precisely because at that price CAP shares were being sold extremely slowly, so much so that, at that rate, reducing CORFO equity in CAP to 51 percent would have taken several years, longer than the government was willing to wait. Therefore, by selling a large package of shares at US$0.25, it could be argued that CORFO received, if anything, a premium on its sale of CAP shares.

However, since at the moment of the actual transaction, the share price in the stock exchange had risen to US$0.38—that is, more than 50 percent over the price fixed for the repurchase operation—many contend in retrospect that CORFO received a lower than market price for its shares. Although it is not fair to judge a decision on the basis of its outcome, we will try to explain some of the factors that might have influenced the behavior of CAP share prices during this period. We highlight two factors in particular:

1. The transaction occurred during a period of general share price increases, which explains over one-half of CAP share price increases during the period under analysis (Table 8.4). As shown in Table 8.4, the relative increase in the price of CAP shares was, at that time, short-lived; the parallel evolution of the general price index of the Santiago Stock Exchange and CAP's share prices was soon reestablished, to vary again only after mid-1987.

2. As a result of the repurchase operation itself, an abnormally high level of demand for CAP shares developed during the March–May 1986 period, which would explain the relative price rise of CAP shares.

Demand could have increased if investors expected significantly higher returns either in the existing operations of privatized SOEs or as a result of investment in new areas. A large part of the general empirical analysis of this first factor, presented in different chapters of this book, does not support this explanation. As a matter of fact, within the Chilean context of competition and hard budgets, SOEs do not seem to have been operating significantly less efficiently than their private sector counterparts during the 1980s (Chapter 7). This is probably reflected in two related sets of phenomena also analyzed as part of the research for this book. On the one hand, share prices were not affected by changes (or the announcement of changes) in the percentage of private sector ownership of the equity of SOEs being privatized. On the other hand, the share price index for SOEs rose less every year from 1985 through 1989, the period when they were being privatized, than did the General Index of Share Prices of the Santiago Stock Exchange. If the market was anticipating an efficiency increase as a result of privatization, share prices should have reflected it, and they obviously did not.

The demand for CAP shares could also have risen relative to other stock for reasons other than expected efficiency gains. For example, at the time, CAP was relatively liquid, even after taking the share repurchase into account, and the prospect of investing that cash in the purchase of its own international debt at market prices (about 60 percent of face value), a possibility that arose soon afterward, promised high rates of return.

It is evident, after the fact, that debt reduction generated sizable capital gains for CAP shareholders.[14] At the time of the share repurchase operation, however, neither state-owned enterprises nor private sector companies were allowed to buy their own debt papers. That is, assuming that this factor explains increased demand for CAP stock, purchasers of CAP shares must have either speculated about such a development or had information not available to the general public or to all investors. In any event, during March and April 1986, CAP stock sales accelerated significantly, and a relatively small number of investors purchased about 20 million shares, almost 6 percent of the new issue. Not surprisingly, given the ample supply of shares at a fixed dollar price, the relative market price of CAP shares experienced a decline.[15] After the stockholders' assembly, the amount of shares to be repurchased was definitely fixed, CAP no longer offered new shares at US$0.25, and CORFO officially decided to take its option; CAP stock prices then rose rapidly until July 1987, both absolutely and relative to the General Index of Share Prices of the Santiago Stock Exchange.

In August 1986, before CORFO officially decided to transfer majority control of CAP to the private sector, the central bank allowed CAP to purchase some of its own debt at international market prices, making use of Chapter XVIII of the central bank charter.[16] During 1988, the central bank again authorized CAP (in which CORFO now had only a minority interest) to purchase its own international debt at market prices. This time, the operation was for US$235 million, carried out making use of clause 5.12 of the recently signed Chilean Debt Restructuring Agreement.[17] With a discount of about 40 percent, these debt repurchases were extremely profitable and were authorized by the government mainly because CAP's debt enjoyed state guarantee, and the government wished to reduce that debt as much as possible.[18] In its decision to allow the 1988 repurchases, the government was probably also influenced by the fact that a relatively large number of private sector companies were buying their own debt abroad, an informal operation that the government allowed as a practical way of reducing the high indebtedness level of Chilean business. In this light the CAP debt repurchase was fair, and it also benefited the state.

In March and April 1986, were only some investors informed about the coming central bank authorization of the CAP to repurchase its own debt at highly discounted market prices? Or were those CAP share purchases basically speculative operations, unrelated to any inside information? The answer to these questions requires research beyond the scope of this book. It is, however, noteworthy that during that period, purchases were concentrated in four groups of companies and persons. One group can be directly or indirectly related to the owners or executives of the Chilean Consolidated Life Insurance Company (almost 8.9 million shares and 44 percent of the total). Another group can be tied to Inversiones Citicorp (more than 6.2 million shares and almost 31 percent of the total). A third group was composed of five stockbrokers (more than 2.6 million shares and about 13 percent of the total). Finally, there were eight private investors (more than 1.6 million shares and about 8 percent of the total). None of these eight investors were CAP executives or public officials nor can they be directly related to those officials, although it is of course impossible to know for certain who ordered the purchase of the shares bought by the stockbrokers. The transfer of shares to the first group was partly in exchange for the AFP El Libertador and partly to settle a debt.

In any event, after July 1986 CAP share prices fell rapidly relative to the General Index of Share Prices of the Santiago Stock Exchange, reestablishing their "normal" relationship. Only in 1988, about a year and a half after the share repurchase operation and more or less in step with the second foreign debt repurchase, did the spectacular relative price rise of CAP stock begin.

The Privatization of ENDESA: A Gift from CORFO to Future Shareholders?

One of the most interesting privatizations carried out in the late 1980s was that of the National Electricity Company (ENDESA), for two reasons. ENDESA is one of the country's largest enterprises and the largest electric power producer: in 1988, it generated approximately 57 percent of the total electric power produced in Chile. In addition, this company had been state property since its creation in December 1943. It had been widely accepted that electric power companies should be in the hands of the state, as they were considered natural monopolies. Today, technological change allows for competition in parts of that business, and regulation allows socially efficient private ownership, within the context of a worldwide movement in favor of private property, even for those sectors traditionally considered to be exclusively state domain. Chile has not escaped this trend. By October 1989, CHILMETRO, CHILGENER, CHILQUINTA, Pilmaiquén, and Pullinque, all companies involved in electricity generation, transmission, or distribution, were completely privatized, and ENDESA was 90 percent privately owned (see Chapter 4).

This section will analyze the privatization of ENDESA, including such issues as change in the rules of the game with respect to the electric power sector, the evolution of company policy both before and after privatization, and the present distribution of ENDESA equity.

Characteristics of the electric power sector

To put the privatization of ENDESA in context, we will begin by describing the main characteristics of the electric power sector and of ENDESA specifically.[19]

Three stages may be distinguished in the process of delivering electric power to users: generation of electric power, absorbing about 51 percent of the total costs of the process; transmission of electric power, absorbing about 11 percent of the cost; and distribution of power, absorbing the remaining 38 percent. In Chile, the first two stages occur together, and there are no legal restrictions on the vertical integration of all three stages, which could be advantageous from a management point of view and may favor minimal generation costs.[20]

At this writing, there are eleven companies devoted to the generation and transmission of electric power, among which ENDESA, CHILGENER, Colbún-Machicura, and Pehuenche are the most important;[21] twenty-three distributing companies, including the present and former subsidiaries of ENDESA and of CHILECTRA;[22] two companies, the Electric Company of Aysén (EDELAYSEN) and the Electric Company of Magallanes (EDELMAG), that cover all three stages; several self-producers; and fourteen electric power cooperatives.

Characteristics of ENDESA

ENDESA was created by the government in 1943, as a subsidiary of CORFO, to develop the production, transmission, and distribution of electric power and to fulfill the country's National Electrification Plan. The role of ENDESA did not change until 1980, when its statutes were reformed to establish a new objective: ''to exploit the production, transmission, distribution, and supply of electric power, for which purpose it may obtain, acquire, and enjoy the respective concessions and benefits.'' In 1985 the statutes were again reformed, broadening the company's objectives to include the development of consultancy activities in the field of engineering, related to its social purposes, both in the country and abroad. In 1988, this last point was modified, adding ''to offer consultancies in the fields of engineering and of company management, in all their specialities, both in the country and abroad.'' The purpose of this statutory modification was to exploit the company's comparative advantages in the field of electrical engineering, given its highly qualified personnel.

The country changed significantly in the late 1970s and 1980s and so did ENDESA. It was administered for profit maximization, without any state contributions or privilege.[23]

ENDESA's principal advantage is that it supplies electrical power, for which demand has constantly increased at a rate somewhat higher than GDP. Nevertheless, although the demand risk is low, the supply risk is high. In the event of droughts, operational costs will grow substantially, but tariffs may not. Obviously, this effect is enhanced by an inadequate tariff legislation for these extreme cases. At any rate, company results are extremely sensitive to tariff regulations.

Another of ENDESA's characteristics lies in the fact that the investment required to implement an electric power plant is significant in relation to the size of the Chilean capital market. Therefore, present legislation allows electricity-generating companies to demand reimbursable financial contributions from clients interested in greater installed capacity. Alternatively, the electricity-generating companies must secure loans abroad, with accounting losses in the event of local currency devaluations. The devaluation of 1982 brought about a 10 percent negative return on capital, while ENDESA obtained operational profits. Again, in 1985, heavy losses were incurred as a consequence of two consecutive devaluations and the end of the "preferential" dollar. These losses were absorbed by a reduction of the company's equity capital.[24] Table 8.5 presents relevant indicators of ENDESA's performance.

Preparations for privatization

During the 1980s, the Chilean electric power sector underwent the most radical changes in its history. In the span of fifteen years, this sector went from being an almost fully state-owned conglomerate of a few large companies to an almost completely private set of companies, many of which are juridically independent, managed according to private efficiency criteria, that is, with the objective of maximizing profits.[25]

The reforms of the Chilean energy sector began, as for the rest of the economy, in 1974, as part of the radical political and economic changes discussed earlier. In 1979, the government decided that SOEs would no longer receive special benefits. In exchange, they were granted greater flexibility in current operations, but not in investment decisions. Moreover, authorities decided that SOEs should not broaden their scope of action but should concentrate on those specific activities for which they had been created. In consequence, they were to transfer to the private sector all activities not directly related to their main line of business.[26]

By the end of 1980, marginal cost pricing was established in the electricity-generating sector, leaving aside previous criteria that had set prices to ensure a 10 percent return on accounting equity. Prices were also freed for the supply of energy to industrial clients (users that require an installed capacity over 2,000 kilowatts per hour).

That same year, a decentralization process began through which ENDESA's electricity distribution units were transformed into limited liability companies owned by CORFO and ENDESA. Later, they were transformed into open stock companies. This process is in itself quite interesting and deserves some commentary.

TABLE 8.5
Evolution of ENDESA's Performance, 1979–1989

	1979	1980	1981	1982	1983	1984	1985	1986	1987	1988	1989
Investment/equity (%)	8.9	13.3	13.2	16.5	16.3	22.3	18.7[a]		15.8	4.6	15.6
Ratio of indebtedness to investment	0.3	0.6	0.4	0.9	0.5	0.9	0.9[a]		0.3	2.1	1.6
Ratio of total debt to equity	0.3	0.4	0.5	0.9	0.9	1.2	2.5[a]		0.7	0.6	0.7
Ratio of long-term debt to equity	0.3	0.3	0.3	0.8	0.8	1.0	2.3[a]		0.6	0.5	0.6
Ratio of current liabilities to current assets	0.9	1.3	1.9	1.1	1.0	1.2	0.5[a]		0.4	0.4	0.4
Profits/equity (%)	2.4	4.5	3.0	−10.4	6.4	2.4	−19.4[a]		4.9	12.3	7.3
Operational income/equity (%)	1.8	3.3	3.9	6.7	7.7	8.5	14.6[a]		8.7	10.7	7.9
Taxes paid/gross profits (%)	19.8	44.2	46.3	—[b]	5.0	41.2	—[a,b]		0.0	0.1	0.2
Dividends/profits (%)	n.a.	78.5	72.4	0.0	0.0	9.0	−13.5[a]		92.5	18.0	25.2
Personnel	4,270	4,018	2,828	2,728	2,705	2,813	2,950	2,905	2,928	2,925	2,980
Annual real tariff increase (%)	14.6	4.5	−2.8	19.2	n.a.	n.a.	−2.8	−7.7	11.7	19.1	11.7

n.a. = not available
a. Average figures for 1985 and 1986.
b. Although there was a net loss, income tax was paid.
SOURCE: ENDESA annual reports.

The purpose of this division was to improve the company's overall economic efficiency through the creation of independent cost centers, managed separately, which would permit the identification of stages or geographical zones generating losses. Previously, these units had been managed centrally, with limited autonomy. Because of their size and geographical dispersion, they were very difficult to control.[27] Later, once the privatization process had started, some of these companies merged because they were too small to be sold independently (for a better understanding of the evolution of ENDESA's subsidiaries, see Table 8.6).

TABLE 8.6

Evolution of ENDESA's Subsidiaries, 1980–1989 (shares held by ENDESA as percentage of total shares)

Company	1980	1981	1982	1983[a]	1984	1985	1986	1987	1988	1989
EMEC[b]	99.7	99.7	99.7	99.7	99.7	99.7				
EMELIG[b]	99.7	99.7	99.7	99.7	99.7	99.7				
EMEL[c]	99.5	99.5	99.5	99.5	99.5	99.5				
EMELAT[d,e]		99.7	99.7	99.7	99.7	99.7	93.8			
EMECO[c,d]		99.6	99.6	99.6	99.6	99.6				
EMELMA[c,d]		99.5	99.5	99.5	99.5	99.5				
EDELNOR[d,f]		100.0	100.0	100.0	100.0	100.0	98.3	97.4	91.0	
EDELMAG[d,g]		99.9	99.9	99.9	99.9	99.9	96.8	7.9		
EDELAYSEN[d,g]		99.9	99.9	99.9	99.9	99.9	99.8	8.0	10.4	
Pullinque[h]			100.0	100.0	100.0	100.0	100.0			
Pilmaiquén[i]			99.7	99.7	99.7	99.7				
Colbún-Machicura[j]			97.1	100.0	100.0	100.0				
IPSEN Ltda.			90.0	90.0	90.0	90.0	90.0	90.0	90.0	0.1
INESA								97.0	97.0	0.01
Pehuenche								29.5	30.0	27.1
EMELARI									91.0	
ELECSA									91.0	
ELECDA									91.0	

Blank cell indicates that ENDESA held no shares in the company.
a. The first nine companies listed here were transformed into a stock company in 1983.
b. EMEC and EMELIG were merged in 1986, with the former buying 100 percent of the latter's shares. Later EMEC was sold to Ingeniería y Maquinarias Ltda.
c. EMECO, EMELMA, and EMEL were merged in 1986, with EMEL buying 100 percent of the shares of the other two. Later EMEL was sold to workers of ENDESA and its subsidiaries, EMEC and Colbún-Machicura, at 47 percent of its book value.
d. Company was not a subsidiary yet.
e. EMELAT was sold to the company made up by EMEL, workers of ENDESA and its subsidiaries, and Colbún-Machicura in 1987.
f. EDELNOR was sold to CORFO in 1989.
g. These companies were sold to CORFO at book value in 1987.
h. Pullinque was sold to Golan S.A. in 1987.
i. Pilmaiquén was sold to Inversiones IMSA in 1986.
j. In 1983 Colbún-Machicura was dissolved by law and became part of ENDESA. When ENDESA was privatized, Colbún-Machicura was again set up as an independent corporation, with its shares held by CORFO.
SOURCE: ENDESA.

In 1982, ENDESA was registered as an open stock company, controlled by the Superintendency of Securities and Insurance, with the price of shares determined in the local stock exchanges. This transformation gave the company an important advantage, because, according to government policies, SOEs could acquire Treasury notes or central bank bonds only with prior authorization of the Ministry of Finance, while stock companies could participate freely in the capital market. That same year, the government decided that as a matter of policy ENDESA should give priority to new sources of financing, by, for example, issuing bonds and preferential shares. It also decided that (1) the operations of the company and its subsidiaries should be regulated by the market; (2) new power plants should be constituted as subsidiaries or mixed companies, with a majority in private hands; and (3) the generation subsidiaries, Pullinque and Pilmaiquén, should be sold.[28]

In 1983, Decree Law 1 established a Reimbursable Financial Contributions system, which involved handing over company shares to private agents in exchange for financing of specific investments in additional capacity needed for energy sales to new customers. This measure, like others mentioned above, implied a gradual process of privatization—that is, the flow of new equity was privatized instead of the stock itself.[29]

In 1986, CORFO split Colbún-Machicura from ENDESA. In addition, about US$500 million of ENDESA debt was capitalized with the purpose of preparing it for subsequent privatization, a heavily criticized operation to be analyzed in detail below. That same year, several ENDESA subsidiaries were merged and sold to the private sector and to ENDESA workers and other company subsidiaries (Table 8.6).

As of December 31, 1987, ENDESA had divested its subsidiaries EMEC, EMEL, EMELIG, EMECO, EMELMA, FRONTEL, Pilmaiquén, Pullinque, and SAESA and sold to CORFO its subsidiaries EDELAYSEN and EDELMAG. All of these operations implied privatizing parts of the old ENDESA. These divestitures were carried out through biddings at auction with the exception of EMEC, sold to its workers.

The sale of ENDESA

Company staff strongly criticized the privatization of ENDESA from the beginning. They argued that electric power was an indispensable good and that, in its distribution, redistributive criteria should be considered, which the private sector would probably not do. The error in this view lay in confusing ownership with who establishes tariffs and how.

In any event, on July 27, 1987, preferential shares were offered to workers of ENDESA and subsidiaries, at a price of 13 pesos per share, with a deadline of September 17 of that same year. Given the opposition mentioned above, initiating the privatization process with the sale of shares to workers at a low price and on credit was politically a sound decision, since labor capitalism was the least-criticized mode of privatization and workers could gain by buying those shares.

As a result of this offer, 93 percent of workers purchased 6.1 percent of the company. These purchases were financed by way of advanced payment of severance pay, 3.2 percent of capital to 3,564 workers; CORFO credits, 1.9 percent of capital to 1,530 workers; and own funds, 0.9 percent of capital to 623 workers.

After these sales to workers, the divestiture process continued, and the results are summarized in Tables 8.7 and 8.8. Table 8.7 shows the divestiture sequencing of the main electric power sector firms, of which

TABLE 8.7
Electric Power Sector Divestiture, 1986–1989 (percentage divested)

Company	December 1986	December 1987	December 1988	October 1989
CHILMETRO	63	100	100	100
CHILGENER	35	100	100	100
CHILQUINTA	63	100	100	100
ENDESA	0	9	54	93 (Dec.)
Pilmaiquén	100	100	100	100
Pullinque	0	100	100	100
Colbún-Machicura	0	0	0	0
Pehuenche	0	0	0	32

SOURCE: CORFO.

TABLE 8.8
Equity Distribution of ENDESA, 1986–1989

	1986	1987	1988	1989	1990
Number of shareholders	306	5,138	37,901	63,629	51,833
Share controlled by the ten largest shareholders (%)	100	96	68	39	38
CORFO's share in ENDESA equity (%)	99.0	90.7	46.2	7.1	1.0

SOURCE: ENDESA.

ENDESA is the main company. By 1989, the divestiture of the Chilean electric power sector was nearly complete.

ENDESA faded almost fully out of CORFO control (Table 8.8). This occurred through the creation of subsidiaries, all but one also divested, and through additional sales of CORFO shares, broadening ENDESA's shareholder base so that the vast majority of ENDESA workers became shareholders, while AFPs, an indirect form of popular capitalism, controlled up to 21.9 percent of the firm's equity by the end of 1989.

In September 1987, CORFO signed a share distribution agreement, allowing the sale of stock to AFPs.[30] On September 28 and 29, for example, 476,470 shares were sold to the AFPs (0.006 percent of capital) at 16 pesos per share.

Starting in October 1987, shares were widely offered throughout the country at a price of 15 pesos per share, with November 15 set as a purchase deadline. AFPs acquired 3.7 percent of ENDESA's capital at that time. Nearly 8.5 percent of company ownership was divested, and 15,000 popular capitalists were created. On November 16, sales to the public were reopened, attracting 2,740 new popular capitalist shareholders, who acquired 0.96 percent of the company.

In February 1988, AFPs acquired an additional 10.6 percent of ENDESA in the Santiago Stock Exchange, at a price of 15.7 pesos per share. With this sale, CORFO fulfilled the terms of the share distribution agreement, which had obliged it to sell 30 percent of its equity. Between March 1988 and January 1989, CORFO sold 53.9 percent of ENDESA's equity to public employees and members of the armed forces at 16.5 pesos per share, within the framework of Laws 18,681 and 18,747 that authorize the use of severance pay advances.[31]

The eventual success of the initially unpopular privatization of ENDESA might have been based on at least two factors. In the first place, appropriate sequencing was probably of paramount importance for ensuring full privatization and the irreversibility of the process. In the second place, initiating the sale of shares among the firm's workers had the double advantage of building support for the government's privatization effort, while simultaneously stimulating the rest of the private sector to invest, because the perceived risk of reverse privatization was reduced.

Consequences of the privatization of ENDESA

In the case of ENDESA, the central objectives of privatization were to increase efficiency, distribute property, and collect funds for the state. In this section, we will analyze the degree to which these and other objectives have been fulfilled, together with any undesired consequences of privatization.

Changes in efficiency. As we have already noted, after 1974 government economic policies forced public enterprises to improve efficiency. ENDESA's operational return (operational income/equity) increased from 2 percent in 1979 to 9 percent in 1987 (Table 8.5). In 1988, the first year with a private sector majority, operational returns rose to 11 percent, but this increase was basically unrelated to privatization. To achieve an actual relative increase in efficiency after privatization, ENDESA's executives would have had to seek cost reductions, beyond those that were usually sought by its staff, given service tariffs established by law. Significant cost savings did not take place, however, until after the 1990 change in its Board of Directors, which allowed the representation of Enersis to play a significant role in the management of the company. Until then only relatively minor changes in personnel and management style had taken place after privatization. Total returns also increased significantly in 1988 (from 5 percent to 12 percent), but debt reduction goes a long way in explaining these results.

ENDESA did not diversify its activities after privatization, at least until the change in its Board of Directors in 1990, with the exception of its creation of engineering consultancy services, which it could have offered even under state control.[32] Some other privatized companies, however, considerably increased their returns on capital by investing in other areas, a strategy they could not follow while in the public sector.

ENDESA suffered negative consequences from the attempt to achieve efficient financing, because in order to be classified as a company whose stock could be purchased by an AFP, it had to maintain a relatively high ratio of current assets to current liabilities. This high ratio, normal for most industrial and commercial concerns, is in large part determined by the inventory level held. Compliance with this ratio is particularly difficult for an electric power company, however, since electricity cannot be stored as inventory (Table 8.5).

Changes in investment decisions.   The freedom to decide on the use of funds, a consequence of privatization, has created a conflict between economic and social efficiency, illustrated in the following examples. Electricity tariffs are established on the basis of the level of the Laja Lake: the higher the level of the lake, the lower marginal electricity costs, and therefore the lower electricity tariffs will be. ENDESA recently learned that this lake is leaking. Investing to stop that leak might be profitable from a social point of view, but ENDESA is not willing to invest to make the lake leakproof because it would increase the lake's level and thus decrease energy tariffs, making such a project apparently unprofitable from a private point of view. Moreover, in 1988, the rate of investment was significantly reduced (Table 8.5) when a large investment planned for

Pehuenche was postponed, possibly because of political uncertainty. These reactions, failing to fix the leak and postponing the construction of Pehuenche, were consistent with both state and private enterprise behavior under the existing rules in Chile, which induced SOEs to operate as if they were private.

Changes in ownership concentration. Because of the strategy used, the privatization of ENDESA actually helped spread ownership of the company's equity capital.[33] ENDESA equity stock sales to workers and to other private investors stimulated the spreading of equity. The decision to stimulate institutional capitalism was of paramount importance in this endeavor. This mode required that the only shares that could be sold to AFPs were those of companies whose equity was not owned in individual packages larger than 20 percent of total shares.

Currently, the largest shareholder of ENDESA is Enersis, a holding company that controls CHILMETRO, the largest electricity distribution company in Chile.[34] This situation implies an important degree of vertical integration among the two largest companies in the sector, which could eventually affect regulation as a result of pressures exerted by this powerful interest group. This arrangement, however, may also have positive aspects, since the operations of both institutions are mainly complementary and improved rationalization may justify the move. In fact, a public service enterprise mood prevailed in ENDESA until the 1990 change of its Board of Directors. The aggressive business strategies of Enersis should now be able to induce some changes in management approach, which, of course, could not have been transformed by privatization decrees alone. To the extent that it has been fairly described here, pressure on the administration to improve rationalization should be positive for the economy. Other pressures to tilt regulation in the concern's favor are of course not desirable and suggest the need for effective antitrust legislation.

Changes in labor policies. The most significant changes in personnel occurred during the 1973–1981 period, as a consequence of new rules applied to public enterprises and the creation of ENDESA subsidiaries. No major changes have occurred since the end of 1989, which constitutes another illustration of our conclusion in Chapter 6 that there is no inherent relationship between privatization—as defined here—and unemployment.

The debt novation operation

The privatization of ENDESA has been heavily criticized, not only because it is a traditional SOE producing a basic public service, but also because of the debt-reducing operation carried out between CORFO and ENDESA in December 1986 to prepare the company for privatization. Marcel describes that measure in the following terms:

> Less well known, but not less important, is the operation that, in practice, made ENDESA's privatization possible. This operation consisted of the novation of ENDESA's foreign currency debts in favor of CORFO in exchange for a package of newly issued shares. This operation would have implied a substantial transfer of capital from CORFO to ENDESA through the overvaluation of the price of ENDESA shares. With this and the sudden fall in ENDESA's debt-equity ratio, its shares were obviously more attractive to private potential buyers (Marcel 1989a:36–37).

That the reduced indebtedness made the shares of ENDESA more attractive is obvious, but that CORFO lost with the operation is not clear at all.

The restructuring of ENDESA had two main objectives: (1) to separate the Colbún-Machicura hydroelectric complex from ENDESA, a procedure probably designed to prepare for the subsequent privatization of both concerns; and (2) to restructure both companies so that they would be on a solid financial and economic footing.[35]

ENDESA's long-term debt-equity ratio had risen from 1.02 in 1984 to 2.18 in 1985. This increase of more than 100 percent was the consequence of new debts contracted in 1985 and the effect of the devaluation of the domestic currency together with the end of the preferential dollar. The latter two factors implied a large drop in the company's net worth. The effect of a devaluation on foreign-denominated debt is obvious. Given the relatively high proportion of such debt in the economy, after the 1982 devaluation, the government made foreign currency available at a preferential (lower than official) exchange rate to service foreign debts. But since debts had to be accounted for at the official exchange rate (instead of the preferential rate at which those debts were being serviced), the government allowed enterprises to offset the implicit accounting loss of such a procedure by setting up an asset account, equivalent to the amount of the debt valued at the difference between the official and the preferential rate. When the government suddenly discontinued the preferential rate in 1985, ENDESA and all other affected Chilean enterprises were obliged to write off that asset account, reducing their net worth accordingly. The effect on ENDESA was devastating.

In addition, the separation of Colbún-Machicura harmed ENDESA's financial structure. Colbún-Machicura's assets were transferred at book value, and its liabilities were allocated in such a way that its long-term debt-equity ratio would not exceed 1.5 (Table 8.9). That is, debt was transferred less than proportionally from ENDESA to Colbún-Machicura.

TABLE 8.9

Separation of Colbún-Machicura and Capital Contribution to ENDESA, 1984–1986 (millions of US$)

	ENDESA 1984	ENDESA 1985	Colbún-Machicura 1986	ENDESA 1986 (post-separation)	ENDESA 1986 (post-capitalization)
Assets					
Current assets	157	230	28	202	202
Fixed assets	2,302	2,113	649	1,464	1,464
Other assets	496	174	1	173	173
Total assets	2,955	2,517	678	1,839	1,839
Liabilities and equity					
Current liabilities	201	125	12	113	110
Long-term liabilities	1,393	1,639	391	1,248	754
Equity	1,361	753	275	478	975
Total liabilities and equity	2,955	2,517	678	1,839	1,839

SOURCE: ENDESA.

The strongly criticized capitalization operation was then carried out to improve ENDESA's financial condition. It involved floating shares for US$500 million, which were purchased by CORFO. To pay for the float, CORFO acquired ENDESA's debt for an equivalent sum. As a result, the long-term debt-equity ratio fell to 0.77. Critics of the operation argue that although the debt reduction amounted to US$500 million, the market value of the shares purchased by CORFO was lower at that time, and thus CORFO sustained a loss of capital. In fact, the shares subscribed by CORFO to carry out the mentioned operation were valued at 28.92 pesos, which was clearly above any price actually paid before or after the flotation except for February 1987, shortly after the operation (Table 8.10).

Who benefited and who lost in this operation? A first glance would indicate that CORFO lost and ENDESA shareholders benefited. However, it is important to analyze the initial and final situations of shareholders in both institutions. At the time of the operation, ENDESA belonged almost 100 percent to CORFO, which in turn was the property of the government of Chile. Thus, if CORFO had lost, the state would have lost, and if ENDESA had benefited, the state would also have benefited. In this sense, the operation would be neutral from the point of view of equity and would only have consisted in a transfer between "companies" belonging to the same owner.

Nevertheless, analysis must go further, since ENDESA was later privatized. Thus, it is necessary to analyze the impact of this operation

TABLE 8.10

Price of ENDESA Shares at Stock Exchange, 1985–1989 (pesos)

Month	1985	1986	1987	1988	1989
January		11.8	28.0	15.5	16.2
February		11.8	29.3	15.9	19.0
March		11.8	25.0	15.9	20.3
April		11.8	23.0	14.9	21.2
May		6.4	20.0	13.1	22.6
June		9.6	19.3	14.1	18.6
July		20.0	14.5	13.8	19.1
August		20.0	18.3	14.1	18.0
September	11.8	18.0	15.7	13.6	20.2
October	11.8	9.5	14.5	13.9	20.1
November	11.8	16.0	14.5	14.5	18.8
December	11.8	19.0	15.2	13.9	21.0

Blank cell indicates no transaction.
NOTE: These are closing prices for each month, adjusted for dividends and new stock issues.
SOURCE: Santiago Stock Exchange.

on the subsequent privatization. Under the assumption that the Chilean capital market is reasonably efficient, the impact on the state's equity again would have been nil. If the debt-equity operation had not been carried out, and ENDESA had been privatized anyway, revenues from ENDESA share sales would have been lower, because the company would have been more indebted and more financially risky—so much so that the reduction in revenues would have been at best exactly equal to, or more likely, larger than, that incurred by CORFO as a result of the operation.

In addition, the debt reduction operation had the advantage of reducing the likelihood of a reversal of the privatization, which could easily have happened given ENDESA's high indebtedness. The experience of the debt-led privatizations during the 1970s is eloquent enough.

NINE

Lessons from Privatization in Chile

By way of summary, we have compiled our responses to questions that are frequently asked about the conditions for and effects of privatization. Most of these questions are technical in nature, and our answers are based on statistical and econometric tests that we performed in the course of gathering evidence for this book. As a whole, the replies sum up the main lessons of the Chilean privatization process.

Is Successful Privatization Possible in a Less-Developed Country?

Based on the Chilean experience, the answer appears to be a firm yes, at least as far as middle-income countries are concerned. Between 1974 and 1989—that is, under the military government—more than 550 of the largest state-controlled enterprises were divested. In addition, more than 50 percent of the arable land, the administration of the social security system, a high proportion of the educational and health systems, and several other significant activities were transferred to the private sector. At the end of that period, a highly centralized mixed economy had been transformed into a modern market economy, and a new government from the political opposition has repeatedly declared the private sector to be the engine of growth of the Chilean economy. Although on a different scale and with other means, the new government is even continuing the process.

Imperfect markets

Although markets are more imperfect in developing countries than in developed countries, the Chilean experience confirms that they can function well enough to generate fair transfer prices (Chapter 5) and to induce relatively efficient operation of the privatized enterprises (Chapter 7). This latter factor, however, depends on the economic and policy framework within which they will operate. Free internal markets, competition—made possible to a large extent by opening up the economy to international trade—and effective regulation of natural monopolies seem to have been enough to generate a socially useful private sector in Chile (Chapter 2).

Resources for privatization

The necessary resources for privatization always exist, even in a developing country. Chile's experience in that respect could not be more eloquent. To begin with, privatization is simply the transfer of existing resources from the public to the private sector and, as such, does not require additional resources from a national point of view.

Share giveaways. State-owned enterprises (SOEs) can be divested by giving shares to private citizens, which, of course, implies a redistribution of resources between sectors. A giveaway can be implemented in many ways. In Chile it took the form of popular capitalism (Chapter 4), through which medium- and high-bracket taxpayers acquired, for all practical purposes gratuitously, shares of some large commercial banks, pension fund administration companies (AFPs), and electricity-generating and -distributing companies. To the extent that SOEs generate a negative cash flow because of inefficient operations, which is unfortunately often the case in developing countries, privatization not only does not require additional resources, but in fact saves them.

If the SOEs are run relatively efficiently and if the stock is given away, privatization might reduce the public sector's net revenue flow, forcing it to reduce expenditures, raise taxes, or sell SOE stock. In a poor country, divesting to foreigners might allow the public sector to maintain its expenditure programs without affecting private investment.

Divestitures to foreigners. During the 1980s, Chile invited foreigners to participate in the privatization process. At the beginning of that process, Chile had the highest per capita foreign debt burden in Latin America, most of it owed by an excessively indebted private sector. Part of the solution to the indebtedness problem was found in debt-equity swaps, which made privatization possible after the state had assumed a large part of the private debt. This could have put absolute control of an excessively large number of enterprises into foreign hands, which might have generated a negative political reaction. Prudence, however, prevented such a result. Instead, authorities created a number of companies in which control is shared between local entrepreneurs and foreigners, and others in which the intention of the foreign shareholders is to gradually divest their interests (these are usually companies belonging to foreign commercial banks heavily exposed to Chile). The competitive framework, or set of regulations where required, has also contributed to making foreign ownership of enterprises more acceptable, eliminating the fear of exploitation by multinational corporations.

The pitfalls of debt-led privatizations.   In most countries poor in liquid assets, there is a tendency to divest by granting credit to purchasers of SOE shares. The Chilean experience in this respect was a disaster. During the 1970s, that is, during the First Round of privatizations, the government used a bidding process to divest controlling interests in a high proportion of its SOEs on credit, usually with a small down payment and up to twelve installments. These credits were generally guaranteed only by the SOE shares being divested. This arrangement led to the emergence of highly leveraged businesses, dominated by a number of financial conglomerates, and subject to moral hazard, which often took excessive risks in order to service their debts. During the early 1980s, as a consequence of the economic crisis, these businesses and conglomerates became insolvent, producing a financial crisis and aggravating the general economic crisis. As a result, the government took over a number of important financial institutions and through them regained control of previously privatized SOEs. The First Round of privatizations was thereby largely reversed (Chapters 2 and 4). Granting credit had allowed the government to receive higher prices for SOE stock than it would otherwise have obtained, but at a high risk of reversal of the whole process.

The government learned its lesson. During the Second Round, it sold controlling SOE stock on a cash basis to persons or institutions with high solvency, thereby eliminating the moral hazard implicit in debt-led privatizations. At the same time, however, it sold minority interests, widely spread, on credit. Examples of this kind of operation were the divestitures of the Provida and Santa María AFPs where Bankers Trust and Aetna Insurance Co., respectively, held controlling interests with the remainder sold through popular capitalism, and of the National Electricity Company (ENDESA), where shares were sold on credit to all employees of the public sector, including the armed forces (Chapter 4). This kind of credit sale to minority shareholders, guaranteed only by the shares transacted, did produce a normal rate of default on the installments but had no impact on the enterprises divested or the economy. They might, however, have had a positive effect on savings (Chapter 4), since many of these small investors probably invested for the first time in financial assets and therefore probably substituted for consumption.

The scope of privatization

It is usually argued that, within the context of a market economy, developing countries should privatize enterprises of a commercial nature (such as industry, agriculture, and mining), with the possible exception of "strategic" enterprises (those providing a very high percentage of exports, for example). The Chilean experience suggests that the range of enterprises and activities that can be successfully privatized is much wider. Chile privatized most public utilities (public transportation, electricity generation and distribution, telephone and other communication services, some ports and most port services, gas distribution and some gas-producing operations, some water-distribution services, garbage collection, and many others), as well as a substantial proportion of social services (including education, health, pensions, and housing). State land was also divested (Chapter 4). In the case of some public utilities (natural monopolies) and social services, the Chilean experience suggests that adequate regulation and control, together with the right economic policies, are essential for achieving the desired results in terms of efficiency and resource allocation. The Chilean experience can be generalized to conclude that almost any activity can be conveniently privatized, as long as the appropriate regulations are in place. These regulations must generate a competitive environment among agencies to ensure efficiency and to set the right prices, in order to produce the desired allocation of resources.

What Conditions Are Necessary for a Successful Privatization?

The Chilean experience suggests a number of conditions that must be met, besides those implicit in the above comments, for the successful implementation of privatization policy. These are mainly political and institutional in nature. Privatization is, after all, a political process with economic consequences.

Leadership

Most successful privatization policies have been led by a person or a small group of people determined to implement the policies at almost any price, as in the case of Margaret Thatcher in Great Britain. Chile is no exception. In this case, President Pinochet himself strongly supported the policy, probably for political reasons (Chapter 3). In fact, after the 1983 reversals, he was willing not only to reprivatize the enterprises that had fallen again under government control (the odd sector), but also to decisively deepen the process by privatizing public utilities and other traditional SOEs not touched during the First Round. Within the economic sphere, leadership was equally strong. The head of the economic team, unconditionally supported by the so-called Chicago Boys, was firmly behind the privatization policies.

Initial political support

Even under an authoritarian regime, the desire of the leaders to privatize, no matter how strong, is probably not enough to achieve as wide and deep a process as prevailed in Chile. Public support from opinion leaders and interest groups is essential. In Chile, privatization was initially supported by the public, which, after the 1973 military coup, clearly favored the restoration of hundreds of nationalized and state-managed enterprises to the private sector (Chapter 3). Without this support, the process probably never would have taken off. That support existed not so much for ideological reasons, but as a fundamental reaction to the conditions that had led to the sociopolitical and economic crisis of the early 1970s, which threatened individual freedom and generated economic chaos.

Means of gaining additional support

Strong leadership and initial support are not enough to explain the depth and smoothness of the privatization process in Chile, which, after all, extended over a seventeen-year period. During that time the government took a number of actions that did not always enhance public support for privatization, but which, on balance, turned out to be sufficiently positive for it to accomplish the vast majority of its divestiture objectives.

Transparent transactions and appropriate sequencing.   On the negative side, insufficiently transparent privatizations and, especially during the First Round, poor timing stand out. Insufficient transparency might not have affected either the price or stock allocations of the vast majority of the privatizations significantly, because the relevant investors were adequately informed, but it did provide grounds for criticism. Most divestitures of the First Round took place before the rules of the game were clearly defined and when the economy was still quite unstable, probably contributing to the privatization reversals of the early 1980s and to "low" divestiture prices.[1] These low prices and their effect on public sector wealth and revenues generated most of the controversy around the privatization policy of the military regime.

A favorable institutional and policy environment.   Continuing support for the government's privatization policy was a function of the effectiveness of the divested enterprises. During the 1950s and 1960s, when the government was closing the economy to international trade and introducing other protective measures, the public image of private enterprise had rapidly deteriorated. A majority of Chileans came to see such enterprise as exploiting customers and workers and not fulfilling a social purpose. During the early 1970s, however, the public image of SOEs also deteriorated, perhaps even more than that of its private counterpart. Chileans perceived SOEs as inefficient and saw them as being used by the government to favor political allies. This situation made possible the drastic divestitures of the mid-1970s, which had to result in efficient enterprises, serving the public well, or a negative reaction would have set in. Within a market economy, efficient and socially useful private enterprises go hand in hand with a competitive environment and appropriate regulation of monopolies (natural or not). Therefore, economic authorities gave the highest priority to fullfilling these conditions and succeeded (Chapter 2), strengthening the likelihood of completing the privatization program and diminishing the likelihood of a policy reversal.

In practice, the government policy of reducing public sector expenditures as much as possible, permitting significant income tax reductions in the 1980s and reducing real interest rates, contributed to a general increase in share prices in the stock exchange. The ensuing capital gains made by private shareholders in those SOEs being privatized induced others to join the process.

Labor and popular capitalism.   During the Second Round the government hoped to achieve property distribution objectives while also gaining significant support for further privatization. To these ends, it used labor and popular capitalism. As a rule, it would start privatizing traditional SOEs by offering stock of the enterprise to be divested to all workers (including executives) at slightly below the market price (Chapters 4 and 5), to be paid for with the advanced severance pay in such a way that those workers who took the offer could not lose. Whenever such an offer was made, most workers accepted it and thereafter became strong supporters of privatization. A similar case can be made for popular capitalism, which allowed the government to gain support for its divestiture policy among thousands of middle-class professionals, most of whom had not invested significantly in financial assets before and did not represent an interest group in the traditional sense of that term, but were important shapers of opinion.

Institutional investors

The Chilean privatization process, especially during the Second Round, was accompanied by the spectacular development of the capital market (Chapter 6). This process was fed by privatization and also provided support for it. During the Second Round, more often than not, the government would first divest relatively large packages to workers, AFPs (formally through the Santiago Stock Exchange), and other important investors, in order to transfer enterprise control to the private sector. It would then auction small packages in the stock exchange until the enterprises were 100 percent privatized. This procedure required a relatively well-functioning capital market, but also contributed to its growth. The empirical analysis in Chapter 5 of the divestiture prices of ten traditional SOEs suggests that, over time, the government was able to sell its stock on ever more favorable terms, a fact that may be related to the growth of the capital market itself.

The growth of that market is also related to the privatization and concomitant transformation of the pension system in Chile (Chapter 4). The new capitalization system, adopted at the beginning of the 1980s, implies competitive management of huge funds (totaling about 25 percent of GDP by early 1991 and growing fast), a proportion of which are invested in stock. These funds did acquire about 25 percent of the shares of those traditional SOEs in which they were allowed to invest and are trading them actively. The lesson here is that the institutional structure generated large financial funds, which made a decisive contribution to the development of the capital market and thereby made divestiture of significant packages of stock in some of the largest Chilean corporations possible through the stock exchanges.

How Long Does It Take to Carry Out a Massive Privatization Process?

As mentioned, the Chilean privatizations took seventeen years, and there are still enterprises and activities that could be privatized, some very significant, like the National Copper Corporation (CODELCO). The first divestiture to be completed was that of Sigdo Koppers, an engineering firm belonging to the Steel Company of the Pacific (CAP) that was sold to its executives. The last privatization was that of ENDESA, the large electricity-generating company whose shares were widely spread among its work force, other public sector employees, and private investors. More often than not, countries with a significant entrepreneurial sector also have heavily protectionist and interventionist economic policies, so that privatization, to be successful, must go hand in hand with sweeping institutional reforms. The lesson seems to be that privatization takes time, although perhaps not necessarily as much as in the case of Chile.

In theory and practice, preparing SOEs for privatization is usually a time-consuming and difficult task. In Chile, this preparation was accomplished for all practical purposes as a by-product of general policies designed to make the whole economic system more efficient. The government forced most SOEs, even during the mid-1970s, to operate like private enterprises with a hard budget (Chapter 8). To this end, SOEs were obliged to take the legal form of open corporations (if they had not already done so) and submit regular financial information to supervisory bodies. They also had to become self-financing and, during the 1980s, distribute 100 percent of their profits as dividends. At the same time, the government would not allow them to diversify their lines of operation and, especially in the 1970s, would approve new investments only in exceptional cases. Since the whole system was made competitive, these policies virtually forced efficient operation on Chilean SOEs (Chapter 7). The government contributed to this effect with nondiscriminatory pricing policies, even in the case of public utilities, and with noninterference management practices.

Does Privatization Affect Employment?

The empirical analysis of the Chilean case, as described in Chapter 6, suggests that the change in ownership associated with privatization does not affect employment levels per se but that the drive to increase efficiency levels, of which privatization might be a tool, does. We reach this conclusion because SOEs and private enterprises in Chile were subject to nearly the same rules of the game after the military takeover. As a result, SOEs adjusted their employment levels downward faster, if anything, than privatized enterprises, to establish normal productivity levels, after the abnormal Allende years. Furthermore, privatized enterprises increased employment significantly faster than SOEs, once the boom of the late 1970s started, a phenomenon that can easily be explained by government restrictions on SOE diversification and expansion. That is, the lesson of the Chilean experience suggests that employment reductions in SOEs with excess employment are associated with efficiency gains, no matter how the reductions are achieved. Privatization, perhaps the most effective means of increasing efficiency in the medium and long term, is only one method of employment rationalization. Although privatization might tend to reduce employment to its optimum level per unit of output, instead of maintaining the excess employment levels common in SOEs, this does not imply that such a policy will increase overall unemployment in the economy. Both theory and the Chilean experience during the Second Round of divestitures actually suggest the contrary (Chapter 2), as long as the economic policy framework of the country is adequate.

Moreover, privatization can lead to an important degree of worker participation in ownership of capital and control of divested SOEs (Chapter 4). Through labor capitalism, and popular capitalism in the case of ENDESA, many workers have become shareholders in privatized SOEs. In some cases, workers have become so enthusiastic about these investments that they have gone into debt in order to purchase stock packages beyond those to which they were entitled by the privatization system itself. In addition, through the AFPs, workers came to participate indirectly in the ownership and control of some of the large privatized traditional SOEs.[2] As a result, in several of these enterprises the board of directors is majority-controlled by worker representatives, and in some others workers have significant representation on the board. Almost without exception, these worker representatives are highly qualified professionals, oriented to maximizing financial returns for the enterprises they control. The lesson here is that workers seem to have accepted their dual role as workers and as capitalists easily.[3] Of course, the significant capital gains obtained since privatization and the high dividend rates of return on their initial investments, which have come about with the economic recovery of the second half of the 1980s, have helped. It remains to be seen how these worker-capitalists will react when macroeconomic conditions change.

How Does Privatization Affect Government Wealth and Revenues?

Although these two effects are related, we will discuss the lessons learned with respect to each of these factors separately.

Privatization and government wealth

Privatization will enhance national wealth only if the privatized SOEs operate more efficiently in the private sector, from the point of view of either internal efficiency or allocative efficiency. With privatization, government wealth might initially be positively affected by an internal efficiency gain but negatively affected by a divestiture that takes place at lower than market prices, either because the government decides to give away stock or to subsidize stock divestitures or because divestiture is not transparent enough or is patently fraudulent. The final outcome will, of course, depend on the use of funds collected from privatization. If those funds are consumed by the government, privatization will almost by definition be associated with a loss of government wealth.[4] If the funds are totally reinvested, the final outcome can in principle range all the way from a significant loss of wealth to a gain equivalent to the national gain resulting from the increase in internal efficiency.

The issue of gains or losses in government wealth resulting from privatization has drawn the most critical attention in Chile. Since this seems to have been a subject of concern almost everywhere governments have privatized, Chapter 5 is devoted entirely to that issue. Estimates of the short-run impact on government wealth (before expenditure of revenues from privatization) were made on the basis of a sample of ten large traditional SOEs divested during the Second Round of privatizations.[5] The total long-run impact was then estimated for each round on the basis of actual government expenditure policies.

The first important lesson to be drawn is that, even in a country poor in liquid capital, shares can be divested at fair market values as long as there is private sector confidence in the economy, the right institutions are created and developed (in this case the new pension fund system), and foreign investment is welcomed. The financial analysis of Chapter 5 suggests that, as a group, the ten SOEs of the sample probably divested at fair market prices,[6] except for those shares sold to workers and popular capitalists, which were divested with an intentional subsidy to spread ownership and gain support for the process. Those who complain that this was not the case tend to compare divestiture stock prices (fixed and paid years ago, when macroeconomic conditions were not as buoyant as today) with either book values or recent market prices, both of which are irrelevant as far as past market prices are concerned.

The Chilean case also shows that the final effect on wealth depends on government expenditure policy. During the First Round the government maximized revenues from SOE divestitures, since there was no giveaway and no subsidies, and credit was granted in favorable conditions to purchasers to make the shares as attractive as possible. It can be inferred, however, that the loss of public sector wealth was about equivalent to the value of the divested state enterprises, even before the government assumed part of the debt of the private sector when the crisis of the early 1980s broke out, because the government used divestiture revenues to increase social expenditures (on health, education and private sector housing).

During the Second Round government expenditure policy had changed, and so did the impact of the privatizations on public sector wealth. It can be inferred in this case that revenues from privatization, somewhat diminished because of the giveaways and subsidies implicit in some of the divestiture modes used, were reinvested largely in public works. As a result, the public sector loss of wealth was reduced to about the amount of the giveaways and subsidies referred to above.

Privatization and government revenues

Privatization affects government revenues in several ways. To begin with, the process alters the timing of revenues. This is most evident in cash sales, in which, assuming relatively well-functioning capital markets, governments anticipate the future cash flows they might have received from SOEs. In addition, revenues tend to increase if the privatized SOEs are expected to be run more efficiently by the private sector, assuming these enterprises are divested at fair market prices. Revenues tend to diminish, however, if sales proceeds are consumed by the public sector or invested in non-revenue-producing projects.

In the Chilean case, divestiture did reduce expected government revenues, if one takes a sufficiently short view. At the time of privatization, especially during the Second Round, SOEs were run relatively efficiently and the government obliged them to distribute 100 percent of their profits, while its contribution to their new investments was relatively limited. That is, SOEs were generating net revenues for the government, in addition to taxes. However, during the First Round revenues from divestiture had been consumed by social expenditures, and during the Second Round they were in part invested in non-revenue-producing public works. As a result, once the SOEs were divested, and the government had spent the sale proceeds, it continued to receive little more than the tax revenue from the privatized enterprises. Thus the government suffered a net expected revenue loss.

If one takes a longer view, however, the answer is not so clear. If we ignore CODELCO, which has not been privatized, and taxes, which if anything are expected to generate large revenues from divested enterprises, the Chilean government had since the 1940s made net investments in its enterprises, taken as a group. In this sense Chile was no different from the majority of other developing countries, although its SOEs were consistently run relatively well and the prices of its products, especially those of the large public utilities, were not too heavily subsidized. In this light, privatization has relieved the public sector from having to contribute net resources to its enterprise sector. That is, from the narrow point of view of the public sector, privatization probably allowed the government to increase the level of expenditures in the social sector and in public works while it was divesting SOEs and after that to increase the level of discretionary expenditures from what they would have been without divestiture.

Other public sector activities

The privatization of the administration of pension funds and of aspects of public housing and health administration have contributed to a more efficient use of the resources devoted to these social services by the public sector. This increased efficiency is sometimes reflected in more services for the same amount of resources (in housing, for example). In other cases it has meant better service (in health and pensions). In general it has generated incentives for better resource allocation, reducing pressure for unlimited increases in government expenditures in those areas.

Does the Chilean Privatization Experience Suggest Ways to Avoid Policy Reversals?

The answer is yes. As mentioned, Chile suffered a major reversal of many of the most important privatizations carried out during the debt-led divestitures of the 1970s. The lesson is obvious: debt-led privatizations, together with stock prices determined as a result of an auction process, yield relatively high stock prices but tend to induce moral hazard. Capital-poor purchasers take high risks in order to pay installments, and their low capital base is fragile. In a business slump, the number of privatized enterprises that go broke is large, and a social problem arises, making government intervention perhaps even desirable. In Chile, this happened during the recession of the early 1980s, when management of a relatively large number of previously privatized enterprises was indirectly taken over by the government, giving rise to the odd sector. Economic and political conditions were such that these enterprises were soon privatized again, but this may not always be the case.

The Chilean privatizations also suggest that a necessary condition for the general acceptance of the privatization process is a high degree of social usefulness of the privatized enterprises. They will tend to be useful as long as they operate in a competitive environment or are adequately regulated.

Does Privatization Lead to More Efficient Enterprises?

Unfortunately, the econometric evidence presented in Chapter 7 does not allow a definite reply one way or the other. Data gathered from financial ratios of balance sheets and income statements suggest that private sector enterprises are somewhat more profitable than SOEs, but differences, although statistically significant, are small. This result does not confirm the majority expert opinion and, to a certain extent, inferences that can be made from economic theory.

These differences from expected results have two possible explanations. One is related to the size and composition of the sample and the number of observations. The number of SOEs that could be included in the formal statistical analysis is relatively small, and the activities of these enterprises are very different from those included in the relatively large sample of private sector enterprises. Moreover, data were only readily available for the 1980s, which limited the number of observations. All these factors might have acted to blur, from a statistical point of view, underlying differences in efficiency.

More important perhaps is the fact that the general framework under which SOEs were operating during the period of analysis was about the same as that for private sector enterprises, and therefore one should not expect significant differences in behavior between these two categories of enterprises.[7] This does not mean that ownership is irrelevant or that the form of the framework is independent of the ownership structure. In fact, the two are probably highly interrelated. We can easily show both theoretically and through the experience of Chile and other countries that in the long run Congress and public officials will tend to alter an SOE regulatory framework such as that existing in Chile during the 1980s in order to take advantage of the possibilities offered by such alterations to grant political favors such as employment and goods and services at subsidized prices.

Is a Massive Privatization in a Developing Country Possible Only under an Authoritarian Political Regime?

The answer to this question lies in the realm of opinion. Chile's program could probably not have been carried out under a regime of a different nature. At the time, no developing country, with the possible exception of Bangladesh, had any experience with massive privatization, and it was still generally accepted in Latin America that public utilities and basic infrastructure enterprises had to be run by governments. The recent reaction against centralized economies in Central Europe was still years away. In fact, the First Round of the Chilean privatization program was already completed when Great Britain began its own highly influential process. In that sense, Chile was breaking new ground, very much against accepted development ideology. Democratic regimes are by nature conservative, and institutional change is slow. Therefore, under existing conditions, the massive privatization that took place in Chile probably required an authoritarian regime, although under today's conditions democracy in all likelihood reduces the possibility of a reversal.

This does not mean that today massive privatization cannot take place in Central Europe under emerging democracies or that significant divestitures cannot occur in Latin America under democratic regimes. In Central Europe, privatization is part of the process of democratization itself, and in Latin America ideological conditions have changed radically. Influenced by the reality of its present economic conditions, by the example of some of its own countries such as Chile, Costa Rica, and Mexico, and by the developments in Central Europe, Latin America is turning toward a development strategy that favors more open economies and in which the private sector is the main engine of economic growth. Within this political context, privatization (although perhaps not on as massive a scale as in Chile or Mexico) can take place in a Western-style democracy. Countries like Costa Rica and Great Britain have demonstrated that it is possible.

Enterprises with State Participation in 1970, 1973, 1983, and 1989

1970

Subsidiaries of CORFO

1. Empresa Forestal Arauco Ltda.
2. Forestal Pilpilco S.A.
3. Industrias Forestales S.A. (INFORSA)
4. Celulosa Constitución (CELSO)
5. Celulosa Arauco
6. Industria Nacional de Cemento S.A. (INACESA)
7. Empresa Pesquera Arauco S.A.
8. Empresa Pesquera Tarapacá S.A.
9. Pesqueras Unidas S.A.
10. Pesquera Indo S.A.
11. Manufacturas de Neumáticos S.A. (MANESA)
12. Sociedad Chilena de Fertilizantes Ltda. (SOCHIF)
13. Fábrica de Acido Sulfúrico S.A. (FASSA)
14. Empresa Electrónica Nacional Ltda. (ELECNA)
15. Empresa Nacional de Computación e Informática Ltda. (ECOM)
16. Sociedad Agrícola CORFO Ltda. (SACOR)
17. Industria Azucarera Nacional S.A. (IANSA)
18. Sociedad de Operaciones Agropecuarias S.A. (SOCOAGRO)

19. Empresa Nacional del Carbón (ENACAR)
20. Empresa Nacional de Energía (ENDESA)
21. Compañía Chilena de Electricidad S.A.
22. Implementos Agrícolas Ransomes Chilena Ltda.
23. Maestranza y Fundición Antofagasta
24. Compañía Acero del Pacífico S.A. (CAP)
25. Industria Conjuntos Mecánicos Aconcagua S.A.
26. Hotelera Nacional S.A. (HONSA)
27. Chile Films S.A.
28. Empresa Nacional de Telecomunicaciones S.A. (ENTEL)
29. Cuero y Curtiembre del Norte
30. Centro de Estudios Metalúrgicos Ltda.
31. Empresa Minera Mantos Blancos S.A.
32. Compañía Sudamericana de Fosfatos S.A. (COSAF)
33. Empresa Nacional de Semillas S.A.
34. Empresa Nacional de Frigoríficos S.A. (ENAFRI)
35. Sociedad Lechera Nacional (SOLECHE)
36. Sociedad Auxiliar de Cooperativas Ltda. (SACOOP)
37. Vinos de Chile S.A. (VINEX)
38. Minera Carolina de Michilla S.A.
39. Minera Chañaral Taltal S.A.
40. Hormigones Industrializados (VIBROCRET)
41. Petroquímica Chilena S.A.
42. Química Alquil S.A.
43. Astilleros del Norte S.A.
44. Frontel S.A.
45. Sociedad Austral de Electricidad S.A. (SAESA)
46. Sociedad Química y Minera de Chile (SOQUIMICH)

Other state-owned enterprises

1. Empresa Nacional de Petróleo (ENAP)
2. Empresa Nacional de Minería (ENAMI)
3. Ferrocarriles del Estado (FFCC)
4. Empresa Portuaria de Chile (EMPORCHI)
5. Empresa Marítima del Estado (EMPREMAR)
6. Línea Aérea Nacional (LAN)
7. Empresa de Correos de Chile
8. Empresa de Comercio Agrícola (ECA)
9. Empresa de Obras Sanitarias (EMOS)
10. Empresa de Obras Sanitarias V Región (EOS V Región)
11. Polla Chilena de Beneficencia (POLLA)
12. Instituto de Seguros del Estado (ISE)

13. Televisión Nacional de Chile (TVN)
14. Radio Nacional de Chile (RNCH)
15. Empresa Transporte Colectivo del Estado (ETCE)
16. Astilleros y Maestranza de la Armada (ASMAR)
17. Fábricas y Maestranza del Ejército (FAMAE)
18. Empresa Periodística La Nación
19. Laboratorio Chile
20. Planta Faenadora de Carnes Lo Valledor S.A.
21. Copper Mines

Other financial institutions

1. Corporación de Fomento a la Producción (CORFO)
2. Banco del Estado

1973

Subsidiaries of CORFO

A. *CORFO majority shareholders with over 50 percent*
   1. Empresa Forestal Arauco Ltda.
   2. Forestal Pilpilco S.A.
   3. Papelera del Pacífico Ltda. (PADELPA)
   4. Industrias Forestales S.A. (INFORSA)
   5. Bosques e Industrias Madereras S.A. (BIMA)
   6. Industrias de la Madera S.A. (IMPREGMA)
   7. RALCO S.A.I. de Maderas
   8. Celulosa Constitución S.A. (CELSO)
   9. Celulosa Arauco S.A.
   10. Complejo Forestal y Maderero Panguipulli Ltda.
   11. Maderas y Materiales de Construcción S.A.C. (MCM)
   12. Elaboradora de Maderas y Sintéticos Ltda.
   13. Sociedad Agrícola y Forestal Lebu Ltda.
   14. Sociedad Forestal y Maderera Chiloé (FOMACHIL)
   15. Fábrica Nacional de Loza de Penco S.A. (FANALOZA)
   16. Compañía de Industrias y Maderas S.A. (CIMSA)
   17. Refractarios Lota Green S.A.
   18. Cemento Cerro Blanco de Polpaico S.A.
   19. Industria Nacional de Cemento S.A. (INACESA)
   20. Fábrica de Cemento El Melón S.A.
   21. Empresa Pesquera Arauco S.A.

22. Productos Congelados del Mar Ltda. (PROMAR)
23. Conservera CORFO-Quellón Ltda.
24. Empresa Pesquera Tarapacá S.A.
25. Sociedad Terminales Pesqueros Ltda. (SOTEPES)
26. Compañía Pesquera Aysén Ltda.
27. Sociedad Pesquera Guanaye S.A.
28. Pesqueras Unidas S.A.
29. Pesquera Indo S.A.
30. Pesquera Iquique S.A.
31. Manufacturas de Neumáticos S.A. (MANESA)
32. Sociedad Chilena de Fertilizantes Ltda. (SOCHIF)
33. Fábrica de Acido Sulfúrico S.A. (FASSA)
34. Empresa Nacional de Explosivos S.A. (ENAEX)
35. Sociedad Química y Minera de Chile (SOQUIMICH)
36. Empresa Electrónica Nacional Ltda. (ELECNA)
37. Rema Rittig S.A.
38. Industrias de Radio y Televisión S.A. (IRT)
39. Empresa Nacional de Computación e Informática Ltda. (ECOM)
40. PROALIM Ltda.
41. Sociedad Agrícola CORFO Ltda. (SACOR)
42. Cecinas Valdivia S.A. (Ex-Loewer)
43. Empresa Nacional Avícola Ltda. (ENAVI)
44. Cecinas Til Ltda.
45. Empresa de Desarrollo Ganadero Ltda.
46. Industria Azucarera Nacional S.A. (IANSA)
47. Embotelladora Andina S.A.
48. Alimentos Purina S.A.
49. Sociedad de Operaciones Agropecuarias S.A. (SOCOAGRO)
50. Sociedad Productora de Alimentos Ltda. (SOPROA)
51. Algodones Hirmas S.A.
52. Textiles Iquitex Ltda.
53. Sociedad Industrial de Los Andes S.A. (SILA)
54. Empresa de Comercio Exterior Textil Ltda.
55. Empresa Nacional del Carbón (ENACAR)
56. Empresa Nacional de Energía (ENDESA)
57. Compañía Chilena de Electricidad S.A. (CHILECTRA)
58. Empresa de Fabricación y Reparación Maquinaria Agrícola Ltda. (ENFREMA)
59. Industria Manufacturera de Maquinaria Agrícola e Industrial S.A.I.C. (MAGRINSA)
60. Industria Maquinaria Agrícola CORFO Ltda. (IMACOR)
61. Implementos Agrícolas Ramsomes Ltda.
62. Empresa de Tractores y Repuestos Ltda. (ENATIR)

63. Empresa CORFO-SEAM Ltda.
64. Industria Farmacéutica de CORFO Ltda. (FARMACORFO)
65. Sociedad Exploraciones Mineras Ltda.
66. Empresa Minera Aysén SCM
67. Sociedad Explotadora de Minerales de Cal Ltda. (SOMINCA)
68. Sociedad Aurífera Flores CORFO
69. Compañía Minera Tamaya S.A.
70. Compañía Minera Amolana
71. Astilleros CORFO Ltda.
72. Empresa Nacional de Instrumentos de Precisión Ltda.
73. Maestranza y Fundición Antofagasta S.A.
74. Fábrica Nacional de Máquinas y Herramientas Ltda. (FANAMHE)
75. Fábrica de Maquinarias Mohrfoll S.A.
76. Níquel y Bronce Sudamericana S. A. (NIBSA)
77. Compañía de Acero del Pacífico S.A. (CAP)
78. Fábrica Electrónica S.A. (FEMSACO)
79. Empresa Asesora Comercial Automotriz Ltda. (EMAC)
80. Industria Conjuntos Mecánicos Aconcagua S.A. (CORMECANICA)
81. Industria Automotriz Arica Ltda. (CORARICA)
82. Automotriz CORFO Citroen S.A.
83. Empresa Nacional de Tapicería Ltda. (ENATAP)
84. INDUSCAR Ltda.
85. ENARA Ltda.
86. Sociedad Industrial Siam di Tella S.A. (SIAM)
87. Empresa de Inversiones Consumo Corriente
88. Turismo Bío-Bío
89. Empresa Editora Nacional Quimantúa Ltda.
90. Hotelera Nacional S.A. (HONSA)
91. Compañía Chilena de Navegación Interoceánica S.A.
92. Chile Films S.A.
93. Compañía Nacional de Teléfonos S.A. (CONATEVAL)
94. Compañía Sudamericana de Vapores S.A.
95. Empresa Nacional de Comercialización y Distribución S.A. (DINAC)
96. Empresa Nacional de Telecomunicaciones S.A. (ENTEL)
97. Sociedad Turismo Chiloé–CHILOTUR Ltda.
98. Empresa Nacional de Trabajadores Artesanales Ltda.
99. Cuero y Curtiembre del Norte
100. Envases del Pacífico S.A. (Ex–FRUGONE)
101. Empresa Vía Sur Ltda.
102. Centro de Estudios Metalúrgicos Ltda.

B. *CORFO majority shareholders with 10 to 50 percent*
1. Fundición y Elaboración de Metales S.G.M. S.A.
2. Termo Metalurgia S.A.
3. Maderas y Sínteticos S.A. (MASISA)
4. Tejidos Caupolicán S.A.
5. Fábrica de Paños Oveja Tomé S.A.
6. Empresa Minera Mantos Blancos S.A.
7. Manufacturas de Cobre S.A. (MADECO)
8. Compañía Minera Caleta del Cobre S.A.
9. Compañía Cervecerías Unidas S.A.
10. Compañía Industrial Indus S.A.
11. Compañía Refinería de Azúcar S.A.
12. Fábrica de Fideos Carozzi S.A.
13. Industria Nacional de Neumáticos (INSA)
14. Compañía Sudamericana de Fosfatos S.A. (COSAF)
15. Compañía de Teléfonos de Chile S.A. (CTC)
16. Enoteca de Chile Ltda.
17. Sociedad de Ferias y Exposiciones Ltda.
18. Cristalerías de Chile S.A.

C. *CORFO majority shareholders with 10 percent or less*
1. Automotriz Carriel Sur S.A.
2. Fábrica de Envases S.A. (FESA)
3. Comercial Gascon S.A.
4. Compañía Industrial y Comercial del Pacífico Sur S.A.
5. Industrias Varias S.A.
6. Inmobiliaria Portillo S.A.
7. Agencias Graham S.A.
8. Sociedad Constructora Establecimientos Educacionales S.A.
9. Sociedad El Tattersall S.A.
10. Sociedad Constructora Establecimientos Hospitalarios S.A.
11. Compañía de Muelles Población Vergara S.A.
12. Sociedad Comercial Saavedra Benard S.A.
13. Sociedad Inmobiliaria San Cristobal S.A.
14. Compañía Comercial S.A. (CICOMA)
15. Industrias Generales y Complementarias de Gas S.A. (INDUGAS)
16. Compañía General de Electricidad Industrial S.A.
17. Compañía de Gas de Concepción S.A.
18. Compañía de Gas de Valparaíso S.A.
19. Compañía de Petróleos de Chile S.A.
20. Sumar S.A.
21. Yarur S.A.
22. Compañía Industrial Hilos Cadena S.A.

23. Sociedad Agrícola La Rosa de Sofruco S.A.
24. Consorcio Nieto S.A.
25. COIA S.A.
26. Compañía Chilena de Tabaco S.A.
27. Compañía de Fósforos
28. Chiprodal S.A.
29. Farmoquímica del Pacífico S.A.
30. Compañía Industrias Chilenas S.A. (CIC)
31. Fábrica de Enlozados S.A. (FENSA)
32. Manufactura de Metales S.A. (MADEMSA)
33. Aceros Andes S.A.
34. Compañía Industrial El Volcán S.A.
35. Vidrios y Cristales Lirquén S.A.
36. Cemento Bío-Bío S.A.
37. Pizarreño S.A.
38. Forestal Quiñenco S.A.
39. Forestanac C.S.
40. Papeles y Cartones S.A.
41. Maderas Cholguán S.A.
42. Laminadora de Maderas S.A.
43. Ganaderos Tierra del Fuego S.A.
44. Sociedad Ganadera Laguna Blanca S.A.
45. Minera Valparaíso S.A.
46. Compañía Naviera Arauco S.A.
47. Industria Nacional de Rayón S.A. (RAYONHIL)
48. Elaboradora de Productos Químicos SINTEX S.A.
49. Pesquera Robinson Crusoe S.A.

D. *CORFO minority shareholders*
　1. Sociedad de Fomento y Mejoramiento Urbano Ltda.
　2. Empresa Nacional de Semillas S.A.
　3. Empresa Nacional de Frigoríficos S.A. (ENAFRI)
　4. Sociedad Lechera Nacional (SOLECHE)
　5. Sociedad Auxiliar de Cooperativas Sacoop Ltda.
　6. Vinos de Chile S.A. (VINEX)
　7. Industria de Viviendas El Belloto Ltda.
　8. Minera Carolina de Michilla S.A.
　9. Minera Cerro Negro
　10. Minera Chañaral Taltal S.A.
　11. Vibrocret S.A.
　12. ENADI Ltda.
　13. Embotelladora Concepción Ltda.
　14. Industria Nacional de Flotadores Ltda. (FLOTEX)

15. Petroquímica Chilena S.A.
16. Química Alquil S.A.
17. Compañía Consumidores de Gas de Santiago S.A. (GASCO)
18. Compañía de Teléfonos de Coyhaique S.A.
19. Astilleros del Norte S.A.
20. Pesquera Coloso S.A.
21. Marco Chilena S.A.

E. *Subsidiaries of CORFO-controlled subsidiaries*
1. Agencias Universales S.A.
2. Agencias Graham S.A.
3. Distribuidora Gibbs S.A.
4. Distribuidora Williamson Balfour S.A.
5. Empresa Nacional de Aceites Ltda.
6. Biriplast Ltda.
7. Ilesco Ltda.
8. Dinacem Ltda.
9. Empresa de Prototipos Ltda.
10. Armco S.A.I.
11. Equiterm S.A.
12. Prodinsa S.A.
13. AZA S.A.
14. Fundición Libertad S.A.
15. Inmar S.A.
16. Indac S.A.
17. Indesa S.A.
18. Mademeq S.A.I.C.
19. Maestranza Cerrillos Ltda.
20. Maestranza Maipú
21. Maestranza Lo Espejo Ltda.
22. Mestranza Santa Mónica Ltda.
23. Manganesos Atacama S.A.
24. ESI Ltda.
25. Socometal S.A.
26. Ingeniería del Pacífico Limitada
27. Extrumetal S.A.
28. Inchalam S.A.
29. Sociedad de Ingeniería S.A.
30. Sigdo Koppers S.A.
31. Compañía de Productos de Acero S.A. (COMPAC)
32. Frontel S.A.
33. Sociedad Austral de Electricidad S.A. (SAESA)

34. Corpesca S.A.
35. Minera Las Chivas SCM

F. *Subsidiaries of CORFO subsidiaries*
   1. Petroquímica Dow S.A.
   2. Sociedad Industrial Pizarreño S.A.
   3. Unidades y Complementos de Refrigeración S.A. (CORESA)

State-managed CORFO-related companies

1. Aceite y Alcoholes Patria S.A.
2. American Screw S.A.
3. Aluminio Las Américas S.A.
4. Acumuladores Helvetia
5. Asociación Fox Warner
6. Conservería Agrícola e Industrial Cisne Ltda.
7. Academia Studium y Liceos de Recuperación
8. Aluminios y Enlozados Fantuzzi S.A.
9. Aguas Minerales Cachantún S.A.
10. Barraca La Frontera
11. Barraca Los Canelos
12. Industria Eléctrica Edmundo Benard Ltda.
13. Compañía Chilena de Representaciones AGA S.A.
14. Confecciones Burger S.A.C.I.
15. Cobre Cerrillos S.A. (CECESA)
16. Compañía Industrial Metalúrgicas S.A. (CIMET)
17. Cristalerías Toro S.A.
18. Compañía Compradora de Maravilla S.A. (COMARSA)
19. Conservas Copihue S.A.
20. Cantolla y Compañía Ltda.
21. Cristavid S.A. (CRISTAVID)
22. Compañía Productora Nacional de Aceites S.A. (COPRONA)
23. Cummins Distribuidora Diesel S.A.
24. Compañía Industrial de Tubos de Acero S.A. (CINTAC)
25. Captaciones de Aguas Subterráneas Ltda. (CAPTAGUA)
26. CALAF S.A.
27. Industria Textil Confecciones Arica S.A.
28. Conservas Aconcagua S.A.
29. Componentes Eléctricos S.A. (COELSA)
30. Compañía de Stencil S.A.
31. Columbia Pictures of Chile Inc.
32. Cinema International Co. Ltda.

33. Canteras Lonco Ltda.
34. Calzados Topzy Ltda.
35. Cine Central
36. Cine Huérfanos
37. Cine Florida
38. Cine Cervantes
39. Cine City
40. Cine York
41. Cine El Golf
42. Cine Oriente
43. Cine Huelén
44. Compañía Minera de Exportación S.A. (COMINEX)
45. Constructora Cerrillos Concepción Ltda.
46. Citroen Bío-Bío Ltda.
47. Contratistas Cormolén Ltda.
48. Constructora Miguel Calvo Ltda.
49. Calzados Florentina Ltda.
50. Cimtram y Quiroga Ltda.
51. Calzados Verona Ltda.
52. Comando Nacional contra la Inflación Ltda. (CONCI)
53. Carburo y Metalúrgica S.A.
54. Compañía Pesquera Taltal S.A.
55. Compañía Electrometalúrgicas S.A. (ELECMETAL)
56. Fundición Metalúrgica José Kamet S.A.
57. Compañía Pesquera Camanchaca Ltda.
58. Compañía Pesquera Pedro de Valdivia S.A.
59. Compañía Pesquera Llanquihue S.A.
60. Compañía Pesquera Kon-Tiki S.A.
61. Compañía Chilena de Tejidos S.A. (CHITECO)
62. Dow Química S.A.
63. Distribuidora de Repuestos Automáticos S.A. (DISTRA)
64. Ingeniería Industrial Edwards y Cerutti S.A.
65. Electrón Chilena S.A.
66. Empresa Distribuidora Juan Yarur S.A.C.
67. Establecimientos Gratry Ltda.
68. Editorial Nacimiento Ltda.
69. Estructuras Metálicas Arca de Noé Ltda.
70. Estructuras Ruiz Ltda.
71. Elaboradora de Vinos el Ingenio Ltda.
72. Estación de Servicios Germán Mayo
73. Estación de Servicio Tristán Matta
74. Electromécanica Arica S.A.
75. Electroquímicas Unidas S.A.

76. Estructuras Metálicas Monsevelli Ltda.
77. Astilleros y Maestranza Las Habas S.A.
78. Aceros y Cuchillerías S.A. (ACSA)
79. Distribuidora de Alimentos King Ltda.
80. Empresa Conservera Perlak S.A.
81. Fábrica de Envases de Papel de Aluminio S.A. (ALUSA)
82. Fábrica de Confecciones el AS Ltda.
83. Fábrica de Materiales Eléctricos S.A. (ELECTROMAT)
84. Fábrica de Confecciones Ronitex S.A.
85. Fábrica de Productos de Loza Blanza Ferriloza S.A.
86. Fundición de Aceros SIMA Ltda.
87. FEBRATEX S.A.
88. Fábrica de Paños Continental S.A.
89. Fábrica de Resortes SUR Ltda.
90. Fábrica de Muebles Arcadio Beltrán Ltda.
91. Fábrica Nacional de Oxígeno Ltda.
92. Fábrica de Muebles Sindumet Ltda.
93. Fábrica de Tejidos Evita e Iruña Ltda.
94. Fábrica de Muebles Roma Ltda.
95. Fábrica de Tejidos Plumatex Ltda.
96. Fábrica de Envases E. Chamy Ltda.
97. Sociedad Agrícola e Industria Farmio Chilena S.A.
98. Ford Motor Company
99. Ferreterías Montero S.A.
100. Fábrica Hormigón Pre-Mezclado Ready Mix S.A.
101. Fábrica de Confites Rosemblut y Compañía. Ltda.
102. Fábrica de Camisas Samur e Hijos Ltda.
103. Granja Avícola Cerrillos Ltda.
104. Gas Lisur S.A.
105. Fundación de Viviendas Hogar de Cristo
106. Hilandería Andina S.A.
107. Hilados y Paños de Lana Comandari S.A.
108. Industria Cerrajera Deva Ltda.
109. Ingeniería Electromecánica Airolite S.A.
110. Industrias Electrónicas Codensa S.A.
111. Ingeniería y Construcción Metálica S.A. (FERROCRET)
112. Industria de Complementación Electrónica S.A. (INCESA)
113. Industria Metalúrgica Incopa S.A.
114. Industria Procesadora de Acero S.A. (IPAC)
115. Industria Metalúrgica Española S.A. (INDUMET)
116. Industria del Aluminio S.A. (INDALUM)
117. Industria Chilena de Soldadura S.A. (INDURA)
118. Sociedad Industria Metalúrgica S.A. (INMETAL)

119. Integradora Electrónica de T.V. S.A. (INELSA)
120. Industria Nacional de Pistones Ltda. (INAPIS)
121. Industria Electrónica Andina S.A.
122. Industria Maderera San Carlos
123. Industria Chilena de T.V. S.A. (CHILEVISION)
124. Industria KORES Ltda.
125. Instituto Profesional John Kennedy
126. Industria Textil Pollak Hnos. S.A.
127. Industrias Alejandro Riquelme
128. Industrias Electrónicas Maxwell
129. Industria de Pinturas Ceresita S.A.
130. Industria Textil Jacard y Pérez
131. Industria Cerrajera Ferromet
132. Industria Montero Ltda.
133. Industria de Corcho Velásquez
134. Industria Maderera de la Sociedad Puyehue
135. Industria de Corcho Pedro Torrens
136. Laboratorio INTERIFA Ltda.
137. Importadora Mellafe Y Salas S.A.
138. Industrias Conserveras Parma
139. Industrias Conserveras Unidas Perlak S.A.
140. Sociedad Industria Componentes de T.V. S.A. (SINTEL)
141. Industrias Metalúrgicas Sorena S.A.
142. Laboratorio Sanderson S.A.
143. Laboratorio Geka S.A.
144. Laminadora de Maderas S.A. (LAMINSA)
145. Industria Maderera Leopoldo Miguel e Hijo Ltda.
146. Lanera Austral S.A. (Coquimbo)
147. Muebles Easton Chile Ltda.
148. Mangueras Schiaffino S.A.
149. Modelería Metalúrgicas Ltda. (MODETAL)
150. Manufacturas de Repuestos Automotrices Pedreros S.A. (MAPESA)
151. Molinos y Fideos Luchetti S.A.
152. Mina La Torre
153. Mina La Fortuna
154. Mina El Molle
155. Mina Julia Taltal
156. Mina Palqui
157. Mina El Enchufe
158. Mina La Culebra
159. Mina La Africana
160. Compañía Molinera Santa Rosa
161. Molino San Bernardo

162. Molino Talca
163. Molino Ideal
164. Molino San Francisco
165. Molino San José
166. Sociedad Molinera y Panadera Ltda. (SOMOPAN)
167. Molino Maipú
168. Molino San Miguel
169. Molino Puente Alto
170. Molino San Pedro
171. Molino Linderos
172. Molino Rengo
173. Molino Caupolicán
174. Molino San Juan
175. Molino Koke
176. Molino La Compañía
177. Molino Maipo
178. Industria Metalúrgica Sylleros Ltda.
179. Matadero Industrial San Miguel Ltda.
180. Maestranza Jemo Ltda.
181. Maestranza Ali Ltda.
182. Maestranza Standard Ltda.
183. Maestranza Valenzuela Ltda.
184. Maestranza General Velásquez Ltda.
185. Metalúrgica Cerrillos Concepción S.A.
186. Mecánica Concepción Ltda.
187. Muebles Galaz S.A.C.I.
188. Muebles Mortonffy S.A.
189. Metro Goldwin Mayer
190. Manufacturas Chilenas de Caucho S.A.
191. Manufacturas Textiles de Arica S.A. (MANUTEXA S.A.)
192. Matadero de Aves Viluco
193. Pinturas Técnicas S.A. (PINTESA)
194. Planta Elisa de Boldos
195. Planta de Elaboración La Patagua
196. PREFACO Ltda.
197. Pinturas El Adaga S.A.
198. Productos de Goma Vulco S.A.
199. Química Industrial S.A.
200. Recauchados Charler Ltda.
201. Radio Taxi 33
202. Rayón Said, Industrias Químicas S.A.
203. Sociedad Agrícola y Lechera de Loncoleche S.A.
204. Sociedad Productora de Leche S.A. (SOPROLE)

205. Sociedad Industrias Eléctricas Nacionales S.A. (SINDELEN)
206. Electrónica Satel S.A.
207. Sindelen Electrónica S.A.
208. Soldaduras González
209. Línea Interprovincial Transportes Ltda. (LIT)
210. Salinas y Fabres S.A.C.I. (SALFA)
211. Sociedad Pesquera Stelaris S.A.
212. Sociedad Pesquera San Antonio S.A. (SOPESA)
213. Sociedad Construcciones Navales S.A. (SOCUNAVE)
214. Sociedad Agrícola Hacienda Venecia Ltda.
215. Textil Bamvarte S.A.
216. Textil Sabal S.A.
217. Textil Progreso S.A.
218. Textil Laban S.A.
219. Técnica Industrial S.A. (TISOL)
220. Textiles Artela S.A.
221. Textil Sudamericana Ltda.
222. Tejidos Caupolicán S.A.
223. Tejidos Salvador S.A. (COTESA)
224. Tapas, Bebidas y Envases Crown Cork de Chile S.A.
225. Textiles Deik Junis S.A.
226. United Artists South American Corp.
227. Viña Concha y Toro S.A.
228. Viña Santa Carolina S.A.
229. Fábrica de Confecciones Beytía
230. Criadero de Aves Las Pataguas
231. Grandes Almacenes Populares
232. Figueroa y Alemparte S.A. (FIGALEM)
233. Empresa Constructora Desco S.A.
234. Viviendas Económicas Desco Ltda.
235. Empresa Constructora Tecsa S.A.
236. Empresa Atevo Bolsi Ltda.
237. Empresa Constructora Autopista de Valparaíso (ECAVAL)
238. Empresa Constructora Belfi S.A.
239. Super Rogas
240. Sociedad Agrícola y Forestal Alphine
241. Sodima S.A.
242. Fábrica de Chuicos Cóndor
243. Industria Agrícola y Maderera Neltume Ltda.
244. Industria Metalúrgica Aconcagua
245. Industria Montespino
246. Fábrica de Tejidos de Punto El Abanico
247. Sociedad Industrial de Parquet Ltda. (SIP)

248. Manuplastic
249. Sociedad Marítima Guillermo Prochelle
250. City Servi
251. Mina Rebote
252. Empresa Eléctrica de Quintero Ltda.
253. Maestranza M. Mundy Ltda.
254. Fábrica de Confecciones Miriam
255. Astilleros Ahrend Ltda.
256. Accesorios de Automóviles Zeus S.A.
257. Litografía Nuestro Tiempo Ltda.
258. Maderas Monte Verde
259. Central Maderera Alaska
260. Planta Minera Aconcagua
261. Fábrica Casas Prefabricadas Raúl Acosta
262. Planta Relave del Río Salado
263. Mina Delirio
264. Distribuidora Notrogas S.A.
265. René Rosati B.
266. Fundición Mecánica Bodilla
267. Mina San Pedro
268. Mina Los Maquis
269. Compañía Industrial de Tratamientos de Minerales
270. Mina Lo Aguirre
271. Mina Los Maquis Norte
272. Empresa Hidrófila Chilena Ltda.
273. Planta Lixiviadora de Cobre Sta. Hortensia
274. Mina Buena Esperanza
275. Mina Cerrado
276. Bahía Arica
277. Compañía Minera Dos Amigos
278. Restorán Nogaró
279. Recauchajes y Gomas Santiago Ltda.
280. Minas Cerrillos y Tralca
281. Club Hípico S.A.
282. Asociación Dueños de Taxis Segundo Ltda.
283. Canteras Kinguer
284. Terminal Buses Chañaral
285. Empresa Ostrícola Belmard Ltda.
286. Sociedad Forestal Siberia S.A.
287. Compañía Marítima Técnica Ltda.
288. Mina Tránsito
289. Empresa de Turismo Ltda. Far West
290. Laboratorio Supra

291. Viña San Carlos
292. Mataderos de Aves Ltda. (MAVETA)
293. Estructuras Martín
294. Construcciones Económicas Copreva Ltda.
295. Sociedad Productora y Distribuidora de Maderas (SOPRODIMA)
296. Planta Beneficadora de Metales A. Gálvez
297. Sociedad Maderera Fénix Ltda.
298. Productos ATV Ltda.
299. COCAVI Ltda.
300. Cooperativa Campesina de Marchigüe
301. Sociedad Cooperativa Agropecuaria de Quillón Ltda.
302. Molinera Punta Arenas
303. Industria de Confites Ro-Ro Ltda.
304. Molinera del Norte S.A.
305. Pesquera Chilena S.A.
306. Sociedad del Lino La Unión S.A.
307. Fábrica Chilena de Sederías Viña del Mar S.A. (SEDAMAR)
308. Fábrica de Confecciones Velarde S.A.
309. Forestación Nacional S.A. (FORESNAC)
310. Muebles Novart S.A.
311. Industria Nacional de Prensados y Construcciones Ltda.
     (INAPRECO)
312. Manufactura de Esmeriles y Abrasivos S.A. (ISESA)
313. Termometalúrgica de Valdivia S.A.
314. Fundición y Maestranza Austral S.A.
315. Sociedad Nacional de Oleoductos Ltda. (SONACOL)
316. Sociedad Química Nacional S.A. (SOQUINA)
317. Metalúrgica Vulco Ltda.
318. Gildemeister S.A.
319. Importación y Comercio S.A. (IMCO)
320. Guías y Publicidad de Chile S.A.
321. Transportes Miguel Calvo y Compañía Ltda.
322. Financiera Automotrices
323. Ferias de Ganado
324. Distribuidora de Cigarrillos de Santiago y Valparaíso
325. Distribuidora de Películas

Banks related to CORFO

1. Chile
2. Español
3. Talca
4. O'Higgins
5. Israelita

6. Osorno y La Unión
7. Continental
8. Sud Americano
9. Crédito e Inversiones
10. Nacional del Trabajo
11. Austral
12. Concepción
13. Edwards
14. Regional de Linares
15. Constitución
16. Llanquihue
17. Curicó
18. Fomento de Valparaíso

Other state-owned enterprises

1. Empresa Nacional de Petróleo (ENAP)
2. Empresa Nacional de Minería (ENAMI)
3. Ferrocarriles del Estado (FFCC)
4. Empresa Portuaria de Chile (EMPORCHI)
5. Empresa Marítima del Estado (EMPREMAR)
6. Línea Aérea Nacional (LAN)
7. Empresa de Correos de Chile
8. Empresa de Comercio Agrícola (ECA)
9. Empresa de Obras Sanitarias (EMOS)
10. Empresa de Obras Sanitarias V Región (EOS V Región)
11. Polla Chilena de Beneficencia (POLLA)
12. Instituto de Seguros del Estado (ISE)
13. Televisión Nacional de Chile (TVN)
14. Radio Nacional de Chile (RNCH)
15. Empresa Transporte Colectivo del Estado (ETCE)
16. Astilleros y Maestranza de la Armada (ASMAR)
17. Fábricas y Maestranza del Ejército (FAMAE)
18. Empresa Periodística La Nación
19. Laboratorio Chile
20. Planta Faenadora de Carnes Lo Valledor S.A.
21. Sociedad de Transporte Marítimo Chiloé-Aysén Ltda. (TRANSMARCHILAY)
22. Pesquera Nueva Aurora
23. Copper Mines

Other financial institutions

1. Corporación de Fomento a la Producción (CORFO)
2. Banco del Estado

1983

Subsidiaries of CORFO

1. Compañía Chilena de Electricidad
2. Compañía Acero del Pacífico S.A. de Inversiones (CAP)
3. Compañía de Teléfonos de Coyhaique S.A.
4. Compañía de Teléfonos de Valdivia S.A.
5. Compañía de Teléfonos de Chile (CTC)
6. Empresa Nacional del Carbón (ENACAR)
7. Empresa Nacional de Energía (ENDESA)
8. Empresa Nacional de Computación (ECOM)
9. Empresa de Telecomunicaciones (ENTEL)
10. Industria Azucarera Nacional (IANSA)
11. Empresa Nacional de Explosivos (ENAEX)
12. Sociedad Química y Minera de Chile (SOQUIMICH)
13. Sociedad Agrícola CORFO (SACOR)
14. Compañía Chilena de Litio
15. Complejo Forestal y Maderero Panguipulli Ltda.
16. Sociedad Factibilidad Celulosa Panguipulli
17. Compañía Chilena de Navegación Inteorceánica (CCNI)
18. Fabricación de Viviendas Económicas Prefabricadas Ltda.
19. Empresa Minera Aysén Ltda.
20. Sociedad Constructora de Establecimientos Educacionales S.A.
21. Estudios Cinematográficos de Chile S.A.
22. Hotelera Nacional S.A.
23. Telex-Chile

Banks related to CORFO

1. Continental

Other state-owned enterprises

1. Empresa Nacional de Petróleo (ENAP)
2. Empresa Nacional de Minería (ENAMI)
3. Ferrocarriles del Estado (FFCC)
4. Empresa Portuaria de Chile (EMPORCHI)
5. Empresa Marítima del Estado (EMPREMAR)
6. Línea Aérea Nacional (LAN)
7. Empresa de Correos de Chile
8. Empresa de Comercio Agrícola (ECA)
9. Empresa de Obras Sanitarias (EMOS)

10. Empresa de Obras Sanitarias V Región (EOS V Región)
11. Polla Chilena de Beneficencia (POLLA)
12. Instituto de Seguros del Estado (ISE)
13. Televisión Nacional de Chile (TVN)
14. Radio Nacional de Chile (RNCH)
15. Empresa Transporte Colectivo del Estado (ETCE)
16. Astilleros y Maestranza de la Armada (ASMAR)
17. Fábricas y Maestranza del Ejército (FAMAE)
18. Empresa Periodística La Nación
19. Laboratorio Chile
20. Sociedad de Transporte Marítimo Chiloé-Aysén Ltda. (TRANSMARCHILAY)
21. Sociedad Agrícola y Servicios Isla de Pascua Ltda. (SASIPA)
22. Corporación Nacional del Cobre de Chile (CODELCO)

Other financial institutions

1. Corporación de Fomento a la Producción (CORFO)
2. Banco del Estado

1989

Subsidiaries of CORFO

1. Comercializadora de Trigo S.A. (COTRISA)
2. Empresa Eléctrica de Aysén S.A. (EDELAYSEN)
3. Empresa Eléctrica Colbún-Machicura S.A. (COLBUN)
4. Empresa Eléctrica del Norte Grande S.A. (EDELNOR)
5. Empresa Marítima del Sur S.A. (EMPREMAR SUR)
6. Transporte por Containers S.A. (TRANSCONTAINER)
7. Empresa Minera Aysén Ltda. (EMA)
8. Empresa Nacional del Carbón S.A. (ENACAR)
9. Carbonífera Victoría de Lebú S.A. (CARVILE)
10. Isapre del Carbón S.A. (ISCAR)
11. Empresa de Servicios Sanitarios de Tarapacá S.A.
12. Empresa de Servicios Sanitarios de Atacama S.A.
13. Empresa de Servicios Sanitarios de Coquimbo S.A.
14. Empresa de Servicios Sanitarios del Libertador S.A.
15. Empresa de Servicios Sanitarios del Maule S.A.
16. Empresa de Servicios Sanitarios del Bío-Bío S.A.
17. Empresa de Servicios Sanitarios de la Araucanía S.A.
18. Empresa de Servicios Sanitarios de Los Lagos S.A.

19. Empresa de Servicios Sanitarios de Aysén S.A.
20. Empresa de Servicios Sanitarios de Magallanes S.A.
21. Empresa de Transporte Ferroviario S.A. (FERRONOR)
22. Empresa de Transporte de Pasajeros Metro S.A.
23. Sociedad Agrícola SACOR Ltda. (SACOR Ltda.)
24. Zona Franca de Iquique S.A. (ZOFRI)

Other state-owned enterprises

1. Empresa Marítima S.A. (EMPREMAR)
2. Empresa Metropolitana de Obras Sanitarias (EMOS)
3. Sociedad Agrícola y Servicios Isla de Pascua Ltda.
4. Sociedad de Transporte Marítimo Chiloé-Aysén Ltda. (TRANSMARCHILAY Ltda.)
5. Polla Chilena de Beneficencia S.A. (Polla)
6. Empresa Nacional de Petróleo (ENAP)
7. Empresa Nacional de Minería (ENAMI)
8. Empresa de Comercio Agrícola (ECA)
9. Empresa Portuaria de Chile (EMPORCHI)
10. Correos y Telégrafos
11. Ferrocarriles del Estado (FFCC)
12. Empresa Obras Sanitarias V Región (EOS)
13. Radio Nacional de Chile (RNCH)
14. Empresa Periodística "La Nación"
15. Fábrica y Maestranza del Ejército (FAMAE)
16. Astilleros y Maestranza de la Armada (ASMAR)
17. Televisión Nacional de Chile (TVN)
18. Línea Aérea Nacional (LAN) (only as minority shareholder)
19. Corporación Nacional del Cobre de Chile (CODELCO)

Other financial institutions

1. Corporación de Fomento a la Producción (CORFO)
2. Banco del Estado

APPENDIX B

Market and Sale Prices of a Sample of Privatized Firms

TABLE B.1
Market and Sale Prices of ENTEL Shares, 1986–1989 (annual summary)

	1986	1987	1988	1989[a]	Total
Number of shares sold	27,501,987	2,778,840	27,127,055	32,263,301	89,671,183
Percentage sold	29.69	3.00	29.29	35.41	97.39
Estimated market price (UF)	2,292,715	352,231	4,066,304	6,164,039	12,875,288
Actual sale price (UF)	1,245,594	283,083	2,788,020	4,754,565	9,071,262
Price gap					
UF	1,047,121	69,148	1,278,283	1,409,474	3,804,026
Percentage	45.67	19.63	31.44	22.86	29.54

a. Includes sale to FAMAE in May 1989.
SOURCE: Authors' estimates.

TABLE B.2

Market and Sale Prices of CTC Shares, 1986–1989 (annual summary)

	1986	1987	1988	1989[a]	Total
Number of shares sold	7,130,368	49,661,660	220,038,290	103,551,683	380,382,001
Percentage sold	1.96	12.30	47.60	14.80	76.66
Estimated market price (UF)	211,518	1,821,059	7,931,978	4,483,380	14,447,935
Actual sale price (UF)	156,594	1,983,528	9,463,429	3,897,207	15,500,758
Price gap					
UF	54,924	-162,469	-1,531,451	586,173	-1,052,823
Percentage	25.97	-8.92	-19.31	13.07	-7.29
Interest subsidy (%)	0.00	0.00	0.00	1.23	0.39
Total price gap (%)	25.97	-8.92	-19.31	14.30	-6.90

a. Includes a term sale (Law 18,747) to public employees.
SOURCE: Authors' estimates.

TABLE B.3

Market and Sale Prices of CAP Shares, 1986–1987 (annual summary)

	1986	1987	Total
Number of shares sold	4,500,235	84,518,852	89,019,087
Percentage sold	3.01	56.55	59.56
Estimated market price (UF)	138,381	3,214,287	3,352,668
Actual sale price (UF)	113,414	2,274,917	2,388,331
Price gap			
UF	24,967	939,369	964,337
Percentage	18.04	29.22	28.76

SOURCE: Authors' estimates.

TABLE B.4

Market and Sale Prices of ENDESA Shares, 1987–1989 (annual summary)

	1987[a]	1988[b]	1989	Total
Number of shares sold	1,808,612,244	5,658,384,000	295,653,900	7,762,650,144
Percentage sold	22.8	71.4	3.7	97.9
Estimated market price (UF)	6,150,651	23,515,991	1,168,750	30,835,392
Actual sale price (UF)	6,855,440	21,178,751	1,249,679	29,283,870
Price gap				
UF	-704,789	2,337,240	-80,929	1,551,522
Percentage	-11.46	9.94	-6.92	5.03
Interest subsidy (%)	7.71	2.07	0.00	5.92
Total price gap (%)	-3.75	12.01	-6.92	10.95

a. Includes a term sale through popular capitalism, November 12, 1987.
b. Includes a term sale (Laws 18,681 and 18,747) to public employees.
SOURCE: Authors' estimates.

TABLE B.5

Market and Sale Prices of SOQUIMICH Shares, 1986–1988
(annual summary)

	1986	1987	1988	Total
Number of shares sold	61,478,519	31,088,546	22,210,907	114,777,972
Percentage sold	49.79	25.20	17.99	92.98
Estimated market price (UF)	4,788,234	2,704,977	2,059,501	9,552,712
Actual sale price (UF)	2,765,245	2,391,403	2,079,860	7,236,508
Price gap				
UF	2,022,989	313,574	−20,359	2,316,204
Percentage	42.25	11.59	−0.99	24.25

SOURCE: Authors' estimates.

TABLE B.6

Market and Sale Prices of CHILGENER Shares, 1986–1988
(annual summary)

	1986	1987	1988	Total
Number of shares sold	4,617,799	7,225,852	2,919,664	14,763,315
Percentage sold	29.75	46.54	18.80	95.09
Estimated market price (UF)	1,265,392	1,953,101	695,848	3,914,342
Actual sale price (UF)	822,780	1,613,133	627,794	3,063,708
Price gap				
UF	442,612	339,968	68,054	850,634
Percentage	34.98	17.41	9.80	21.73

SOURCE: Authors' estimates.

TABLE B.7

Market and Sale Prices of CHILMETRO Shares, 1986–1987
(annual summary)

	1986	1987	Total
Number of shares sold	5,027,755	44,948,899	49,976,654
Percentage sold	43.54	38.13	81.67
Estimated market price (UF)	2,862,118	3,090,041	5,952,159
Actual sale price (UF)	1,702,793	2,355,982	4,058,775
Price gap			
UF	1,159,325	734,059	1,893,384
Percentage	40.51	23.76	31.81

SOURCE: Authors' estimates.

TABLE B.8

Market and Sale Prices of CHILQUINTA Shares, 1986–1987 (annual summary)

	1986	1987	Total
Number of shares sold	1,543,186	1,290,910	2,834,096
Percentage sold	44.44	40.42	84.86
Estimated market price (UF)	661,021	691,914	1,352,935
Actual sale price (UF)	369,428	639,160	1,008,588
Price gap			
UF	291,593	52,754	344,347
Percentage	44.11	7.62	25.45

SOURCE: Authors' estimates.

TABLE B.9

Market and Sale Prices of IANSA Shares, 1986–1988 (annual summary)

	1986	1987	1988	Total
Number of shares sold	719,929,290	79,762,641	1,111,488,500	1,911,180,400
Percentage sold	30.16	3.34	46.56	80.06
Estimated market price (UF)	454,056	52,333	1,417,570	1,923,959
Actual sale price (UF)	187,695	33,169	1,462,463	1,683,327
Price gap				
UF	266,360	19,164	−44,893	240,632
Percentage	58.66	36.62	−3.17	12.51

SOURCE: Authors' estimates.

TABLE B.10

Market and Sale Prices of Laboratorio Chile Shares, 1986–1988 (annual summary)

	1986	1987	1988	Total
Number of shares sold	58,570,069	69,206,013	114,974,601	242,750,683
Percentage sold	23.43	27.68	45.99	97.10
Estimated market price (UF)	164,852	195,792	591,330	951,973
Actual sale price (UF)	90,154	180,862	531,590	802,606
Price gap				
UF	74,698	14,929	59,740	149,367
Percentage	45.31	7.63	10.10	15.69

SOURCE: Authors' estimates.

TABLE B.11

Market and Sale Prices of ENTEL Shares Sold to Workers, April 1988

	April 1988
Number of shares sold	11,578,498
Percentage sold	12.50
Estimated market price (UF)	1,604,905
Actual sale price (UF)	1,340,259
Price gap	
UF	264,646
Percentage	16.49

Source: Authors' estimates.

TABLE B.12

Market and Sale Prices of CTC Shares Sold to Workers, April 1987 to March 1988 (monthly summary)

	April 1987	May 1987	June 1987	September 1987	March 1988	Total
Number of shares sold	24,420,771	417,049	412,276	7,348,894	15,600,000	48,198,990
Percentage sold	6.0	0.1	0.1	1.8	3.5	11.5
Estimated market price (UF)	843,050	14,315	14,580	276,712	604,465	1,753,121
Actual sale price (UF)	775,641	12,963	17,917	311,992	595,770	1,714,281
Price gap						
UF	67,409	1,352	–3,338	–35,280	8,697	38,840
Percentage	8.00	9.44	–22.90	–12.75	1.44	2.22

Source: Authors' estimates.

TABLE B.13

Market and Sale Prices of CAP Shares Sold to Workers, December 1986
to February 1987 (monthly summary)

	December 1986	February 1987	Total
Number of shares sold	4,500,235	12,000,000	16,500,235
Percentage sold	3.01	8.56	11.57
Estimated market price (UF)	138,381	416,686	555,067
Actual sale price (UF)	113,414	394,451	507,865
Price gap			
UF	24,968	22,235	47,203
Percentage	18.04	5.34	8.50

SOURCE: Authors' estimates.

TABLE B.14

Market and Sale Prices of ENDESA Shares Sold to Workers, March 1988

	March 1988
Number of shares sold	47,535,000
Percentage sold	6.0
Estimated market price (UF)	1,519,147
Actual sale price (UF)	1,500,404
Price gap	
UF	18,743
Percentage	1.2

SOURCE: Authors' estimates.

TABLE B.15

Market and Sale Prices of SOQUIMICH Shares Sold to Workers, January
1986 to March 1988 (monthly summary)

	January 1986	December 1986	January 1987	March 1988	Total
Number of shares sold	3,154,594	2,271,542	10,077,568	6,774,520	22,278,224
Percentage sold	2.55	1.84	8.16	5.48	18.03
Estimated market price (UF)	165,301	197,596	751,688	652,108	1,766,694
Actual sale price (UF)	108,068	100,068	441,544	627,910	1,277,591
Price gap					
UF	57,233	97,529	310,144	24,198	489,104
Percentage	34.62	49.36	41.26	3.71	27.68

SOURCE: Authors' estimates.

TABLE B.16
Market and Sale Prices of CHILGENER Shares Sold to Workers, July 1986

	July 1986
Number of shares sold	363,696
Percentage sold	2.34
Estimated market price (UF)	107,685
Actual sale price (UF)	58,495
Price gap	
UF	49,190
Percentage	45.68

SOURCE: Authors' estimates.

TABLE B.17
Market and Sale Prices of CHILMETRO Shares Sold to Workers, November 1986 to August 1987 (monthly summary)

	November 1986	June 1987	August 1987	Total
Number of shares sold	366,870	347,894	2,349,731	3,064,495
Percentage sold	3.14	2.93	20.0	26.07
Estimated market price (UF)	226,597	234,614	1,643,447	2,104,658
Actual sale price (UF)	119,875	155,202	1,109,909	1,384,986
Price gap				
UF	106,722	79,412	533,538	719,672
Percentage	47.10	33.85	32.46	34.19

SOURCE: Authors' estimates.

TABLE B.18
Market and Sale Prices of CHILQUINTA Shares Sold to Workers, December 1986 (monthly summary)

	December 1986
Number of shares sold	21,940
Percentage sold	1.0
Estimated market price (UF)	18,725
Actual sale price (UF)	9,348
Price gap	
UF	9,377
Percentage	50.1

SOURCE: Authors' estimates.

TABLE B.19

Market and Sale Prices of IANSA Shares Sold to Workers, November 1986 to November 1988 (monthly summary)

	November 1986	January 1988	November 1988	Total
Number of shares sold	376,179,524	122,961,830	196,625,535	695,766,889
Percentage sold	15.76	5.15	8.24	29.15
Estimated market price (UF)	237,252	92,374	363,352	692,978
Actual sale price (UF)	92,776	79,743	371,229	543,748
Price gap				
UF	144,476	12,630	−7,877	149,230
Percentage	60.89	13.67	−2.16	21.53

SOURCE: Authors' estimates.

TABLE B.20

Market and Sale Prices of Laboratorio Chile Shares Sold to Workers, May 1986 to November 1988 (monthly summary)

	May 1986	May 1987	November 1988	Total
Number of shares sold	347,270	31,250,000	31,250,000	62,847,270
Percentage sold	0.14	12.5	12.5	25.14
Estimated market price (UF)	985	88,529	175,154	264,668
Actual sale price (UF)	1,072	64,782	127,762	193,615
Price gap				
UF	−87	23,747	47,392	71,053
Percentage	−8.83	26.82	27.06	26.85

SOURCE: Authors' estimates.

APPENDIX C

Multivariate Analysis Applied to Efficiency Comparisons

with Sebastián de Ramón

Multivariate analysis can be used to find out if differences exist in the behavior of different groups of enterprises, such as public, private, privatized, or any subset of these. First, we must test normality of distributions of variables to insure the appropriateness of the multivariate method to be used. Second, we will apply discriminant analysis to find out if each category of firms chosen constitutes a compact group with characteristics of its own. Third, we will use canonic discriminant analysis to discover the attributes producing greater differentiation (discrimination) among groups.

The sample of variables used in this analysis comprises nine financial ratios (R1 to R9) for the period 1980 to 1987 and in some cases a tenth (R10); when R10 is included the analysis does not cover the subperiod 1980–1982 because of a lack of information for that particular ratio. The financial ratios are as follows:

R1: inventories/total assets

R2: investment in related companies/total assets

R3: operational results/total assets

R4: financial expenditures/debt

R5: total benefits/total assets

R6: distributed dividends/total assets

R7: current liabilities/total liabilities

R8: long-term liabilities/total liabilities

R9: debt/total assets

R10: investment/total assets

R1 and R10 are related to investment; R4, R7, R8, and R9, to indebtedness; R2, to relations with other enterprises; and R3, R5, and R6, to efficiency. The sample of firms has been assembled into groups as follows:

Group 1: eighty-two private enterprises that have always been in private hands

Group 2: sixteen private firms, managed by the state in 1982–1983 and privatized thereafter; these firms have been known as the odd sector

Group 3: twelve enterprises that were originally private and then were legally acquired by the public sector and privatized during the period 1975–1982

Group 4: fourteen originally private firms that were either state-managed or expropriated during the period 1971–1973 and returned in an unrequited manner to the private sector after 1974

Group 5: twelve traditionally public enterprises divested after 1984

Group 6: eight traditionally public firms that have remained in the public sector

Test of Distribution of Variables

The first step in the analysis consists of examining the type of probabilistic distributions from which variables R1 to R10 are issued. In particular, we have to verify that the distribution for each group or category 1 to 6 is a normal multivariate for the ten ratios.

Let $\vec{\mu}$ be the vector of expected values for the ten ratios and Σ the variance-covariance matrix of the variables:

$$\vec{\mu}^{\,T} = (E[R_1], E[R_2], \ldots, E[R_9], E[R_{10}]) = (\mu_1, \mu_2, \ldots, \mu_{10})$$
$$\vec{R}^{\,T} = (R_1, R_2, \ldots, R_9, R_{10})$$
$$\Sigma = E[(\vec{R} - \vec{\mu})(\vec{R} - \vec{\mu})^T]$$

We will use the test χ^2 (Pearson 1990) to find out in which measure the variables chosen proceed from a normal multivariate distribution, that is, to find out if we can accept the null hypothesis:

$$H_0: \vec{R} \rightsquigarrow N_v(\vec{\mu}, \Sigma)$$

Thus, the normalization of variables is required in order to generate an aggregate of variables $\vec{Z} = (Z_1, Z_2, \ldots, Z_9, Z_{10})$ with:

$$\vec{Z} \rightsquigarrow N_v(\vec{0}, 1)$$

that is, one variable Z, a linear combination of the ten ratios, which, if the null hypothesis is correct, will be derived from a normal multivariate distribution of mean 0 and variance 1. Each Z_i will be a random variable normally distributed with zero mean and unit variance.

$$H_{01}^{\dagger}: Z_i \rightsquigarrow N(0,1)$$

Let S be a matrix such that $\Sigma^{-1} = SS^T$. We define Z by mean of such transformation. It is clear that the new variable is a vector of random variables, independent and with normal distribution of mean 0 and variance 1.

For our sample, to estimate $\vec{\mu}$ and Σ, we will take for each group:

$$\vec{R}_M = \frac{1}{n} \sum_{i=1}^{n} \vec{R}_i$$

$\vec{R}_i$ is observation i of the variables.

$$\Sigma_M = \frac{1}{n-1} \sum_{i=1}^{n} (\vec{R}_i - \vec{R}_M)(\vec{R}_i - \vec{R}_M)^T$$

S is a 10×10 matrix such that $SS^T = \Sigma_M^{-1}$. We estimate S as the Cholesky decomposition of the inverse of the variance-covariance matrix.

The test is applied to each variable Z and consists in comparing the empirical distribution with the theoretical one; the latter is assumed to be normal of mean 0 and variance 1. The line is divided into $k + 1$ intervals with the numbers $a_1, a_2, \ldots, a_k$, and values are estimated for $\Theta_i = P[a_i \le x_i < a_{i+1}]$ for the theoretical probability. On this basis, we build the variable:

$$c = \sum_{i=1}^{k+1} \frac{(n_i - n\Theta_i)^2}{n\Theta_i}$$

where n_i is the number of observations in the empirical distribution that fall into the interval $[a_i, a_{i+1}]$ and n, the total number of observations in the sample. This variable c is computed for each Z_i. Given the convergence of distributions, c is a $x^2 - k$ degrees of freedom—distributed variable. If c takes a value greater than the critical point ($\alpha\%$ level), we could reject the hypothesis that the distribution Z_i is normal with mean 0 and variance 1. If so, it would be questionable that the distribution of the original variable be a multivariate normal.

Table C.1 presents the results of the test applied to the normalized variables Z. We use ten intervals to test the distribution of the sample for each group. For the level 95 percent the critical point is 19.7; for the level 97.5 percent the rejection zone comprises the values greater than 21.9.

It is important to note that for the test we used nine variables Z_i, when ten should have been taken, given the original number of variables. The reason is that, in the process of normalization, the dimension of the problem—the space covered by the ten original variables $(R_1, R_2, \ldots, R_{10})$—is reduced. In other words, it is possible to show the information contained in the ten original variables in only nine variables. The results show a tendency to the no-normality in some components. Groups 1, 5, and

TABLE C.1
Normality Tests

Group	Observations	c_1	c_2	c_3	c_4	c_5	c_6	c_7	c_8	c_9
					$R1, \ldots, R9$					
1	315	84.6	66.8	57.3	42.1	17.2	47.6	24.3	54.1	74.9
2	63	49.3	22.3	25.0	8.7	26.0	21.8	4.9	15.8	27.2
3	48	34.4	67.4	28.1	9.1	8.2	11.2	16.0	16.9	31.8
4	58	12.0	7.7	11.3	12.0	5.7	17.5	11.7	14.4	16.2
5	43	68.8	52.3	39.5	11.0	12.5	62.6	27.8	9.0	31.6
6	32	63.7	142.1	44.3	8.7	17.3	35.5	19.8	28.0	5.3
					$R1, \ldots, R10$					
1	630	85.8	62.6	56.2	28.7	12.9	49.0	23.3	51.0	90.5
2	127	23.2	12.2	17.8	17.8	18.2	23.6	6.7	15.9	25.0
3	96	33.5	47.7	22.4	10.7	8.3	12.3	8.5	18.3	15.9
4	114	9.6	8.1	9.7	8.4	11.9	12.7	3.4	19.3	8.4
5	86	58.9	65.2	35.1	8.1	11.6	60.3	18.4	6.3	14.6
6	64	52.6	108.5	45.2	3.5	6.3	83.4	26.6	26.2	6.4

SOURCE: Authors' estimates.

6 (private, privatized, and public enterprises) show the greatest values for the statistic. This fact is important especially for group 1, since this group is represented by the highest number of firms and, consequently, can give more reliable results for the relevant test. However, this no-normality is not absolute, and we do not reject the null hypothesis for many of its components. On the other hand, the test used allows acceptance of the null hypothesis for the original variables when it is accepted for variables $Z_1, Z_2, ..., Z_9$, but it does not allow rejection of variables $R_1, R_2, ..., R_{10}$ when we have rejected it for normalized variables. No doubt the rejection of the normality of some components of vector Z_i is an alert with respect to the distribution of the financial ratios, our main variables.

The test developed here has only illustrative value, since it does not allow rejection of the hypothesis on the original variables. On the other hand, any test on the distribution of the ratios would require recognizing the expected value and variance of variables, and for these, estimates that can affect the result of the test are the only ones available.

Other factors could also be exerting some influence on the results of the test; these are the changes occurring through time within any group of firms. However, it is not possible to realize a temporal analysis of the variables, given that samples, with the exception of group 1, are too small. The idea is to ensure that variables have a reasonable behavior and to use the discriminant and canonic analysis to discover if, despite the change within groups over time, it is possible to find planes within which each group is significatively distant from the other.

Finally, a possible way to enhance the results in canonical analysis is to find a nonlinear tranformation of the original ratios, such as $Ln(R_i + \text{constant})$, where the "constant" must be small, have smoothing properties for the distribution of the variables, and be such that the new variables maintain its economic features. This is possible if the constant is small.

Multivariate Analysis

Given the high number of ratios chosen—at least nine—it may be convenient to reduce the number required to describe any group, thereby diminishing the dimension of the problem. This reduction will depend on the existing correlation between variables.

The matrix of correlation between variables is given by

$$R = D^{-1/2} V D^{-1/2},$$

where V is the matrix of dispersion and D is the diagonal of V.

$$R = \begin{bmatrix} 1 & r_{21} & \ldots & r_{n1} \\ r_{12} & 1 & \ldots & r_{n2} \\ \cdot & & \cdot & \cdot \\ \cdot & & \cdot & \cdot \\ \cdot & & \cdot & \cdot \\ r_{1n} & r_{2n} & \ldots & 1 \end{bmatrix}$$

The test of the hypothesis used to determine the existence of a correlation is:

$$H_0 : \rho = 0$$
$$H_1 : \rho \neq 0$$

The t-student statistic is given by:

$$t_0 = \frac{\rho_{ij} \sqrt{n-2}}{\sqrt{1-\rho_{ij}^2}} \rightsquigarrow t(n-2),$$

where ρ_{ij} is the partial correlation coefficient of i with j and n is the number of observations. The critical point of comparison is, at α percent level, the value that gives this percentage in a t-student distribution – (n – 2) degrees of freedom.

The results appear in Table D.1. The only significant correlations (89 percent) are those of R7 (current liabilities/total liabilities) with R9 (debt/total assets) and R5 with R7; the correlation of R3 with R7 is not significant. The elimination of two variables would not reduce the dimension of the problem in any significant way. Consequently, they will not be taken out of the discriminant analysis.

Discriminant analysis

The application of this method permits the classification of any individual firm in one particular group based on variables that supposedly contain information on the group to which this firm really belongs (private, public, privatized, etc).

The lineal discriminant is given by:

$$W_{ij} = R^T S^{-1} (\overline{R}_i - \overline{R}_j) - \frac{1}{2} (\overline{R}_i + \overline{R}_j)^T S^{-1} (\overline{R}_i - \overline{R}_j)$$

where $\overline{R}_i$ is the vector of means of group i and R^T is the vector of new observation $(R_1, R_2, \ldots, R_{10})$, and

$$S^{-1} = \frac{1}{N - k} \sum_{j=1}^{k} \sum_{i=1}^{n_j} (R_j - \overline{R}_j)(R_j - \overline{R}_j)^T$$

where N is the total number of observations and k is the total number of groups.

The rule of classification is the following:

assign R to the population i, if $W_{ij} > 0 \; \forall \; j \neq i$. For example, if we have three groups 1, 2, and 3:

$$W_{12} = R^T S^{-1} (\overline{R}_1 - \overline{R}_2) - \frac{1}{2} (\overline{R}_1 + \overline{R}_2)^T S^{-1} (\overline{R}_1 - \overline{R}_2)$$

$$W_{13} = R^T S^{-1} (\overline{R}_1 - \overline{R}_3) - \frac{1}{2} (\overline{R}_1 + \overline{R}_3)^T S^{-1} (\overline{R}_1 - \overline{R}_3)$$

$$W_{23} = R^T S^{-1} (\overline{R}_2 - \overline{R}_3) - \frac{1}{2} (\overline{R}_2 + \overline{R}_3)^T S^{-1} (\overline{R}_2 - \overline{R}_3)$$

X classifies as population 1 if $W_{12} > 0$ and $W_{13} > 0$; population 2 if $W_{12} < 0$ and $W_{13} > W_{12}$; and population 3 if $W_{13} < 0$ and $W_{12} > W_{13}$. This classification can be expressed in terms of the distance Mahalanobis.

$$D_i^2 = (R - \overline{R}_i)^T S^{-1} (R - \overline{R}_i)$$

X is assigned to population i if $D_i^2 = \min [D_i^2, ..., D_k^2]$. Then

$$W_{ij} = -\frac{1}{2} D_i^2 + \frac{1}{2} D_j^2$$

and the rule of decision is assign R to the population i, if $D_i^2 < D_j^2 \; \forall \; j \neq i$.

The results are presented in Table 7.1 in Chapter 7 and Tables D.2 through Table D.6 in Appendix D.

Canonical variate analysis

To better ascertain possible differences among groups of firms, we apply canonical variate analysis. Like discriminant analysis, it allows us to determine (1) if each group is self-contained and if differences exist among groups and (2) which of the variables (ratios) used allows better discrimination among groups.

Formally, this method consists in maximizing l with respect to b where $l = (b^T B b)/(b^T W b)$.

Defining

$$T = \sum_{j=1}^{k} \sum_{i=1}^{n_j} (R_{ij} - \overline{R})(R_{ij} - \overline{R})^T$$

as the matrix of correlation of groups with the mean, and:

W matrix of correlation within groups
B matrix of correlation between groups will be

$$B = T - W = \sum_{j=1}^{k} n_j (\overline{R}_j - \overline{R})(\overline{R}_j - \overline{R})^T$$

where $\overline{R}_j$ is the mean of group j

$$\overline{R}_j = \sum_{i=1}^{n_j} R_{ij}/n_j$$

and $\overline{R}$ is the total mean

$$\overline{R} = \sum_{j=1}^{k} \sum_{i=1}^{n_j} R_{ij}/n$$

$$n = \sum_{i=1}^{k} n_j$$

R_{ij} is variable i of group j; n_j is the number of observations of group j; $i = 1,...,n_j$ number of variables; and $j = 1,...,k$ number of groups.

Conceptually, λ maximizes the distance between groups and at the same time minimizes the distances within groups. An alternative to represent this maximization is to solve equation $(W^{-1}B - \lambda|)b = 0$ for λ and b.

Once b is obtained, the canonical variate functions can be built. The first one explains the greatest variance among groups and is a weighted average of the distinct variables (ratios) used in the analysis

$$Can_1 = Y = b_1 R_1 + b_2 R_2 + ... + b_P R_P$$
$R_1,...,R_P$: financial ratios.

The variance of Can_1

$$VAR_B(Can_1) = b^T VAR_B(R_1, ..., R_P)b$$

It can be demonstrated that $VAR_B(Can_1) = b^T Bb$, which is maximum, and, $VAR_W(Can_1) = b^T VAR_W (R_1, ..., R_P)b$, where $VAR_W(Can_1) = b^T Wb$, which is minimum. Then b maximizes the variance among groups and minimizes it within groups. It can be extracted $q = min(p,k) - 1$ of canonical variables. In our case, at most five canonical variate functions can be obtained (the number of groups minus one). However, Can_1 delivers the combination of ratios which discriminate "best" among categories. Can_2 will represent the second best, and so on. Consequently, the method used here will present graphs only in the space Can_1 and Can_2, expecting that the different groups will be centered in different coordinates.

Further, from the observation of the structure of the canonical variate functions, variables that better discriminate among groups can be inferred: they are those with a higher correlation with the axis given by b.

To conclude, a test of the hypothesis will be realized to insure that existing differences among groups are significant:

H_0: $\mu_1 = \ldots = \mu_k$
H_1: at least, one mean significantly different

We define

$$L = \frac{[W]}{[T]}$$

$$r_E = \frac{ms - \frac{p \cdot (k - 1)}{2} + 1}{p \cdot (k - 1)} \cdot \frac{1 - \sqrt[s]{\Lambda}}{\sqrt[s]{\Lambda}}$$

where

$$m = n - 1 - \frac{p + k}{2} \text{ and } s = \sqrt{\frac{p^2 - (k - 1)^2 - 4}{p^2 + (k - 1)^2 - 5}}$$

where k is the number of groups; p is the number of variables (ratios); and n is the number of observations.

The statistic r_E is distributed approximately as Fisher (Rao 1952) with parameters

$$(p \cdot (k - 1), ms - \frac{p \cdot (k - 1)}{2} + 1)$$

If $r_E < r_c$ Æ H_0 is not rejected. If $r_E > r_c$ Æ H_0 is rejected.

The results of the test are presented in Table C.2. H_0 is rejected in each case.

TABLE C.2
Test of Hypothesis

Case	R1,...,R9		R1,...,R10	
	r_E	r_c	r_E	r_c
1-2-3-4, 5-6	7.4780	1.88	6.6189	1.83
1-2-3-4, 5, 6	4.9535	1.60	4.6532	1.57
1,2-3-4-5, 6	12.2427	1.60	13.1782	1.57
2, 3, 4, 5	9.7766	1.49	10.8372	1.46
1-3-4, 2, 5-6	13.1198	1.60	13.6855	1.57
1, 6	9.9977	1.88	8.2224	1.83
1, 2, 3, 4, 5, 6	9.4900	1.42	10.1903	1.36

SOURCE: Authors' estimates.

Consequently, it can be concluded that the differences among group means are significant or else that groups can be discriminated, although the degree of difference cannot be inferred from them.

A second test over distances between classes will be made. This is a T^2-Hotelling test over distances, based on the Mahalanobis distances. Table C.3 presents the groups that are significantly discriminated—at 95 percent level—for each case.

TABLE C.3

Significant Distances between Groups

Groups		R1, . . . , R9				
1-2-3-4, 5, 6	5-6	—	—	—	—	—
1, 2-3-4-5, 6	1,2-3-4-5	—	—	—	—	—
2, 3, 4, 5	2-3	2-4	2-5	3-4	3-5	4-5
1-3-4, 2, 5-6	1-3-4,2	2,5-6	—	—	—	—
1, 2, 3, 4, 5, 6	1-2	1-4	2-3	2-4	2-5	2-6
1, 6	3-4	3-5	3-6	4-5	4-6	5-6
		R1, . . . ,R10				
1-2-3-4, 5, 6	5-6	—	—	—	—	—
1, 2-3-4-5, 6	1,2-3-4-5	—	—	—	—	—
2, 3, 4, 5	2-3	2-4	2-5	3-4	3-5	4-5
1-3-4, 2, 5-6	1-3-4,2	2,5-6	—	—	—	—
1, 2, 3, 4, 5, 6	1-2	1-4	2-3	2-4	2-5	2-6
1-2-3-4, 5-6	3-4	3-5	3-6	4-5	4-6	5-6

SOURCE: Authors' estimates.

APPENDIX D

Statistical Tables and Figures

TABLE D.1
Partial Correlation Coefficients, R1–R9 and R1–R10

	R1	R2	R3	R4	R5	R6	R7	R8	R9	
					R1–R9					
	R1	**R2**	**R3**	**R4**	**R5**	**R6**	**R7**	**R8**	**R9**	
R1	1.00	−0.16	0.27	0.03	0.08	0.04	0.03	0.03	0.04	
R2	−0.16	1.00	0.00	−0.01	0.11	0.09	−0.09	−0.11	−0.13	
R3	0.27	0.00	1.00	−0.09	0.49	0.21	−0.05	0.02	−0.02	
R4	0.03	−0.01	−0.09	1.00	−0.09	−0.01	0.00	0.01	0.00	
R5	0.08	0.11	0.49	−0.09	1.00	0.22	−0.50	−0.16	−0.52	
R6	0.04	0.09	0.21	−0.01	0.22	1.00	−0.02	−0.10	−0.09	
R7	0.03	−0.09	−0.05	0.00	−0.50	−0.02	1.00	−0.02	0.89	
R8	0.03	−0.11	0.02	0.01	−0.16	−0.10	−0.02	1.00	0.41	
R9	0.04	−0.13	−0.02	0.00	−0.52	−0.09	0.89	0.41	1.00	

	R1	**R2**	**R3**	**R4**	**R5**	**R6**	**R7**	**R8**	**R9**	**R10**
					R1–R10					
R1	1.00	−0.16	0.27	0.03	0.08	0.04	0.03	0.03	0.04	0.00
R2	−0.16	1.00	0.00	−0.01	0.11	0.09	−0.09	−0.11	−0.13	−0.01
R3	0.27	0.00	1.00	−0.09	0.49	0.21	−0.05	0.02	−0.02	0.03
R4	0.03	−0.01	−0.09	1.00	−0.09	−0.01	0.00	0.01	0.00	0.00

continued

TABLE D.1 continued
Partial Correlation Coefficients, R1–R9 and R1–R10

	R1	R2	R3	R4	R5	R6	R7	R8	R9	R10
					R1–R10					
R5	0.08	0.11	0.49	−0.09	1.00	0.22	−0.50	−0.16	−0.52	−0.03
R6	0.04	0.09	0.21	−0.01	0.22	1.00	−0.02	−0.10	−0.09	0.02
R7	0.03	−0.09	−0.05	0.00	−0.50	−0.02	1.00	−0.02	0.89	−0.04
R8	0.03	−0.11	0.02	0.01	−0.16	−0.10	−0.02	1.00	0.41	0.02
R9	0.04	−0.13	−0.02	0.00	−0.52	−0.09	0.89	0.41	1.00	−0.03
R10	0.00	−0.01	0.03	0.00	−0.03	0.02	−0.04	0.02	−0.03	1.00

SOURCE: Authors' estimates.

TABLE D.2
Discriminant Analysis of Groups 1-2-3-4 and 5-6

A priori classification	Classification based on R1–R9		
	Group 1-2-3-4	Group 5-6	Total
Group 1-2-3-4			
Number of firms	703	267	970
Percentage	72.5	27.5	100.0
Group 5-6			
Number of firms	72	78	150
Percentage	48.0	52.0	100.0
Total			
Number of firms	775	345	1,120
Percentage	69.2	30.8	100.0

A priori classification	Classification based on R1–R10		
	Group 1-2-3-4	Group 5-6	Total
Group 1-2-3-4			
Number of firms	475	133	608
Percentage	78.1	21.9	100.0
Group 5-6			
Number of firms	51	43	94
Percentage	54.3	45.7	100.0
Total			
Number of firms	526	176	702
Percentage	74.9	25.1	100.0

SOURCE: Authors' estimates.

TABLE D.3

Discriminant Analysis of Groups 1, 2-3-4-5, and 6

A priori classification	Classification based on R1–R9			
	Group 1	Group 2-3-4-5	Group 6	Total
Group 1				
Number of firms	401	145	85	631
Percentage	63.5	22.9	13.5	100.0
Group 2-3-4-5				
Number of firms	106	233	86	425
Percentage	24.9	54.8	20.2	100.0
Group 6				
Number of firms	25	8	31	64
Percentage	39.1	12.5	48.4	100.0
Total				
Number of firms	532	386	202	1,120
Percentage	47.5	34.5	18.0	100.0

A priori classification	Classification based on R1–R10			
	Group 1	Group 2-3-4-5	Group 6	Total
Group 1				
Number of firms	242	88	65	395
Percentage	61.3	22.3	16.5	100.0
Group 2-3-4-5				
Number of firms	61	137	69	267
Percentage	22.9	51.3	25.8	100.0
Group 6				
Number of firms	15	3	22	40
Percentage	37.5	7.5	55.0	100.0
Total				
Number of firms	318	228	156	702
Percentage	45.3	32.5	22.2	100.0

SOURCE: Authors' estimates.

TABLE D.4
Discriminant Analysis of Groups 1-3-4, 2, and 5-6

A priori classification	Classification based on R1–R9			
	Group 1-3-4	Group 2	Group 5-6	Total
Group 1-3-4				
Number of firms	504	147	190	841
Percentage	59.9	17.5	22.6	100.0
Group 2				
Number of firms	27	74	28	129
Percentage	20.9	57.4	21.7	100.0
Group 5-6				
Number of firms	63	18	69	150
Percentage	42.0	12.0	46.0	100.0
Total				
Number of firms	594	239	287	1,120
Percentage	53.0	21.3	25.6	100.0

A priori classification	Classification based on R1–R10			
	Group 1-3-4	Group 2	Group 5-6	Total
Group 1-3-4				
Number of firms	354	75	98	527
Percentage	67.2	14.2	18.6	100.0
Group 2				
Number of firms	25	44	12	81
Percentage	30.9	54.3	14.8	100.0
Group 5-6				
Number of firms	44	12	38	94
Percentage	46.8	12.8	40.4	100.0
Total				
Number of firms	423	131	148	702
Percentage	60.3	18.7	21.1	100.0

SOURCE: Authors' estimates.

TABLE D.5

Discriminant Analysis of Groups 1-2-3-4, 5, and 6

A priori classification	Classification based on R1–R9			
	Group 1-2-3-4	Group 5	Group 6	Total
Group 1-2-3-4				
Number of firms	583	220	167	970
Percentage	60.1	22.7	17.2	100.0
Group 5				
Number of firms	27	46	13	86
Percentage	31.4	53.5	15.1	100.0
Group 6				
Number of firms	26	12	26	64
Percentage	40.6	18.6	40.6	100.0
Total				
Number of firms	636	278	206	1,120
Percentage	56.8	24.8	18.4	100.0

A priori classification	Classification based on R1–R10			
	Group 1-2-3-4	Group 5	Group 6	Total
Group 1-2-3-4	416	65	127	608
Percentage	68.4	10.7	20.9	100.0
Group 5				
Number of firms	25	17	12	54
Percentage	46.3	31.5	22.2	100.0
Group 6				
Number of firms	16	3	21	40
Percentage	40.0	7.5	52.5	100.0
Total				
Number of firms	457	85	160	702
Percentage	65.1	12.1	22.8	100.0

SOURCE: Authors' estimates.

TABLE D.6

Discriminant Analysis of Groups 2, 3, 4, and 5

A priori classification	Classification based on R1–R9				
	Group 2	Group 3	Group 4	Group 5	Total
Group 2					
Number of firms	49	24	35	21	129
Percentage	37.9	18.6	27.1	16.3	100.0
Group 3					
Number of firms	5	48	13	30	96
Percentage	5.2	50.0	13.5	31.3	100.0
Group 4					
Number of firms	25	15	66	8	114
Percentage	21.9	13.2	57.9	7.0	100.0
Group 5					
Number of firms	7	14	10	55	86
Percentage	8.1	16.3	11.6	63.9	100.0
Total					
Number of firms	86	101	124	114	425
Percentage	20.2	23.8	29.2	26.8	100.0

A priori classification	Classification based on R1–R10				
	Group 2	Group 3	Group 4	Group 5	Total
Group 2					
Number of firms	25	16	27	13	81
Percentage	30.9	19.8	33.3	16.1	100.0
Group 3					
Number of firms	3	27	11	19	60
Percentage	5.0	45.0	18.3	31.7	100.0
Group 4					
Number of firms	10	7	48	7	72
Percentage	21.9	9.7	66.7	9.7	100.0
Group 5					
Number of firms	4	7	8	35	54
Percentage	7.4	12.9	14.8	64.8	100.0
Total					
Number of firms	42	57	94	74	267
Percentage	15.7	21.4	35.2	27.7	100.0

SOURCE: Authors' estimates.

TABLE D.7
Canonic Analysis of Groups 2-3-4-5, 1-3-4, 2, and 5-6

| | Analysis based on R1–R9 | | | | |
| | Group 2-3-4-5 | | | Groups 1-3-4, 2, and 5-6 | |
Ratio	Can_1	Can_2	Can_3	Can_1	Can_2
R1	0.39	0.40	0.56	0.08	0.27
R2	0.62	−0.07	0.08	0.39	−0.50
R3	0.00	0.60	−0.60	0.12	0.30
R4	0.34	0.13	−0.05	0.03	0.00
R5	−0.23	0.65	0.08	−0.54	0.05
R6	−0.22	0.17	0.19	−0.08	0.54
R7	0.12	−0.39	−0.18	0.47	0.26
R8	0.24	−0.63	−0.24	0.68	0.30
R9	0.20	−0.57	−0.27	0.72	0.29

| | Analysis based on R1–R10 | | | | |
| | Group 2-3-4-5 | | | Groups 1-3-4, 2, and 5-6 | |
	Can_1	Can_2	Can_3	Can_1	Can_2
R1	0.41	0.35	0.50	0.11	−0.20
R2	0.56	0.14	0.10	0.21	0.54
R3	−0.05	0.48	−0.65	0.18	−0.32
R4	0.29	0.09	−0.02	0.01	0.06
R5	−0.17	0.64	0.05	−0.52	−0.05
R6	−0.23	0.19	0.14	−0.06	−0.49
R7	0.12	−0.44	−0.11	0.50	−0.14
R8	0.27	−0.68	−0.22	0.76	−0.09
R9	0.20	−0.64	−0.18	0.76	−0.14
R10	0.14	0.05	−0.30	0.02	0.56

SOURCE: Authors' estimates.

TABLE D.8
Canonic Analysis of Group 1-2-3-4-5-6

	Analysis based on R1–R9				
Ratio	Can_1	Can_2	Can_3	Can_4	Can_5
R1	0.32	0.17	0.72	−0.32	0.15
R2	0.43	−0.54	0.28	0.26	−0.08
R3	0.35	0.65	0.32	0.46	−0.34
R4	0.04	−0.06	0.04	0.08	−0.02
R5	−0.33	0.36	0.52	0.48	0.00
R6	0.06	0.50	0.14	0.09	0.59
R7	0.36	0.09	−0.35	−0.43	−0.20
R8	0.64	0.15	−0.36	−0.04	0.26
R9	0.60	0.10	−0.49	−0.30	−0.04
	Analysis based on R1–R10				
Ratio	Can_1	Can_2	Can_3	Can_4	Can_5
R1	0.32	0.00	0.64	−0.40	−0.35
R2	0.30	−0.52	0.38	0.24	0.36
R3	0.46	0.59	0.42	0.44	−0.13
R4	0.01	−0.05	0.02	0.03	0.03
R5	−0.27	0.28	0.64	0.32	0.36
R6	0.08	0.47	0.21	−0.16	0.35
R7	0.38	−0.01	−0.41	−0.22	−0.37
R8	0.70	0.00	−0.34	−0.01	0.27
R9	0.62	−0.03	−0.51	−0.18	−0.22
R10	−0.02	−0.32	−0.03	0.56	−0.36

SOURCE: Authors' estimates.

FIGURE D.1
Ratio of Financial Costs to Total Debt, 1965–1983

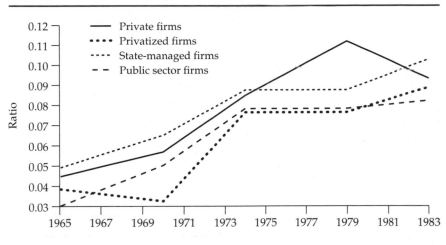

SOURCE: Authors' estimates.

FIGURE D.2
Ratio of Financial Costs to Total Debt, 1980–1987

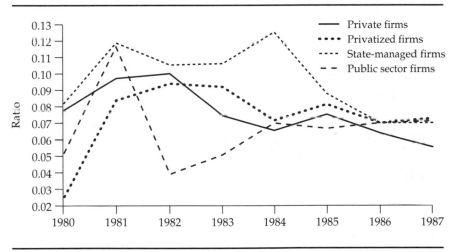

SOURCE: Authors' estimates.

FIGURE D.3

Ratio of Inventories to Total Assets, 1965–1983

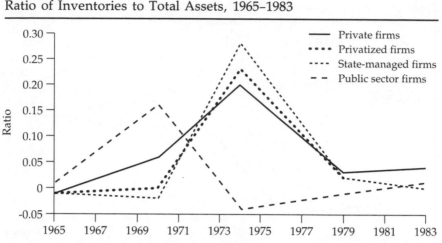

SOURCE: Authors' estimates.

FIGURE D.4

Ratio of Inventories to Total Assets, 1980–1987

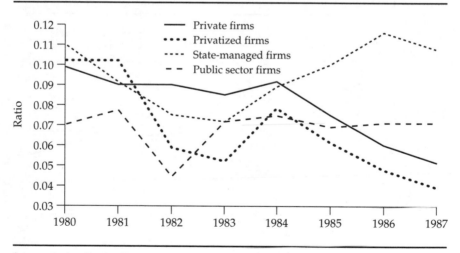

SOURCE: Authors' estimates.

Evolution of Regulations for Three Privatized Sectors

The Telecommunications Sector

The norms that regulated the telecommunications sector until 1982 were based on the Decree with the Force of Law 4 (DFL 4) of July 1959. This decree replaced DFL 244 of 1931. DFL 4, called the General Law of Electric Power Services, governed both the telecommunications and the electric power sectors. In October 1982, Law 18,168, the General Law of Telecommunications, was approved, implying significant reforms to the legislation in force until then.

The telecommunications market

This market differentiates final services from intermediary services. Final services are fixed telephone service, mobile telephone service, telex service, data transmission, and electronic mail. Intermediary services consist of urban lines, interurban connections, and international exits.

Before the sector's reform in 1982, the market was dominated almost exclusively by state-owned national companies with monopolistic positions in their respective sectors. The local telephone service (fixed, because the mobile mode had not appeared yet) was served almost exclusively by the Telephone Company of Chile (CTC), a subsidiary of the State Development Corporation (CORFO). Two private companies constituted the exceptions, the National Telephone Company (CNT) and the Telephone Company of Coyhaique, which operate in the Tenth and Eleventh Regions in the southern part of the country, respectively.[1] Telex and telegram services were provided locally by the state-owned company Correos y Telégrafos and internationally by the International Telephone and Telegraph Corporation (ITT) and Transradio. The National Telecommunications Company (ENTEL), another subsidiary of CORFO, dominated all long-distance international telephone service and most long-distance domestic service.

Since the privatization of all state-owned firms in this sector in 1989, the telecommunications market has contained a number of companies—all of them private—that demonstrate a certain degree of competition. Most noteworthy, however, are the technological innovations being introduced, and the investment plans under way.

The structure of the different submarkets of the telecommunications sector is as follows: In fixed telephone service, there are currently two companies competing with CTC (over 50 percent privatized in 1987), which were created in the late 1980s: Complejo Manufacturero de Equipos Telefónicos (CMET) in the metropolitan region Providencia and Fifth Region, and Compañía de Teléfonos de Manquehue (CTM) in the metropolitan region Las Condes. In their respective markets, their joint relative importance amounts to approximately 6 percent.

Some companies, however, have an exclusive presence in some regions. These are ENTEL (over 50 percent privatized in 1988), which serves Easter Island, and CNT and the Telephone Company of Coyhaique, local companies that continue operating in the Tenth and Eleventh Regions, respectively.

In mobile telephone service (a new submarket), CTC-Celular and the Mobile Telephone Company (CIDCOM) each have about 50 percent of the market. Two other companies, Via TransRadio (VTR) and TELECOM, are entering the market. All of these companies are privately owned.

In telex and telegrams, data transmission, and electronic mail, the following companies (all private) participate in at least one of these services: Telex-Chile (a company created in 1982 and privatized in 1986, which took over the telegraphic services from Correos y Telégrafos), VTR (in 1984, Transradio was incorporated into it), ITT, ECOM, ENTEL, and Chile PAC. The major companies dominating these submarkets are Telex-Chile and VTR.

In domestic long-distance services, ENTEL is now virtually a monopoly. CTC offers this service only between Santiago and Valparaíso, but it will soon provide services to the northern part of the country. VTR and Telex-Chile could enter this market, too (these three companies would use PANMSAT's satellites).

In international long-distance services, ENTEL is the only operating company, being the Chilean signatory of the INTELSAT Agreement.

DFL 4 of 1959 and the telecommunications sector

DFL 4 was in force for the electrical-power-generating and -distributing companies and for the telecommunications sector (including radio communications and broadcasting stations), all of which are given the generic name electric services.

DFL 4 established, in its Title II, the modality of concessions and permits, but determined certain monopolies beforehand:

- "The State has a monopoly on telegraph services within the national territory" (Article 8).
- "The cablegram companies and international telecommunications companies shall only perform public service toward the exterior" (Article 9).
- "Private telecommunications services may be carried out only between those localities of the territory listed in the corresponding concession, and when there is no other service of the same kind between them already provided by the Telégrafo del Estado or another public service telecommunications company" (Article 10).

This decree created the General Administration of Electric and Gas Services, reporting to the Ministry of the Interior. The organization's responsibilities included fulfilling the provisions regarding the sector, reporting on the electric service concession applications, seeing that the obligations established in the concession decrees were complied with, and studying and reporting to the Price Commission on the necessary background data for establishing rates of electric services (Article 159).

The Price Commission was a public organization, chaired by the general director of electric and gas services and made up of representatives of CORFO, the Institute of Engineers of Chile, the Production and Commerce Confederation, and the president of the republic (Article 156). The Price Commission fixed rates "to provide the companies an annual net profit of 10 percent on the current fixed capital of the respective concession" (Article 144).

Other provisions against free competition in this market were the following:

- "The rates of the telephonic, telegraphic and other kinds of telecommunications companies will be applied with a 50 percent discount when providing services to the State or Municipalities" (Article 113).

- "The concessionaires shall maintain . . . a proportion of Chilean employees of no less than 75 percent of the total" (Article 119).
- "In equal conditions, the concessionaires shall use national raw material in all their installations and equipment" (Article 120).

Law 18,168 of 1982

The General Law of Telecommunications covers only the telecommunications sector. The National Telecommunications Policy (1978) serves as background.

Law 18,168 promotes the liberalization of the market and, as argued at the time it was issued, facilitates sector development. Below are some of its most important provisions:

- "All the Republic's inhabitants will have free and equal access to telecommunications and any person may opt for the concessions and permits established by law" (Article 2).
- "The concessions and permits shall be granted without restrictions with respect to quantity and kind of service or to its geographic location and there may be more than one concession or permit of the same kind of service within the same geographical area" (Article 12).
- "The concessionaires of public telecommunications services will have the obligation of establishing and accepting interconnections in accordance with the technical norms given by the Telecommunications Department (which reports to the Ministry of Transport and Telecommunications), so that users have access to all the public services installed" (Article 25).
- "Prices or rates of public telecommunications services and the intermediary services contracted between the different companies, organizations, or persons participating in said services will be freely established by the suppliers of the respective services without prejudice to the agreements that can be made between them and their users" (Article 29).
- The previous paragraph is complemented by the following article: "If the market conditions or regulations were insufficient to ensure free competition or if monopolistic situations or other distortions of the kind should arise, as determined by the Antimonopoly Commission by its own initiative or by third party's request, the Ministries of Transport, Telecommunications, Economy, and Development and Reconstruction may establish, on the basis of such a pronouncement, also at their own initiative or by third party's request, by joint resolution, the maximum prices or rates of those services in that situation" (Article 30).

A comparison of DFL 4 and Law 18,168

It is impossible to dissociate the change in legislation regulating the telecommunications business industry from the new approach toward that sector from 1970 onward. The three companies that dominated the telecommunications sector and that were public property—CTC, Correos y Telégrafos, and ENTEL—experienced deep changes in their operational environment.

First, beginning in 1973, a cost-rationalization process was implemented, along with new price policies, which made efficiency possible in these state-owned enterprises (SOEs).[2] Second, beginning in 1985, a privatization program of these now "efficient" companies was implemented. Telex-Chile was transferred to private hands in 1986, CTC in 1987, and ENTEL had a majority share of private shareholders in 1988.

The privatization of telecommunications in Chile would not have been possible (with any success) if the companies had not improved their efficiency and a change in legislation had not occurred. The fundamental element was Law 18,168 of 1982.

Law 18,168 meant choosing between (1) using telecommunications companies to redistribute national income, an objective that can be read in some norms of DFL 4 (for example Articles 8 and 144), and (2) developing the telecommunications sector in a way compatible with the country's goal of GNP growth, within a strategy of openness to external commercial and financial resources. The second option was chosen.

The telecommunications sector requires large sums for investment, because the projects it needs to carry out are enormous. Likewise, the sector undergoes continuous technological change. Given the restrictions inherent to a balanced budget, attracting the necessary capital requires that ownership of these enterprises be accessible to the private sector (domestic and foreign), which will develop an expansion program to modernize the sector.

Law 18,168, however, reduced the telecommunications companies' potential for growth (although in many telecommunications activities there are increasing returns to scale that encourage the development of "large" companies). By so doing, the law restricted the potential for monopolistic practices. The norms on concessions and permits guarantee the free entrance of companies (Article 12), while the role given to the National Controllers Office allows for control of unfair competition practices in establishing tariffs (Article 30).

In 1987 DFL 1 allowed some legal changes that ended with cross-subsidies among user-groups and established clear tariff mechanisms, thereby paving the way for the privatization of CTC and other state-owned telephone companies.

The many investment plans being implemented by companies like CTC support private sector access to telecommunications, for the purpose of benefiting from the development of telecommunications (at the cost of eliminating the possibility of using the telecommunications companies as redistributive tools in the short term).[3]

With regard to CTC, the adjudication of 151 million shares in January 1988 by the Bond Group (Bond Corporation Holdings Limited and Bond Corporation Holdings International Limited) implied a commitment by this buyer to increase the capital of CTC by an amount equivalent to US$269.8 million.[4]

The CTC 1988–1990 implementation project planned the installation of 183,000 lines and included the Connection Plan, which called for an investment of US$185 million in the installation of 160,000 new lines in thirty Chilean cities. An additional plan for 1989–1992 projected the installation of 468,000 digital lines.[5]

Conclusions

Technological innovation is an inherent characteristic of the telecommunications sector. At the same time, the country's economic development requires a telecommunications network that links the different regions with one another and with the rest of the world. For both of these reasons, it is critical to increase investments and modernize this sector.

Given the channels available to attract the sizable financial resources necessary and given the efficiency and dynamism that the sector must maintain, development of the sector should take place within an environment of competition and private participation (domestic and foreign) in the ownership of the companies.

Law 18,168 of 1982 eliminated all discrimination between domestic and foreign companies, and abolished state monopolies in the sector. In general, this legislation has allowed for competitive development of the telecommunications sector, notwithstanding the safeguarding function of the National Controllers Office.

The Electric Power Sector

In 1982, the changes that the electric power sector had been undergoing since the creation of the National Energy Commission (CNE), were legally formalized.

DFL 1 of June 1982 (which originated in the Ministry of Mining) modifies DFL 4 of July 1959, known as the General Law of Electric Power

Services (which also was in force for the telecommunications sector until October 1982).

The electric power market

The market of the electric power sector distinguishes two activities: (1) the generation and conduction of electric power and (2) the distribution of electric power.

The production of electric power is carried out by two kinds of companies: public service companies,[6] whose business is the sale of electric power, and self-producing companies that generate power for their own use, but which sometimes buy the electric power they cannot produce themselves or sell production surplus. These two kinds of producers are interconnected within geographic areas. There are four geographic areas in the country, within each of which there is competition at the level of large customers.

The distribution of electric power is carried out by individual companies in each territory (with different population density). Therefore, each company is a monopoly in its respective geographic area.

At the beginning of 1980, the electric power market consisted of two large companies, ENDESA and CHILECTRA (both CORFO subsidiaries), which dominated the production and distribution of electric power, respectively, throughout the country. After 1980 ENDESA and CHILECTRA atomized their equity, creating subsidiary companies, which were privatized from 1985 onward.

From ENDESA emerged the following companies (as of December 31, 1988):

- ENDESA parent company: This company was over 50 percent private beginning in 1988. As of December 31 of that year, it had the following subsidiaries: EDELNOR, ELECDA, ELECSA, and EMELARI.
- Private companies: EDELMAG, EMEC, EMECO, EMEL, EMELAT, EMELIG, EMELMA, FRONTEL, Pilmaiquén, Pullinque, and SAESA.
- CORFO subsidiaries related to the ENDESA parent company: EDELAYSEN and Pehuenche. This last company was bought by the ENDESA parent company in 1989, to begin operating in 1991.
- Colbún-Machicura, a CORFO company, which was planned for sale in 1990.

From CHILECTRA came the following:

- CHILGENER, an electric-power–producing company
- CHILMETRO
- CHILQUINTA

All of these new companies were sold to the private sector between 1986 and 1987 (in September 1988, the three were 100 percent private).

Generation and conduction of electric power.   The installed power of the country amounts to 4,015.5 Mw, of which 76.6 percent corresponds to plants belonging to public service companies and the remaining percentage to self-producers. The major companies at a national level are ENDESA and its subsidiaries (45.2 percent),[7] CHILGENER (13.6 percent), and Colbún-Machicura (12.2 percent). These three companies are capable of generating 93 percent of the production needed by public service companies.

Although the above information is of interest, it is more pertinent to make an analysis at the level of the markets in terms of the geographically interconnected areas. The four generation and transmission markets are:

1. the North Interconnected System (SING), which includes the First and Second Regions, with 17.5 percent of the installed electric power of the country
2. the Central Interconnected System (SIC), which includes the area between the Third and Tenth Regions, representing 80.1 percent of national electric power[8]
3. the Aysén Electric Power System, Eleventh Region, which accounts for 0.4 percent of the country's electric power
4. the Punta Arenas Electric Power System, Twelfth Region, which provides 2.0 percent of the national electric power

In the SING, public service enterprises own only 16.2 percent of the installed power in the system (98 percent of that amount is supplied by EDELNOR, an ENDESA subsidiary). The main self-producer is CODELCO.

In the SIC, installed power of public service companies represents 90.8 percent of the system. Three companies are responsible for 95 percent of this percentage: ENDESA (59.4 percent), CHILGENER (18.7 percent), and Colbún-Machicura (16.8 percent).

Energy distribution.   Of total national production (10.673 million kwh) of electric power, 89.2 percent is channeled toward the SIC. From the SIC,

4.701 million kwh are transferred to distributing companies. The main distributing companies are:

- CHILMETRO, which distributes 15.8 percent of the national production and operates in the Metropolitan Region of Santiago
- the Industrial Electric Company (CGEI), which sells 10.7 percent of the country's production between the Sixth and the Tenth Regions
- CHILQUINTA, which sells 3.2 percent of national production in the Fifth Region

Another way of measuring the importance of the distribution companies is through the number of customers. The national total is 2.35 million. The invoices are broken down as follows: CHILMETRO: 42.9 percent; CGEI: 14.1 percent; CHILQUINTA: 11.0 percent; others (more than fourteen companies, among which SAESA of the Tenth Region and EMEC of the Fourth and Fifth Regions stand out): 32.0 percent

The public service electric-power–generating companies are altogether significantly larger than the electric-power–distributing companies. The assets of the former are 5.7 times the assets of the latter. The equity ratio is 4.6 to 1.

On December 31, 1988, 54 percent of the generating companies and 96 percent of the distributing companies were privately owned.

Finally, it is worth noting the sector's sales trend. Between 1975 and 1988, the consumption of electric power in the country increased at an annual rate of 5.3 percent.

DFL 4 of 1959 and the electric power sector

Although we have already analyzed DFL 4 of July 1959 in relation to the telecommunications sector, we will make additional comments on this decree in relation to the electric power sector, to which it also applies.

DFL 4 is made up of nine titles, of which the most pertinent for this analysis are numbers I through III and V through VII.

Title I spells out, among other aspects, the areas covered by this law, including thermo- and hydroelectric–power producing plants, transformation substations, and electric power transmission lines (Article 2). It also defines private and public services (Article 6).

Title II concerns concessions and permits, indicating that electric power concessions can only be granted to Chilean citizens and to organized companies in conformity with the laws of the country (Article 17).

''The concession includes the right to install lines through the air or underground, in streets, public squares, parks, roads and other national property of public use" (Article 19). "Public service concessions do not constitute monopolies. The President of the Republic may, consequently, grant a second electric power service concession in the same territory" (Article 22). "Concession expiration limits will be established by the President of the Republic in the concession decree and may not be extended. This period may not be less than thirty years or more than ninety for public service concessions" (Article 43).

Title III deals with easements (rights to occupy lands). It establishes that "easement lines for transmission and distribution of electric power . . . (. . . of telephone lines, etc.) . . . give the concessionaire the right to install lines by means of posts or underground ducts over someone else's property and to occupy the necessary lands for the conduction of electric power" (Article 87).

Title V establishes, among other provisions, some discriminatory norms in favor of nationals. "Concessionaires must maintain, during the entire period of the concession, . . . a proportion of Chilean employees not lower than 75 percent of the total work force" (Article 119) and, "If in equal condition, the concessionaires will use national raw material in all their installations and equipment" (Article 120).

Title VI indicates the norms regarding rates. These rates should be established "so that they produce a net annual return of 10 percent over fixed capital in force in the respective concession" (Article 144). The setting of rates in the public service electric power companies is the responsibility of the Price Commission, which is made up of the general director of electric and gas services (who chairs it) and four other members appointed by CORFO, the Institute of Engineers of Chile, the Production and Commerce Confederation, and the president of the republic (Articles 155 and 156).

Title VII refers to the General Administration of Electric and Gas Services. Article 158 establishes that "the inspection and supervision of the construction and exploitation of any kind of electric service companies, established or that will be established in the future, will be carried out by this Administration, reporting to the Ministry of the Interior."

Another provision contained in DFL 4 and worth mentioning here is the following: "The rates of the companies supplying electric power will be applied with a 25 percent discount to the consumption of State offices, departments and services, and Municipalities" (Article 113). DFL 4 did not confer monopoly power on the electric power sector, as it did for the telecommunications sector.

Mining DFL 1 of 1982

In June 1982, the Mining DFL 1 was issued in connection with the decree for the electric power sector. Its first article states that this law will rule "the production, conduction, distribution, the regime of concessions, and the rates of the electric power sector and the role of the state in relation to these matters." This decree contains 8 titles that cover 164 articles. We will present the most pertinent titles.

Title I, of a general character, establishes the matters contained in DFL 1, which are those associated with the concessions and permits to operate in the sector, the easements, price regimes, and relationships between the public enterprises and the state (Article 2). In another of its provisions it stipulates that "the application of this law corresponds to the Ministry of the Interior, through the Superintendency of Gas and Electric Services . . . without prejudice to the attributions conferred on the National Energy Commission" (Article 9).[9]

Title II refers to concessions and permits. It states that concessions may be granted only to Chilean citizens and companies (Article 13) and that "other public service distribution concessions may be requested for one part or the totality of the territory of concessions of this kind, already granted" (Article 17). With regard to the duration of the concessions, it is indicated that "the definitive concessions will be granted for an undefined period" (Article 30).

This and the following title deal with the subject of interconnections: "the companies who own electric concessions will be obliged to accept connections between themselves" (Article 32), and "concessionaires of any nature will be obliged to carry out the interconnection of their installations when, based on a report of the Commission, it is determined by means of a supreme decree of the Ministry of the Interior" (Article 81). The provisions regarding easements are presented in Articles 47 to 71. Article 50 is similar to Article 87 of DFL 4 of 1959.

Title IV is dedicated to the norms regarding rates. Article 90 states: "The following electric power supplies will be subject to price fixing: (1) Supplies for final users whose connected power is lower than or equal to 2,000 kilowatts, located in public service distribution concession areas; . . . (2) Supplies for final users of connected power lower than or equal to 2,000 kw, made from generation or conduction installations of an electric power company; . . . (3) Supplies made to electric power companies that do not generate their own supply, in the proportion that these companies, in turn, provide power subject to price fixing; this will apply to electric power systems of more than 1,500 kilowatts of installed generation capacity."

Article 96 states: "In electric power systems with more than 1,500 kilowatts in installed generation capacity, two levels of prices will be subject to price fixing: (1) *Prices at the generation-transmission level.* These prices will be called 'knot prices,' and they will be defined for all generation-conduction substations from which the supply is made. The knot prices will have two components: the price of electric power and the price of input power. (2) *Prices at the distribution level*. These prices will be determined by adding the knot price, established at the point of connection with the distribution installations, and the added value due to distribution costs . . . To the energy supply indicated in Numbers 1 and 3 of Article 90 will be applied the prices of the distribution level. To the energy supply indicated in Number 3 of the same article, will be applied the knot price, if the supply is made from the generation-transmission installations of the company making the sale; and the distribution level prices, if the supply is made from the distribution installations of the company making the sale.''

Articles 97 through 99 refer to the knot prices, which ''must reflect an average in time of the marginal costs of supply at a generation-conduction level for permanent very low risk users'' (Article 97) and ''they will be fixed half-yearly in the months of April and October of each year'' (Article 98). Article 99 deals extensively with the way in which knot prices will be calculated.

Article 105 establishes that ''the price structure at the distribution level considers knot prices established at the spot of connection with distribution installations and the value added for distribution costs, adding them in such a way, by means of formulas that represent a combination of these values, that the resulting price of the power supply corresponds to the cost of usage by the user of the resources at the level of production-transmission and distribution.'' Article 106 gives the method for estimating the value added for distribution costs and, among other aspects, determines the discount rate, which will be equivalent to the social discount rate calculated by the National Planning Office (ODEPLAN).

According to Article 108, ''with the resulting values from the previous article and the corresponding knot prices, the Commission shall structure a series of preliminary basic rates, . . .

''There shall be as many basic rates as the number of companies and distribution sectors defined for each company. If the basic preliminary rates, thus determined, allow the added group of distribution installations of concessionary companies to obtain a rate of return—before taxes on profit—that does not differ in more than four points from the discount rate defined in Article 106, the weighted values added to create them will be accepted.'' Further on, the procedure for estimating the economic rate of return is established.

Title V is devoted to the Superintendency of Gas and Electric Services, ''an organization that reports to the Ministry of the Interior'' and that ''will be in charge of seeing that the law is applied'' (Article 130). Some of the superintendency's responsibilities, indicated in articles 131 to 134, are to see that the current laws and regulations are obeyed; to grant approval certificates for machines, instruments, apparatus, equipment, appliances, and electric material of any kind; and to interpret the rule's provisions and establish the norms in special cases that may appear and that are not expressly contemplated.

A comparison of DFL 4 and DFL 1

Mining DFL 1 of 1982 inherits and improves many of the norms concerning concessions, permits, and easements contained in DFL 4 of 1959. It also maintains the role of the Superintendency of Gas and Electric Services (its previous equivalent was the General Administration of Electric and Gas Services) of the Ministry of the Interior in inspecting and overseeing the sector.

The main differences in this new legal body are the inclusion of institutional support from the National Energy Commission, which coordinates the plans, policies, and norms of the electric power sector and advises the government in these matters, and the overall change in the price policy. DFL 1 also eliminates the norms that discriminated in favor of Chilean nationals and the state contained in the former legislation.

The National Energy Commission has two main functions:

1. It must develop planning capabilities for large generation-transmission projects and coordinate state investments in the electric power sector. This function is carried out by ODEPLAN, which classifies all studies and projects of public companies and institutions according to priority, by means of an Investment Basic Statistics System (SEBI) (National Energy Commission 1989:117).
2. It must carry out the relevant studies to fix prices in the sector, which serve as the basis for the Ministry of the Economy decrees with respect to the electricity rates.

Both the approach and the objectives of the new price policy are different from those of the former legislation. DFL 4 of 1959 restricted the "profits" of the monopolistic electric power companies by establishing a maximum return on capital (10 percent). Thus, the level of rates was to be consistent with their social objective. Mining DFL 1 of 1982 establishes a price policy whose "main objective is to reflect the real costs of efficiently producing, transmitting and distributing the electric power supply" (National Energy Commission 1989:118). The price system distinguishes two power supply areas: that in which there are natural monopoly characteristics (electric power distribution to a large number of clients) and regulated prices and that in which it is possible to create conditions for competition (power supply to large customers) and in which free prices are established.[10]

Conclusions

The electric power sector is a complex market where state regulations are indispensable. Legal prereform regulations and the new legislation are based on both of these characteristics.

Sector supervision was performed by the General Administration for Electric Services and, subsequently, by the Superintendency of Gas and Electric Services. The National Energy Commission also participates in this responsibility, as in others.

State regulation of the electric power market has focused on price policy. Policies put into practice until the mid-1970s differ from those established in 1982 by Mining DFL 1, which distinguishes between sub-sectors with free prices and subsectors with regulated prices. Nevertheless, regulations should not be confused with discretionary intervention, for which concrete and objective technical norms exist to fix prices in areas where natural monopolies tend to form.

The current legislation is neutral as regards public or private property owned by electricity generation and distribution companies. In fact, for this very reason, it made the sale of CORFO-owned property possible.

Privatization of electric power sector companies began in 1985. Electric power distribution companies passed into private hands in 1986 (100 percent in 1987). Sales of electric generation companies went through a slower process, so that by the end of 1989, only EDELAYSEN and Colbún-Machicura remained in CORFO'S power. Only the second of these companies is of a considerable size.[11]

The Commercial Aeronautics Industry

Until 1979, the commercial aeronautics industry was ruled by DFL 221 of May 1931 and DFL 241 of March 1960. Other relevant legislation, in force at the end of the 1970s, was Law 16,436 of 1966 and DFL 3 of 1969.

In March 1979, DL 2,564 was issued. It "dictates norms for air transport and commercial aeronautic services; modifies DFL 221 of 1931, DFL 241 of 1960, and other precepts named." Subsequently, Article 2 of DL 2,564 was modified by Law 18,243 of September 1983.

The commercial aeronautics market

Five different products can be distinguished in this market: domestic passenger transport, domestic cargo transport (cabotage), international passenger transport, international cargo transport, and other aerial services (air taxis and aerial work).[12] The most important products of the sector are domestic and international transport of passengers and cargo.

Domestic passenger services correspond to flights to the main cities in the country (with a demand greater than a certain number of passengers per week and generally at a distance from Santiago equal to or greater than approximately 500 kilometers): Arica, Iquique, Antofagasta, Concepción, Puerto Montt, Punta Arenas, and others.[13] Domestic cargo services present similar characteristics regarding frequency and routes. The majority of airplanes transport cargo and passengers at the same time. The international passenger and cargo service takes place primarily between Santiago and cities in South America, North America, and Europe.

Before the 1979 reform of the sector, fewer airlines operated than at present, and there were fewer flights. Nevertheless, the reform did not represent a drastic change in the sector, as the leading companies in the market are the same and have similar shares of the market.[14]

From 1975 to 1979 the main airlines offering domestic passenger service were the National Airline of Chile (LAN Chile, a public enterprise) and Copper Airlines (LADECO, a private enterprise). LADECO grew during those years both in capacity and in actual traffic. In 1979, LADECO carried 47.9 percent and LAN Chile 51.9 percent of all passengers transported within the country.

In domestic cargo operations, LAN Chile showed a stable share (63.7 percent of traffic) in 1978, and LADECO (14.7 percent) experienced a decrease in its share owing to the emergence in that year of a new private company: Aeronorte (19.8 percent).

In 1976 LADECO and LAN Chile were the only domestic operators also involved in international passenger and cargo transport. The latter had an overwhelming 99 percent and 93 percent share of passenger and cargo traffic, respectively. That year, these two companies carried 34 percent of Chile's international passenger traffic and about 50 percent of its international cargo traffic.

In 1987, almost a decade after the implementation of reforms, the situation was the following: Eight companies operated within the domestic passenger market, all of them private: LADECO, LAN Chile (privatized in 1989), Aeronorte, TAC, A.S.A., A. Guayacán, Aerov. DAP, and Icarosán.[15] All, except the last three, are dedicated to the joint transport of passengers and cargo. Market participation (according to actual passenger traffic) breaks down as follows: LAN Chile, 46 percent; LADECO, 52 percent; and the other operators, 2 percent.

In the domestic transport of cargo, six companies were present: LAN Chile, LADECO, Aeronorte (with an almost negligible volume of activity), Fast Air (a private company, wholly dedicated to cargo), TAC, and A.S.A.

LAN Chile's share of the market, in terms of actual traffic, was 53 percent; LADECO's, 46 percent; and the rest of the operators', 1 percent.

The international transport of passengers was in the hands of the two traditional Chilean companies: LAN Chile (84 percent of traffic) and LADECO (the remaining 16 percent), although LADECO was making evident progress. The Chilean companies carried 32 percent of passenger traffic to and from Chile (a percentage similar to that of 1979).

There have been changes in the international transport of cargo. Fast Air entered the market in 1979, with sustained participation around 30 percent (1987 value). LAN Chile had a share of 66 percent, and LADECO only 4 percent. These domestic companies carry 46 percent of cargo traffic to and from Chile.

Finally, it is interesting to observe the significant changes in the volume of sales in the commercial aeronautics sector during the 1978–1987 period, shown in Table E.1.

DFL 221 of 1931 and DFL 241 of 1960

The two main laws that regulated the sector before the 1979 reform were DFL 221 of 1931 and DFL 241 of 1960. Some articles of Law 16,436 of 1966 and DFL 3 of 1969 will also be mentioned here.

DFL 221 of May 1931 on air navigation improves on DL 675 of 1925. DFL 221 dictates regulations regarding aircraft, pilots, air traffic, airports, and passenger and merchandise transport. Some of the most important articles contained in this decree state that:

• "The State will exercise full and exclusive sovereignty over the airspace that exists over its territory and territorial waters" (Article 22).

TABLE E.1

Average Annual Growth of Sales and Supply in the Commercial Aeronautics Sector, 1978–1987 (percentage)

Type of service	Growth of sales	Growth of supply
Domestic passenger service	3.6	4.9
Domestic cargo service	–1.1	4.4
International passenger service	11.1	n.a.
International cargo service	9.6	n.a.

n.a. = not available.
Source: Civil Aeronautics Board.

- "The navigation of Chilean airships within the national territory will be free, but will be governed by the provisions contained in this Law. The navigation of foreign aircraft will follow the norms established in International Agreements, but foreign aircraft are forbidden to carry either commercial or postal cargo, which is reserved for domestic aircraft" (Article 23).

- "To own a Chilean aircraft, natural or legal citizenship of the Republic is required. If the owner of the aircraft is a Corporation, it must be Chilean, in the sense that it must be legally constituted in Chile and must prove that two-thirds of its social capital permanently belongs to Chilean citizens and that its President and a minimum of two-thirds of its Board of Directors are Chilean citizens" (Article 7).

- "Any aircraft that flies over Chilean territory must have a regulation navigability certificate, issued or revalidated by the State of the nationality to which the aircraft belongs. Chilean aircraft will receive this certificate from the Aeronautics Board" (Article 11).

- "It is forbidden to establish or operate airports without authorization from the Aeronautics Board" (Article 36).

- "Air transport will follow the Commercial Code regulations related to transport by land, lakes, canals, or navigable rivers" (Article 41).

This selection of DFL 221 regulations demonstrates the sovereignty of the state over national airspace, the importance of international agreements, the Aeronautics Board's role as inspector, and legal discrimination in favor of Chilean aircraft.

International agreements contain the regulations and procedures that countries use to organize the industry at an international level. The multilateral agreement known as the Chicago Conference (1944) confirms the sovereignty of each state over its airspace and consecrates bilateral negotiations as the means to establish rights for the use of airspace. The Bermuda Agreement I (1946) presents the foundations for agreements in which countries determine concessions at a bilateral level.

The Aeronautics Board, an organization within the Chilean Air Force, is in charge of regulating the sector, especially in matters relating to the registry of Chilean aircraft, issuance of navigability (aircraft) and aptitude (pilots) certificates, and airport control.

At the end of March 1960, DFL 241 was published. The provisions of this decree establish the administrative dependencies of the Civil Aeronautics Board (JAC) and of the Aeronautics Board, and detail the functions of each of these organizations.

DFL 241 makes the following provisions regarding the Civil Aeronautics Board:

- The "Civil Aeronautics Board is an office of the Ministry of the Economy, Transport Department" (Article 1).
- The JAC "will be responsible for the country's civil aviation" (Article 3). Some of the specific functions are detailed in Article 6 (the following numbers correspond to those of Article 6). It will:

   1. "exercise the management of the country's commercial aviation"

   2. "approve, on the basis of a report from the Aeronautics Board, the general plan for airports and aerodromes"

   5. "authorize the establishment of air transport services in the National territory, both domestic and international, and any other form of commercial air service"

   6. "regulate traffic capacity and approve commercial service flight frequencies"

   7. "propose air transport fares to the President of the Republic"

   8. "inform on and propose projects for international treaties, pacts or agreements related to civil aviation"

   12. "approve, reject or propose modifications of the agreements and pacts adopted by domestic companies among themselves or with international companies with respect to mutual use of facilities"

   13. "approve or propose the adoption of rules, regulations and procedures related to air transport and other commercial aeronautic services"

- Added to Article 7 is the provision that "JAC agreements authorizing the establishment of public passenger or cargo transport air services of a regular character or fixed itinerary, and those who deny or declare their expiration, must be submitted to the approval of the President of the Republic, without impairing the faculty of the Board to grant provisional authorization for six months, while the corresponding concession decree is being dictated."

In relation to the Aeronautics Board, DFL 241 establishes the following provisions:

- "The Aeronautics Board will be an organization of the Chilean Air Force, directly dependent on the Commander in Chief of this Institution, and will be responsible for the enforcement of aeronautic laws and regulations, the direction and promotion of civil aviation activities in their technical aspects, air traffic control in the national territory, and aeronautics security. It is responsible, especially, for the administration and direction of public airports and aerodromes and of services destined to aid and protect aeronautics'' (Article 14).

- The main functions of the Aeronautics Board are found in Article 15. They include the following (numbered as in DFL 241):

    1. "fulfill and enforce the agreements and resolutions of the Civil Aeronautics Board"

    5. "propose to the President of the Republic, for his resolution, the rights and rates for the use of public airports and aerodromes and remaining services and installations destined for air navigation, as established by supreme decree of the Ministry of National Defense"

    6. "grant concessions, leasing rights or other kinds of contracts for land ceded to the Aeronautics Board and for aerodromes and airports"

    10. "maintain a National Register of aeronavigability"

    11. "establish the requirements, study programs and examinations needed to obtain licenses in the necessary areas for the conservation, maintenance and repair of civil aircraft and grant the corresponding certificates or licenses"

    12. "grant certificates or licenses to inspection personnel, flight crews, instructors, auxiliary services and civil aviation infrastructure personnel"

    19. "make plans for the purchase of material needed to operate aeronautics protection and aid services"

    22. "authorize and inspect public and private airports and aerodromes and administer public ones"

In another of its resolutions, DFL 241 confirms Articles 23 and 7 of DFL 221 of 1931. Article 9 of DFL 241 contains the following:

> Air transport of passengers, cargo and correspondence between various points located within the national territory is reserved for domestic aircraft that belong to natural or legalized Chilean citizens.
>
> If the owner or entrepreneur is a corporation or association, it will be considered Chilean only when more than two-thirds of the social capital or association rights belong to natural or legal Chilean persons and its administrators are Chilean in equal proportion.

Other regulations associated with the commercial aeronautics industry help explain the legal context of this sector prior to its reform in 1979. Law 16,436 of February 1966 establishes the areas in which ministers of state and undersecretaries can issue decrees or resolutions. The law spells out which matters are the responsibility of the Ministry of the Economy. Two of these, related to the commercial aeronautics section, are (1) the approval or setting of rates as proposed by the Civil Aeronautics Board and (2) the issuance of cabotage air traffic permits (Article 1, Title VI, points 9 and 10, respectively).

DFL 3 of 1969 establishes the new National Airline (LAN) Organic Law. Some of its main resolutions are:

- "National Airline of Chile is a State-owned commercial company with autonomous administration and independent legal status, domiciled in the city of Santiago, for the purpose of air transport and whatever is directly or indirectly related to said activity, in or out of the country.

  "Furthermore, through it, the functions that the State must perform to reach its objectives of ensuring air transport between different points within the country and abroad are to be fulfilled (Article 1).

- "In each year's National Budget Law, the funds needed to meet the cost of the company's operation of noncommercial and profitable national and international air transport, which the State requires in conformity to Article 1 of this decree with force of law, will be included" (Article 10).

- "National Airline of Chile will be exempt from all kinds of tax and municipal and fiscal contributions, without exception, including taxes on sales and purchases, on sealed paper and stamps, on services when it receives them, and on municipal licenses and others, and will enjoy poverty privileges before the Courts of Justice.

  "Likewise, it will be eligible for benefits and exemptions that legislation has granted or will grant in the future to air transport activities" (Article 12).

- "National Airline of Chile must be consulted prior to the discussion and conclusion of international agreements on air transport or any other act that implies granting of permission or extension of those existing to operate commercially in the country" (Article 13).

- "Personnel from public services, or semi-public services administered autonomously, municipalities, and State-owned companies must acquire their tickets from National Airline of Chile,. . ."

  "Likewise, air cargo belonging to the services or people indicated, except that destined for national defense or from other countries, must be carried on LAN Chile aircraft between the points covered by their regular services and in the measure of their availability" (Article 14).

DL 2,564 of 1979

Decree Law 2,564 (DL 2,564) was published in March 1979. It "dictates norms on air transport and commercial aeronautic services; modifies the Decrees with Force of Law 221 of 1931 and 241 of 1960." It contains the main provisions that reform the sector. The most important subsequent norm, Law 18,243 of September 1982, modifies Article 2 of DL 2,564. DL 2,564 will be presented in this section, including the modification.

To understand the implications of this decree law, it is important to be familiar with the "spirit of the new norms," which is expressed in the introductory sections:

- "Chile . . . requires the availability of air transport services of the highest quality and efficiency at the lowest possible cost, for this relates directly to the development of the country."
- It is necessary to create optimum competitive conditions among all companies interested in Chilean air transport services, for the purpose of achieving the characteristics mentioned above."
- "Said competition supposes freedom of tariffs and minimization of intervention by State authority, in order to guarantee the stability of the norms that regulate air transport."

This legal text is brief and can be divided in two parts: the first, which explicitly establishes the general norms of competition within the sector, and the second, which modifies and revokes provisions contained in DFL 221 of 1931, DFL 241 of 1960, DFL 3 of 1969, and other laws. These amendments have the object of reducing "excessive" sector regulations.

In the first part of DL 2,564, three articles stand out:

1. "Air transport services, either international or cabotage, and all other kinds of commercial aeronautics services may be performed by domestic or foreign companies, as long as they fulfill the security and technical requirements established by the national authorities.

   "It is the responsibility of the Aeronautics Board to establish and control technical requirements and of the Civil Aeronautics Board to establish security requirements" (Article 1).

2. "The norm established in the first clause of the previous article will be applied to foreign aeronautics companies as long as, in the routes they operate, the other States grant similar conditions to Chilean airline companies, when requested.

"If, on some route, another State should limit the conditions for Chilean aircraft or companies' operation of their commercial aeronautic services, the Civil Aeronautics Board may impose temporary suspension, up to 30 days, on any commercial aeronautical services of the companies which operate on said route. . . .

"On the routes in which, by disposition of another State, freedom of fares does not exist, the Civil Aeronautics Board will have authority to establish the fares, . . .

"In the cases in which fares have not been established by the Civil Aeronautics Board, according to the previous clause, commercial aeronautical companies must register fares to be applied with this organization . . .

"The Civil Aeronautics Board, for valid reasons, may end, suspend or limit cabotage services or any other kind of commercial aeronautics services, which take place exclusively within national territory, by foreign companies or aircraft, if in their country of origin, the right to equal treatment of Chilean companies or aircraft is not granted or effectively recognized . . ." (Article 2, replaced by Law 18,243).

3. "If according to international agreement and for reciprocity reasons, only a limited number of international routes or frequencies were made available to domestic carriers, these will be assigned by public tender, following the procedure established in the regulations. The same procedure will be observed when it becomes necessary to reduce the number of frequencies on a particular international route" (Article 3).

The second part of DL 2,564 modifies and revokes previous legislation (for pertinent comparisons see the section on DFLs 221 and 241). For example, it replaces Article 7 of DFL 221. It now says, "The aeronautics authority may allow the registry of aircraft belonging to natural or legal foreign persons, as long as they hold or practice some job, profession or permanent industry within the country" (Article 4a). The phrase "but foreign aircraft are forbidden to carry either commercial or postal cargo, which is reserved for domestic aircraft" is eliminated from Article 23 of DFL 221 (Article 4b). Point 5 of Article 6 of DFL 241 is replaced with the following: "carry out the President of the Republic's decrees on termination, suspension or limitation of foreign air transport companies, dictated for reciprocity or national security reasons" (Article 5).

The main articles revoked are points 6, 7, 12, and 13 of Article 6 and Articles 7, 9, and 10 of DFL 241 of 1960; numbers 9 and 10 of paragraph VI of Article 1 of Law 16,436 of 1966; and Article 14 of DFL 3 of 1969.

DFL 221 and DFL 241 compared with DL 2,564

An adequate comparison between the current and previous legislation ruling the sector must distinguish between international and domestic traffic. The international transport market is, essentially, a market regulated by the will of the countries to reach bilateral agreements, in which nations with larger fleets (many times with some large state-owned airline) have a major influence on the combination of restrictions and permits that countries reciprocally grant.

The new Chilean legislation could not ignore this reality. The new Article 2 of DL 2,564 (Law 18,243) clearly establishes all the areas (international routes, fares, domestic transport) where strict reciprocity must exist between foreign and domestic airlines. As in DFL 241, these matters are responsibilities of the Civil Aeronautics Board.

Apart from the evolution of pertinent laws, changes in the competitive structure of commercial aeronautics at an international level are much in evidence. New developments have arisen from the 1978 and 1980 deregulations in the United States, which subsequently promoted the same philosophy in the international field. At the end of the 1970s, the United States signed more liberal agreements with Belgium and Holland. These agreements are harbingers of the trend toward greater freedom in Europe.

A movement toward decentralization in decision making and less state intervention is also under way. At a domestic level, a comparison between the old and new legislation shows a clear shift toward increased competition and less regulation of the sector. DL 2,564 establishes the freedom to fix fares and minimizes state intervention.

The provisions in favor of more competition and less state intervention are Article 1, which limits the authority to lend air transport services to considerations of a technical nature; Article 4, which eliminates biases in favor of Chilean citizens for licenses and Chilean aircraft for cabotage; and Article 10, which diminishes the responsibilities of the Civil Aeronautics Board, frees fares, and eliminates some provisions that favored LAN Chile, such as the obligation of state employees to use flights from this company exclusively.

Conclusions

The commercial aeronautics industry is now in a situation similar to that of the telecommunications and electric power sectors. The government favors competition, by allowing the free entry of companies to the sector, eliminating captive markets, and altering the relations between the regulating state and the owner state. In situations where competition may be hindered, companies have the option of going before the Antimonopoly Commission (DL 211). Furthermore, the state avoids participating in the economy as owner and regulator at the same time, justifying the divestitures of SOEs. Privatization also fulfills other objectives, such as promoting trust in private property and a subsidiary role for the state.

The privatization of LAN Chile, initiated in 1988 and concluded the following year, was made possible thanks to the major liberalization of this market established by DL 2,564 of 1979.

During the 1980s, the equality of companies before the law allowed private companies to gain markets from LAN Chile, which, although it operates more efficiently than in previous periods, could not maintain its level of participation in the domestic market. This change in participation was accompanied by growth of the domestic passenger market (where the supply has grown even more than sales), and a significant expansion of international passenger and cargo transport.

Summary of Legal Changes in the Recently Privatized Productive Sectors

In the different sections of this appendix, it has been possible to witness how the privatization process becomes part of an evolution common to all privatized productive sectors. The changes in legal norms that rule different economic activities play a leading role in this evolution.

In the telecommunications sector (privatized companies: CTC, ENTEL, and Telex-Chile) Law 18,168 of 1982 replaced DFL 4 of 1959. In the electric power sector (privatized companies: ENDESA, CHILGENER, CHILMETRO, CHILQUINTA, and others), DFL 4 of 1959 was replaced by Mining DFL 1 of 1982. In the commercial aeronautics industry (privatized company: LAN Chile), the issuing of Decree Law 2,564 of 1979 modified the norms established in DFL 221 of 1931 and DFL 241 of 1960. All changes in legislation affecting these sectors led to greater competition.

Other productive sectors that were privatized between 1985 and 1989 were the steel industry (CAP was privatized in 1986), the sugar industry (IANSA was privatized in 1988), pharmaceutical industry (Laboratorio Chile was privatized in 1988), the nitrate industry (SOQUIMICH was privatized in 1986), and the coal industry (Schwager was privatized in 1988).

New legislation also made changes in the coal market. The main modifications were associated with the new 1983 Mining Code, which replaced that of 1932. The 1983 law eliminated the exception regime for coal, making the legal treatment of coal the same as that of other minerals.

Table E.2 gives a brief chronology of the main legal and property modifications in the telecommunications, electric power, and commercial aeronautics sectors since 1973.

TABLE E.2

Chronology of Changes in the Telecommunications, Electric Power, and Commercial Aeronautics Sectors, 1973–1989

	Telecommunications Sector
1973	The state has a monopoly in all telecommunications services (centered in a few companies).
1975–1980	Public telecommunications companies start to pursue efficiency objectives.
1982	New General Telecommunications Law passes (Law 18,168).
1987	DFL 1 eliminates cross-subsidies, clarifies tarification.
1985–1988	Telecommunications companies are privatized: • Telex-Chile (1986) • CTC (1988) • ENTEL (1986)

	Electric Power Sector
1973	The state has a monopoly in electric power companies in a highly concentrated market.
1975–1980	Government adopts goal of increasing efficiency of companies within the sector.
1980	ENDESA begins to subdivide, forming a group of subsidiaries.
1982	The new legislation for the sector is passed.
1985–1989	The electric power companies are privatized: • CHILMETRO and CHILQUINTA (1986) • CHILGENER (1987) • ENDESA (1988) • Pehuenche (1989)

	Commercial Aeronautics Sector
1973	LAN Chile, a state-owned company, has a monopoly on commercial aeronautics.
1979	New rules on air transport and commercial aeronautics are established.
1988–1989	LAN Chile is privatized.

SOURCE: Authors.

NOTES

Chapter 1, "Introduction"

1. The government issues several types of decrees. A decree law (DL) is a law issued by a de facto government. A decree with the force of law (DFL) is a law issued by the executive by virtue of another law granting legislative powers in specific areas to the executive.

2. State-managed firms, or *compañías intervenidas*, are firms in which the government took management control without claiming ownership. These interventions took place in two periods. A little-known decree law issued in 1932 allowed the government to intervene in a company with labor problems that threatened the "normal" supply of goods produced by the company. In 1972–1973, the Allende government used this decree law, generating labor unrest and then taking over management of various companies. In 1982–1983 the Pinochet government intervened in a number of insolvent banks to prevent them from going bankrupt, and these banks in turn took over many holding companies that were unable to service their loans. As a result, the state-managed banks gained control over many commercial, industrial, and mining companies, which collectively became known as "the odd sector."

Chapter 2, "The Economic Framework, 1973–1989"

1. For details on the objectives of the new government, see Hachette 1977.

2. The distinction between means and objectives may be misleading. It will depend on the problem to be solved and its degree of aggregation.

3. See chapters by J. Cauas and S. de Castro in Méndez 1979.

4. See Marshall and Romaguera 1981, Cortés and Sjaastad 1981, and Tokman 1984.

5. After December 1980 legislation was required for any new price control.

6. After 1983, however, a special exchange rate was temporarily established for foreign debt payment.

7. At one time, prohibitions covered about 60 percent of imported and exported goods, through quantitative or administrative restrictions, 10,000 percent prior deposits, and official approval requirements.

8. The freeing of interest rates was expected to encourage savings, equalize interest rates between formal and informal credit segments, and lower the costs of financial instruments. The freer flow of international capital was expected to increase investment and move domestic interest rates closer to international rates. For more details, see Ramos 1986.

9. Other features of the Andean Pact, such as the agreements among members to monopolize the production of specific industrial goods and the high and differentiated customs duties considered for the expected common external tariff, were also serious obstacles to Chile's remaining a full partner in the pact.

10. Shares at current prices point better to the extent of sacrifice in terms of alternative costs (consumption), while the same figures, when expressed in constant prices, allow for a more accurate picture of the intertemporal evolution of "real" investment and, then, of the stock of nonhuman capital. A new methodology, developed by the statistical office responsible for national accounts, may produce new figures for investment, but it is applicable, to date, only to 1986. According to the new results, investment in fixed capital has been underestimated by 3.4 percentage points for that year.

11. The substitution of domestic for foreign savings is analyzed in the Chilean context by Foxley (1985) and Behrman (1976).

12. Social security should be added. However, it would have an impact on private savings only after the end of the period analyzed.

13. This phenomenon has been analyzed by various authors, including Acle (1985) and Edwards and Cox-Edwards (1987).

14. On the basis of evidence gathered from comparative studies, the economic team expected that growth would reduce poverty and eventually inequality. Therefore, they favored measures to ease equality of opportunity to education, health, housing, and the labor market.

15. Riveros and Paredes (1989) and Sapelli (1989) take a fresh look at the issue of unemployment in Chile, which had previously been analyzed superficially under the assumption that employment was essentially demand determined. According to Riveros and Paredes, with the exception of 1974, more than two-thirds of measured unemployment was structural.

16. It included a so-called Labor Plan and a Labor Law Code, whose main features are summarized in this paragraph.

17. Most of the other aspects of the reform would become relevant after 1985.

18. Moral hazard, as used here, refers to an economic agent's increased willingness to take risks when that agent does not bear the full cost of any losses.

19. If other forms of rescue of foreign debt are taken into account, the reduction is even greater, amounting to the equivalent of US$8,987.3 million, or more than 50 percent of the total foreign debt accumulated up to the end of the recession (1984).

20. Tariffs had risen to 35 percent for six months in 1985 and were reduced to 20 percent in 1986.

Chapter 3, "The Ideological and Economic Objectives of Privatization"

1. CORFO is a state-owned and -operated development corporation formed in 1939 and has played an important role in the industrial development of the country.

2. Short (1984), using figures for 1975, gives percentages of 9.4 and 6.6 percent for world and Western Hemisphere countries, respectively.

3. Chileanization meant that the government acquired 50 percent of the large foreign copper companies, mainly through new investments in the mines. Through nationalization the remaining 50 percent was transferred to the public sector without compensation.

4. "Liberal" is used here in its original European sense. During the 1950s and early 1960s, the U.S. Agency for International Development financed an exchange program in economics between the Pontifical Catholic University of Chile and the University of Chicago. As a result, about one hundred Chileans did graduate work at the University of Chicago, and a full-time economics faculty, mostly engaged in research, was established at the Pontifical Catholic University of Chile. The work of these Chilean economists, as well as that of other foreign-trained economists, eventually led to policy recommendations that differed radically from the protectionist and interventionist policies in effect in Chile and most other Latin American countries at the time. When some of these economists were called to participate in the Pinochet government, they became known as the Chicago Boys.

5. Efficiency is used here in the sense of maximization of profits. The government believed that the argument in favor of entrepreneurial activities of the state on the basis of the need to correct market imperfections had been grossly abused, and that it was extremely difficult, if not impossible, to fulfill this role.

6. To begin with, the government would not explicitly or implicitly guarantee such operations.

7. Internal efficiency refers to efficiency within the firm and implies minimum costs for any given product. Although clearly an oversimplification, it is often assumed that private enterprise, as a profit maximization endeavor, is

internally efficient by definition from a technical point of view. Allocative efficiency refers to the distribution of output among different sectors, subsectors,
branches, etc. The usual assumption is that, in the real world, market imperfections always exist that require government intervention. SOEs are one of the
instruments available to government to correct such imperfections.

8. The principal reason was, of course, maximization of revenues.

9. Competition was also introduced to discourage monopoly gains;
bankruptcy law reforms were introduced as part of a package of measures to
control problems generated by the existence of highly indebted conglomerates;
and measures to facilitate takeovers were part of a package of measures designed
to develop the local capital market.

10. The odd sector is the name given to those private sector enterprises, most
of which belonged to conglomerates, that were managed by the public sector after
the government intervened in the financial institutions to which the holding companies of these enterprises were highly indebted in early 1983. The "odd" thing
about these enterprises was that their ownership was not well defined, since they
legally belonged to the private sector, but they were managed by the public sector
as a result of government intervention in banks. In consequence, banks demanded
strict debt service from holding companies, a requirement many of these companies were unable to meet because of the economic crisis and because, to minimize the already enormous expected interest rates, they had been rolling over
their large debt every thirty days. Therefore, those holding companies were taken
over by the state-managed banks and the operational companies were, then,
managed by the public sector.

11. This view is taken in Díaz-Alejandro 1988.

12. See Mandakovic and Lima 1989. The objectives as defined in 1988 were
(1) the elimination or reduction of frequent fiscal deficits caused by SOE operational losses; (2) popular capitalism, or the spreading of ownership through sales
to workers and small shareholders (correlation of the individual with entrepreneurial activity; (3) long-term efficiency of enterprises; (4) diversification of the
AFPs' investments in solid instruments that guarantee a satisfactory pension level
(correlation of the pensioner with the growth of the enterprises); (5) the strengthening of the capital market; (6) expansion and modernization of enterprises through
capital increases instead of debts to the state; and (7) additional resources for the
state and CORFO, with the purpose of financing projects with a high social rate
of return, like private sector promotion credits. From this list, it can be inferred
that the substantive changes were minor with respect to those from 1985.

13. Whether social expenditures are current expenditures or investment can
only be judged on a case-by-case basis. If the gathered funds were used, for
example, to expand infant nutrition programs, and if this was a project with a
high (relative to other projects in the country) social economic rate of return, it
probably should have been carried out, although it might be considered a current
expenditure from an accounting point of view and result in a capital loss
to the state.

14. These were, in fact, also debt-equity swaps, although formally they took a different form.

15. Authorities tried to diversify AFP funds not only by allowing AFPs to purchase privatized companies' stock, but also by permitting them to acquire titles of private companies approved by the Risk Classification Commission. Nevertheless, initially, the pension funds were only allowed to include stock of state-owned enterprises in their portfolio, and of these, only some met the requirements allowing them to be acquired by AFPs. Today AFPs can purchase a significant number of shares of Chilean private corporations and can invest 2 percent of their assets abroad.

16. It is estimated by its chief executive officer that CODELCO has about 3,000 more employees than required. See *El Mercurio,* July 1, 1990. According to Allende the objectives were also destined to "tie the hands" of future authorities, so that they could not introduce substantial modifications to the existing economic system (Monckeberg 1988). But the following question arises: If the idea was to restrict future authorities, why was it not done from the beginning? A probable answer is that there was an increasing fear on the part of the military government of future reverse privatization of large privatized SOEs, with the consequences that this could have on the functioning of an economic system based on private property.

Chapter 4, "The Privatization Process"

1. A complete list of the enterprises privatized in both rounds can be derived from Appendix A.

2. In fact, an intermediate public system was also institutionalized, allowing people to choose medical services at either public or private facilities assigned to the National Health Service.

3. It is impossible to construct a complete list of the odd sector enterprises divested. Nor is it possible to determine divestiture modes and prices for most of these privatizations. Neither the Comisión Progresa (in charge of divesting the enterprises of the so-called Cruzat-Larrain Group) nor the Banco de Chile (responsible for selling the major enterprises of the Vial Group) provided the required information, on the basis that it was private. However, some part of this information can be gathered from newspaper accounts and legal documents, in-depth research beyond the scope of this book. To illustrate the caliber of the enterprises belonging to the odd sector, it is sufficient to indicate that the following were among them: Banco de Chile, Banco Santiago, Banco Concepción, AFP Provida, AFP Santa María, COPEC, Forestal Arauco, INFORSA, CCU, INDUS, Compañía Minera Pudahuel, and CTI.

4. The privatization of the traditional SOEs had really begun in 1982, when the government decided to privatize minority interests in some public utilities, although the process was later interrupted and resumed again only in 1985.

5. Most existing estimates suggested that, for example, the repurchase periods for Banco de Chile and Banco de Santiago would exceed twenty years.

6. This section is based in part on information provided by José Martínez, who was normalization manager of CORFO during the Second Round of privatizations. An active military officer, Martínez has a master's degree in economics from the State University. His master's thesis was an analysis of the First Round of privatizations.

7. An important exception to the general case described here was the privatization of most of the enterprises belonging to the odd sector. These enterprises, except the commercial banks and the AFPs, were privatized either by special commissions (Comisión Progresa) or directly by the state-managed banks (Banco de Chile). Commercial banks and the AFPs other than Banco de Chile, Banco de Santiago, and AFPs Santa María and Provida were privatized using the framework described above.

8. The economic team during the Pinochet regime, also known as the Chicago Boys, was composed of about thirty persons, depending on who defined it and the period of government, in high-level executive positions in the government, usually including the Ministries of Finance and Economics, as well as other ministries in the economic and social area, including the central bank.

9. The ownership of all but a handful of SOEs was concentrated in CORFO in 1973. Although during the 1940–1970 period CORFO accumulated a relatively large number of industrial SOEs, this concentration process was accelerated during the Allende government, which intended to transform CORFO into a large holding company of SOEs. The exceptions were mainly the traditional SOEs created by law, each of which was usually assigned to a sectoral ministry.

10. During the last phase of the privatization process under the military government, this position was held by Cristián Larroulet. Larroulet, who had joined the economic team relatively early after the military takeover, after his graduate studies at the University of Chicago, had, from his advisory position at the Ministry of Economics, contributed to the management policies of the SOEs. Among other things, he established a centralized information system to monitor the performance of these enterprises. His knowledge of the SOEs and of the workings of the government allowed him to play a key role during the Second Round of the Chilean privatization process.

11. The Committee for the Sale of Shares was formed in May 1985 when CORFO, at the urging of Minister of Finance Hernán Büchi, was authorized to divest up to 30 percent of the shares of a number of its main subsidiaries. Sales of these shares were to be made, to a significant degree, to AFPs. The committee's main initial function was to facilitate such sales, eliminating bureaucratic problems that might have been raised either at CORFO or at the Ministry of Labor (Superintendency of AFPs). As mentioned in the text, in practice its functions were broadened considerably. This committee, in a way, followed up on the work of the Committee for the Sale of Assets, formally created in 1982 at the urging of the then Minister of Economics Luis Danús. The Committee for the Sale of Assets was formed by almost the same persons as its informal follower and functioned

until 1983. Given the strong recession that existed in Chile during its existence, the committee was only able to arrange for the sale of the shares of the Chilean Interoceanic Navigation Company (CCNI) and of some other minor assets. However, it prepared and recommended legislation to allow AFPs to buy SOE shares, a key feature of the second stage of the Second Round of privatizations.

12. The committee met every week during 1985, when the last phase of the privatization process under the military government was effectively launched. Over time, these meetings were gradually held less frequently—initially one meeting every fifteen days and perhaps no more than one meeting a month during the first half of 1989. This clearly reflects the lower number of enterprises being privatized, as well as the smooth operation of the privatization process itself. The committee ended its meetings during the last quarter of 1989.

13. One important exception was the case of ENDESA, in which some operations were separated and new enterprises created, with CORFO assuming a high proportion of its debt. Without the latter measure, ENDESA shares could not have been sold to the AFPs, and moral hazard might have affected other purchasers. This case is discussed in Chapter 8.

14. There were, of course, exceptions, especially in the transport sector. The State Railway (FFCC), in spite of rationalization efforts, showed losses all along. The government also took over a large volume of LAN Chile's debt during the first half of the 1980s as part of a reordering process. In other cases, the origin of excessive or high indebtedness tended to lie, at least in part, in the need for foreign exchange to solve balance of payments problems, which the central bank obtained from solvent SOEs, which, in turn, contracted debt abroad. In these cases, the SOEs were highly indebted but also had high levels of foreign currency deposits at the central bank. Good examples of this latter case were CAP and ENDESA.

15. In fact, Carlos Ominami, minister of economics of the Patricio Aylwin government, in a report to Congress denouncing the capital loss of CORFO as a result of privatizations and CORFO credit operations during the military government, highlighted the fact that the government in no way intended to reverse the privatizations.

16. Related to this factor is the fact that, traditionally, a percentage of overseas copper sales has been transferred directly to the armed forces to finance arms purchases. Although the fraction of the sales transferred is established by law, neither this income nor the purchases financed with those resources are reflected in the balance of trade. Moreover, as a way to maintain the "necessary" secret, these imports are not subject to customs duties or inspection.

Chapter 5, "Effects of Privatization on Government Revenues and Wealth"

1. It will be assumed in this chapter that divested shares were paid in cash. This is a realistic assumption for the period 1985–1989, when, with the exception

of ENDESA (69.8 percent) and CTC (95.8 percent), shares were sold for cash. During the previous period, 1974–1982, credit sales were the rule.

2. Equation 2 assumes only one sale made at year zero and intends to evaluate the factors determining the net returns over time and their impact on the present value of net returns to the public sector for the sale of the firm or of the package α_0.

3. While the first assumption is important to determine the effective transfer of funds from public firms to the public sector, the second is required to estimate the relevant tax paid by the private sector on distributed dividends.

4. The five firms were CHILGENER, CHILMETRO, CHILQUINTA, CAP, and IANSA. Laboratorio Chile would require an insignificant increase and thus was not included in the list.

5. The implicit assumption is that public sector expenditures financed with SOE divestiture revenues will not affect wealth distribution.

6. These rates were exceedingly high, averaging almost 28 percent in real terms (after monetary correction) over the 1975–1982 period.

7. Given the high leverage of the holding companies of these conglomerates, stock price fluctuations had significant effects on the net wealth of owners.

8. Nondiversifiable risks related to specific characteristics of divested firms—in production or markets—may arise too. However, they do not differ between the public and private sectors.

9. Another way in which this reverse privatization risk can be viewed is as an increase in the discounting parameter for the private sector with respect to the one used for the public sector. These are just two different ways to say the same thing.

10. It can also be argued that the high rate of return implicit in the repurchase of foreign debt papers implied a high discount rate after 1985 for public investment, similar to that of the private sector.

11. This section is based on Cabrera, Hachette, and Lüders 1989.

12. Given the economic policies followed during the military regime described in Chapter 2, significant efficiency gains should not have been expected. The analysis carried out in Chapter 7 confirms these expectations.

13. In this expression the expected capital gains are already implicitly included.

14. The use of percentage changes in the GDP is based on the fact that fluctuations in the market are markedly procyclic. Nevertheless, because variations in the stock market's profitability, compared with variations in GDP, are higher in the Chilean economy than in the U.S. economy, the use of factor ∂ probably leads to an underestimation of MRP applied in the national market. This fact implies a likely overestimation of the value of divested SOEs for the private sector, that is, a bias in exactly the desired direction.

15. This reduction could result, for example, from a greater diversification of exports and a more efficient use of compensating mechanisms, such as the Copper Stabilization Fund and the international reserves of the central bank.

16. Adjustments must be made based on the company's leverage because the sectoral b's can be used to discount the enterprise's assets flows, but what is of interest here are net worth flows. The b used here included adjustments by the relevant leverage.

17. It is important to note that this retention rate is slightly higher than the current maximum legal one (70 percent). This assumption, therefore, in all likelihood introduces another factor that biases estimates in the desired direction, that is to say, to overestimate the value of the enterprise to the private sector.

18. The main difference between the methodology of Cabrera, Hachette, and Lüders (1989) and that of Marcel (1989a) is that the latter (1) assumes that initial rates of return to calculate the dividend flows are those the companies obtained during 1987 (this implies anticipated knowledge of higher than experienced rates of return for all privatizations before that date), while the former assume that agents have access to information only on monthly actual changes in returns, (2) uses an arbitrary, relatively low, 10 percent discount rate for the evaluation of all privatized SOEs, and (3) uses two fewer years of information, years during which a significant divestiture effort was carried out.

19. See Table 5.5. This cost includes a subsidized long-term credit to buy the shares and a tax deduction. The first is relevant, here, only in the cases of the shares of ENDESA and CTC sold through that mode; the second cost is relevant neither for the ten firms considered in our estimates nor for the rest of the twenty-seven enterprises divested during the period 1985–1989, since it only applied to the sale of shares of four financial institutions (Banco de Chile, Banco de Santiago, AFP Provida, and AFP Santa María) belonging to the odd sector.

20. Income taxes were quite low by national and international standards during the period analyzed. In 1989, as an electoral victory by the opposition to the military regime became increasingly likely, a tax increase became predictable. This fact helps to explain the increase in the estimated difference in 1989 between estimated and actual prices of packages of stocks divested compared with previous years.

21. Growing uncertainties related to the proximity of elections and changes in the political regime may also have reduced the attractiveness of divested stocks.

22. If labor contracts were different between private and public sectors, differences in efficiency could arise with privatization, even if subject otherwise to the same laws. Efficiency changes as a consequence of privatization remain a challenging topic of research only partially tackled in Chapter 7.

23. This argument is really a variant of the efficiency factor.

24. Electricity generation cannot be considered a natural monopoly, as is usually done. Competition can exist.

25. This is certainly an important factor to take into account in the process of privatization, to avoid creating inefficiency and doubtful monopoly rents.

26. Information on government revenues was not available for 1989.

27. No information is available on these two factors.

28. Increases in efficiency, however, would not imply a loss of public net worth.

29. All the papers describing the crisis cited above, plus many others on the Chilean economy of the time, provide possible explanations for the level of the interest rates in the country.

30. In some cases depositors and taxpayers might be the same. This is, however, not generally so, since taxes on interest income are usually avoided in Chile because declaration and payment cannot in practice be enforced by Internal Revenue, because of regulations on secrecy of deposit accounts.

31. There are no reliable estimates of the losses to the government as a result of these operations. At the time of the intervention in the banks in 1982, the government estimated bad loan losses not yet amortized through bad loan provisions at between US$2.5 and US$4.0 billion, of which slightly more than US$1.0 billion were to be covered by financial institution shareholders and other private sector investors. As a result of the rescue operations of the central bank in connection with the financial crisis of the early 1980s, the central bank financed about US$7.0 billion in relief operations with the financial institutions, a high proportion, to make foreign exchange accessible to private sector borrowers at a preferential rate, to reschedule loans to private sector borrowers at lower than market interest rates, and to buy bad loans from the financial institutions. Not all of the latter will be lost, since financial institutions are obliged, as mentioned in the text, to use most of their profits to repurchase the bad loans from the central bank.

32. Fiscal information is not yet available for 1989.

33. The public sector used those proceeds to reduce its debt with the central bank related to the support given by this last institution to the commercial banks to improve their financial situation after 1983.

34. There is a growing discussion on this issue. See, for example, Vickers and Yarrow 1988 on the public sector borrowing requirement.

35. This consideration is irrelevant if the only source of funds for the public sector is the divestiture of public enterprises; this was not the case in Chile and, consequently, this possibility is left aside.

36. It should also be noted that some current expenditures are no different from asset accumulation. In particular, expenditures on education and health classified as current expenditures represent, strictly speaking, human capital accumulation. Consequently, the results presented in Table 5.8 should be interpreted with care.

37. The only author who has tried to estimate that impact (Marcel 1989b) has reached the conclusion that no more than 50 percent of funds obtained through divestiture financed capital accumulation. However, his methodology is essentially based on CORFO's accounting, which denies the fungibility assumption he recognized earlier. Even if one accepts his general approach, its application presents problems that bias his results downward. CORFO's credits to SOE purchases represent new CORFO assets with a positive rate of return and not consumption expenditures. Consequently, most income retained by CORFO on SOE divestiture represents asset accumulation; the part related to the subsidy on credit does not. On the other hand, he assumes that part of deficit financing went into financing a theoretical tax revenue reduction derived from the 1984 tax

reform. This assumption is difficult to support. In the first place, revenues have been increasing in real terms, not decreasing, although part of this improvement is a consequence of the rise in the price of copper (Table 5.8). In the second place, even if tax revenues had been decreasing, if the authorities had decided to reduce revenues in a permanent way, the relevant level of revenues upon which to base an estimate of the distributional impact of deficit financing would be the one given after the tax reform and not before it.

38. The public sector prepaid in 1988 part of a significant debt it had acquired with the central bank, financing the operation with accumulated foreign currency deposited in a Copper Stabilization Fund as a public sector asset.

Chapter 6, "Effects of Privatization on the Capital Market, Savings and Investment, and Employment"

1. See in particular Lüders 1986.

2. See Chapters 2 and 4 for details.

3. This count does not include equity related to the odd sector, which had returned to private sector hands after 1984.

4. The number given for the number of shareholders is the sum of people who bought shares in the privatized SOEs. The number of different persons owning shares may differ from the noted number of shareholders since some may have purchased shares of different SOEs. It is impossible, at this stage, to obtain a precise estimate of them. Bidding at auction and direct sales of SOE equity stimulated the development of the stock exchange and investment banks. The mode implied cash payment, and for that reason, a more careful choice of potential buyers in relation to their financial capabilities. If this mode limited the number of users of the capital market, it stimulated its development through requirements of more precise information: quality versus quantity, both considerations important to strengthen the capital market.

5. The divestitures, the enactment of DL 600, and the opening of the capital account did not coincide fully. The privatization process started two years before both; however, there was considerable overlapping afterward.

6. Foreign competition, however, would reduce profits to be obtained from buying the name of a traditional bank.

7. Several financial institutions—formal and informal—went broke at the end of 1976 and the Bank Osorno y la Unión did so in mid-1977, that is, in the middle of the privatization process of the eleven banks.

8. Stylized facts are a limited number of facts about a phenomenon that, taken together, allow a reasonably clear description of the phenomenon itself.

9. Private savings are obtained from the difference between total and public savings. Since the latter is not available, private savings cannot yet be estimated for 1989.

10. A simple model of rational consumer behavior can justify this argument. It is presented in Hachette and Lüders 1988: Appendix III-I.

11. These opportunities were made more attractive because privatization, from the private point of view, moved the investment schedule to the right.

12. It is necessary to recognize the importance of the upward trend in GDP as a partial explanation of this investment trend.

13. During the Second Round, although privatization tended to stimulate savings more than during the First Round, there seems to have been greater substitution between privatized SOEs and alternative investment projects.

14. External savings appear significant in 1975, when expressed as percentage of GDP. However, GDP had fallen significantly and half the current account balance was financed with foreign reserves.

15. Edwards 1985, Morandé 1988, De la Cuadra and Hachette 1991, and Ramos 1986.

16. It has been argued that the public sector financed a high share of the divestitures between 1974 and 1981. Although apparently true, given loans made to the private sector for that purpose, that sector had for all practical purposes repaid its debt in full by 1982. In order to achieve this result, the private sector obviously had to transfer real resources to the public sector in the form of savings, partly financed by foreign sources.

17. This figure derives from the required increase in efficiency of divested SOEs to avoid any loss in fiscal revenues that could result from privatization (see Chapter 5). It is not, then, an expected increase in efficiency.

18. Between 1979 and 1982, very few enterprises were privatized, while the government continued to receive revenues from First Round divestiture payments of installments.

19. In fact, authorities at the time insisted on two fiscal objectives: to reduce the fiscal deficit and to increase social expenditures (and military, too).

20. Fiscal information is not available for 1989.

21. In addition to market prices, this implies having to face a "hard budget"— that is, any loss can only be financed in the capital market on a voluntary basis.

22. Most time series of production were obtained from the evolution of value added by subsector (sectoral GDP); however, in the case of mining the gross value of production was used, while in the case of manufacturing the index of production of the Society for Factory Promotion (SOFOFA) was used, since it seemed to better explain employment.

23. It is implicitly assumed, then, that disguised unemployment was nonexistent before Allende took over. This is clearly an understatement of the situation.

24. Additional analysis on the composition of samples, along with some conclusions, albeit tentative, are presented in Hachette and Lüders 1988: Appendix III-2.

Chapter 7, "Are Private and Public Enterprises Different?"

1. Sunk costs are resources allocated for a certain use, which cannot be reallocated for any other use.

2. The worst price for assets held by the previous owner of the franchise is the scrap value of assets, while the highest price the new entrant would have to pay for these assets is the replacement value. The difference depends on the importance of sunk costs and the expense of bargaining or arbitration.

Chapter 8, "Two Polemic Cases of Privatization: CAP and ENDESA"

1. In the mid-1970s, the company's assets were 33 percent financed by equity and 67 percent by third-party loans.

2. The general orientation of annual activities of each ministry was detailed in so-called ministerial programs.

3. The debt-capital ratio was 0.89 in 1979.

4. By this time, the government's intention to privatize the company seems to have been clearly established, otherwise this change of social objective would have been contradictory to government policies that did not allow an SOE to carry out activities unrelated directly to its main line of business.

5. It had capital of US$708 and US$676 million in 1981 and 1982.

6. Before the repurchase operation, the private sector (workers and the general public) owned 11 percent of CAP stock.

7. To date, worker-shareholders hold CAP shares individually instead of forming a holding company that controls the shares, an approach taken by workers in many other firms (such as SOQUIMICH, IANSA, LAN Chile, and CHILMETRO). In those cases, workers formed holding companies to obtain credit for the purchase of additional shares, as well as to improve their bargaining position in the board of directors. In the case of CAP, the first reason was irrelevant, since CAP granted its workers credit to buy shares.

8. However, only those who had financed the purchase of shares with their own funds could dispose freely of them; others—the majority—could do so only after prepaying the corresponding credit.

9. The objective of these reschedulings was to improve the balance of payments.

10. The purchase agreement had existed since April 1986.

11. Of course, privatization in itself also contributed to the recovery and growth of the capital market, together with the possibility given to AFPs to invest pension funds in shares and bonds of previously classified companies. See Chapter 6.

12. The price in U.S. dollars of the shares was the same in the stock exchange at that time and was also the same as that offered to private sector shareholders subsequently.

13. See the report presented on this issue by Minister of the Economy Carlos Ominami to Congress in January 1991. If the nominal prices of shares were higher than the market prices, according to CAP's statutes, it was allowed to repurchase its own shares.

14. Table 8.4 shows this significant capital gain. In a rapidly rising market, the CAP shares rose almost four times as fast as average prices in the General Index of Share Prices of the Santiago Stock Exchange between 1986 and 1989.

15. This decline is easily explained given the elastic supply of new stock at US$0.25 in a rapidly rising market.

16. These and other debt reduction operations allowed CAP to reduce its debt by US$147.9 million during 1986 and 1987.

17. Other SOEs, authorized to repurchase their foreign debt in pesos, were ENDESA (US$210 million), ENTEL (US$17 million), ENAEX (US$13 million), and ENAP (US$40 million), all of them majority controlled by the state at the time.

18. During 1987 CAP's debt-equity ratio was reduced from 0.9 to 0.7, and during 1988 it was further reduced to 0.5. As a result, with the decisive contribution of the debt repurchase operations at market prices, CAP was able in about two years to reduce its debt-equity ratio from 0.9 to 0.5.

19. More details on the electric power sector may be found in Appendix E.

20. Obviously, there is an economic limit to this integration determined by the size of the companies involved.

21. ENDESA controls Pehuenche, while Colbún-Machicura is an SOE.

22. One of these, CHILMETRO, is controlled by Enersis, which also owns 11.3 percent of the shares of ENDESA and has a determining influence in that Board of Directors.

23. Nevertheless, it is still argued that ENDESA's operational and investment costs could be significantly reduced through more effective rationalization than that carried out during the period under consideration here. This argument is confirmed by the relatively low rates of return on its investments.

24. A preferential dollar was established for the repayment of existing foreign debt as of May 1982. As a consequence of the reduction in equity capital, the financial year was closed on July 31.

25. Nevertheless, efforts have been made through appropriate legislation to ensure that electric power fees reflect social economic costs.

26. From the beginning of the military government, the idea was set forth that the state should transfer to the private sector disposable assets and activities that would be managed better in private hands. What seems to have changed over time are the criteria for judging which activities should be managed by the state.

27. This process of administrative division occurred in diverse public enterprises and was controlled directly by the government.

28. Pilmaiquén was sold in 1986, and Pullinque in 1987.

29. This process has been unimportant as a measure of privatizations, although it is a way of allowing electricity-generating plants to raise the capital needed to expand their operations.

30. Because of the current legislation, AFPs could not buy shares of a company that had more than 50 percent of its capital concentrated in one shareholder and that did not have at least 10 percent in the hands of minority shareholders. AFPs could, however, sell shares to AFPs even if they did not comply with those requirements, as long as they committed themselves to fulfill the requirements within a given time span.

31. Eventually, 10 percent of those sales were not completed for a variety of reasons.

32. In the 1984 ministerial programs, it is expressly stated that ENDESA could provide engineering services within the country and abroad. It should be noted that the ministerial programs were not necessarily legally enforceable.

33. It is necessary to recall that the mere fact of privatizing is not directly related to ownership distribution; obviously the privatization mode chosen is a key factor.

34. As of December 31, 1989, Enersis officially owned 11.3 percent of the shares of ENDESA, but this percentage has increased since then. AFPs as a group are the most important shareholders, but each individual fund controls less than 5 percent.

35. ENDESA had assumed a commitment with creditors to maintain a certain debt-equity ratio, lower than that of the 1985 balance sheet.

Chapter 9, "Lessons from Privatization in Chile"

1. Many private sector offers probably exceeded those that would have been made had the tariff reform of 1978 and the real interest rate level during the second half of the 1970s been known. Yet the interest rate level was so high at the time of the First Round privatizations that book values exceeded market values by a wide margin in most cases.

2. The control exercised in these cases is interesting, since it is, in fact, limited to ensure that the AFPs invest in efficiently run enterprises. If AFPs do otherwise, their funds will tend to achieve lower rates of return (for similar risks) and shareholders will switch to other funds, which do invest in more efficiently run enterprises. In practice the system is not as responsive as suggested here, but incentives to encourage movement in that direction and adjustments to the system, which occur constantly, should eventually bring it close to the ideal described here.

3. Subsidized prices and employment creation are policies that worker-capitalists can be expected to resist strongly, and since workers are represented in a relatively large proportion of the main Chilean public utilities such policies are unlikely even to be proposed.

4. The exceptions are those cases in which the SOEs had a negative value.

5. These estimates assume that, at the time of privatization during the second half of the 1980s, there was no significant difference in internal efficiency between private and state-owned enterprises. This assumption is based on the econometric work presented in Chapter 7.

6. Stock prices paid in relation to fair market prices estimated do vary significantly from company to company in the sample.

7. This general framework included competition at free-market prices or regulated "true" marginal cost prices, hard budgets, and the absence of government interference in the management of SOEs, except with respect to limits on new investment projects.

Appendix E, "Evolution of Regulations for Three Privatized Sectors"

1. These companies were temporarily nationalized under the Allende government.

2. The price policies consisted of not only rate liberalization, but also the implementation of a "marginal cost" rates criterion and the elimination of crossed subsidies granted through the rates. The ministerial programs forced state-owned companies to finance themselves from 1975 on. Figures from the Budget Department indicate that the ratio of salaries and wages paid by the SOEs (public companies and CORFO subsidiaries) to GNP changed from 4.7 percent in 1973 to 2.3 percent in 1985.

3. It is evident that an obligation of the authorities in the medium term will be to ensure that these companies, when they become larger still, continue to comply with the practices of free competition.

4. The Bond Group won the bid because it offered to pay US$0.76 per share, both for the shares bidded and for those corresponding to the capital increase: 355 million shares.

5. These plans would raise the number of lines installed by CTC at the end of 1992 to 1,200,000.

6. This concept is independent of the public or private property of the company.

7. Another index of the importance of ENDESA and its subsidiaries is the percentage of electric power generation, which in 1988 was 44.8 percent. These shares reached the following values in 1980: power, 54.5 percent, and generation, 52.9 percent.

8. SIC's operation is coordinated by the Centro de Despacho Económico de Carga del SIC (CDEC-SIC), an organization formed by ENDESA, CHILGENER, and Colbún-Machicura.

9. The Superintendency of Gas and Electric Services is ruled by the provisions contained in Law 18,410, published in the *Official Gazette* of May 22, 1985.

Its functions are indicated further on. The National Energy Commission (CNE) was created by Decree Law 2,224 of May 1978. The CNE reports directly to the presidency of the republic and is formed by a council of seven ministers and an executive secretary. The ministers who constitute it are the minister president of CNE, the minister of defense, the minister of mines, the minister of finance, the minister of economy, the minister secretary general of the presidency, and the minister of ODEPLAN. The CNE is responsible for preparing and coordinating the plans, policies, and norms for the proper functioning and development of the electric power sector. It also advises the government in all related matters.

10. See previous section, Articles 90 to 108 of DFL 1 of 1982.

11. Sales information of 1989 is not available. ENDESA (a private company) is presumed to have sold a considerable part of its subsidiaries, and EDELAYSEN was scheduled to be privatized.

12. Aerial work includes the following activities: locating fish, controlling fires, and fumigation.

13. It is interesting to note that (1) given the country's geography, a main network that unites the country from north to south exists; (2) the main routes go between Santiago and some city in the north or south; nevertheless, several routes exist that unite two cities other than Santiago; (3) air taxis cover routes of shorter distances—for example, Santiago–La Serena and Santiago–Talca—or of lower demand—for example, Santiago–Capiapó. One exception is the route Santiago–Concepción, which is served by both medium- and long-range airlines as well as by air taxis.

14. The sector was more competitive in 1979 than it was in the early years of the air navigation industry from the 1930s to the 1950s. For example, Article 2 of DFL 222 of May 1931, which granted legal status to LAN, stated that "the National Airline will have the exclusive right to effect and exploit air transport of all kinds in the territory of the Republic."

15. Although it is probable that the reforms were the main cause of the increasing number of companies, it has not been conclusively shown. On the one hand, a significant increase in demand, associated with higher growth of economic activity, coincided with the reforms. On the other hand, without the reforms, flight supply would not have reacted as rapidly as it actually did.

REFERENCES

Acle, C. 1985. "El Sistema Financiero y el Desarrollo Económico." Thesis, Institute of Economics, Pontifical Catholic University of Chile.

Allende, J. A. 1988. "The Political Economy of Privatizing the State." Working Paper, Department of Political Science, University of Tennessee.

Behrman, R. 1976. *Foreign Trade Regimes and Economic Development: Chile.* Special Conference Series on Foreign Trade Regimes and Economic Development. Vol. 3. National Bureau of Economic Research. New York: Columbia University Press.

Bolsa de Comercio. 1987 to 1989. *Reseña de Valores.* Santiago.

Brealey, R., and S. Myers. 1988. *Principles of Corporate Finance.* New York: McGraw-Hill.

Büchi, H. 1988. "Statement on the State of Public Finance in 1987." *Boletín Mensual* (Central Bank of Chile) (January).

Cabrera, A., D. Hachette, and R. Lüders. 1989. "La Privatización en Chile después de 1985: Se Vendieron o Regalaron las Empresas Públicas? Una Cuantificación." Annual Meeting of Economists, Santiago (November).

Coloma, F. 1988. "Rentabilidad de Distintas Formas de Inversión (1975–1988)." Institute of Economics, Pontifical Catholic University of Chile. Processed.

———. 1989. "Análisis Institucional y Económico del Sector de Telecomunicación en Chile." Institute of Economics, Pontifical Catholic University of Chile. Processed.

Cortés, H., and L. Sjaastad. 1981. "Protección y Empleo." *Cuadernos de Economía,* nos. 54–55. Institute of Economics, Pontifical Catholic University of Chile.

De la Cuadra, S., and D. Hachette. 1991. "Chile." In *Liberalizing Foreign Trade,* edited by D. Papageorgiou, M. Michaely, and A. Choksi. London: Basil Blackwell.

Díaz-Alejandro, C. 1988. "Good-bye Financial Repression, Hello Financial Crash." *Journal of Development Economics* 19.

Edwards, S. 1985. "Stabilization with Liberalization: An Evaluation of Ten Years of Chile's Experience with Free Market Policies, 1973–1983." *Economic Development and Cultural Change* (January).

Edwards, S. and A. Cox-Edwards. 1987. *Monetarism and Liberalization: The Chilean Experiment.* Cambridge, Mass.: Ballinger.

Embassy of the United States in Chile. 1985. "Chile: Economic Trends." Santiago.

Foxley, J. 1985. "Determinantes Económicos del Ahorro Nacional: Chile 1963–1983." *Cuadernos de Economía,* no. 68 (April). Institute of Economics, Pontifical Catholic University of Chile.

Hachette, D. 1977. "Aspectos Macroeconómicos de la Economía Chilena: 1973–1976." Documento de Trabajo no. 55. Pontifical Catholic University of Chile.

———. 1988. "El Ahorro y la Inversión en Chile, un Gran Desafío." In *Desarrollo Económico en Democracia,* edited by F. Larraín. Santiago: Ediciones Universidad Católica de Chile.

Hachette, D., and R. Lüders. 1988. "Aspects of Privatization: The Case of Chile, 1974–1985." Institute of Economics, Pontifical Catholic University of Chile, Santiago. Processed.

———. 1991. "Privatizing the Economy." Institute of Economics, Pontifical Catholic University of Chile, Santiago. Processed.

Harberger, A. 1985. "Observations on the Chilean Economy, 1973–1983." *Economic Development and Cultural Change* 34, no. 3 (April).

Ibbotson, R. G., and R. A. Sinquefield. 1982. *Stocks, Bonds, Bills, and Inflation: The Past and the Future.* Charlottesville, Va.: Financial Analysts Research Foundation.

Investment Steel Company of the Pacific (CAP). 1989. "Antecedentes sobre la Reprivatización de CAP." Santiago. Processed.

———. 1980 to 1989. *Memorias.* Santiago.

Larroulet, C. 1984. "Reflexiones en Torno al Estado Empresario en Chile." *Estudios Públicos* (Winter).

Larroulet, C., and E. Hahn. 1983. "Las Empresas Públicas y Su Respuesta a Diferentes Incentivos: El Caso Chileno entre 1971 y 1981." *Empresas Públicas en Latinoamerica,* edited by J. Kelly de Escobar. Caracas: Ediciones Instituto de Estudios Superiores de Administración.

Lüders, R. 1986. "Lessons from the Financial Liberalization of Chile 1973–1982." World Bank, Washington, D.C.. Processed.

———. 1990. "Institutional Investors, Regulation and Capital Market Development in Brazil." World Bank, Washington, D.C.. Processed.

Mandakovic, T., and M. Lima. 1989. "Privatization in Chile: Management Effectiveness Analysis." In *Privatization and Deregulation in Global Perspective,* edited by D. Gayle and J. Goodrich. Westport, Conn.: Greenwood Press.

Marcel, M. 1989a. "La Privatización de Empresas Públicas en Chile 1985–1988." *Notas Técnicas* (Corporación de Investigaciones Económicas para Latinoamerica, Santiago), no. 125 (January).

———. 1989b. "Privatización y Finanzas Públicas: El Caso de Chile, 1985–88." *Colección Estudios* (Corporación de Investigaciones Económicas para Latinoamerica, Santiago), no. 26 (June).

Marshall, J., and P. Romaguera. 1981. "La Evolución del Empleo Público en Chile 1970–1978." *Colección Estudios* (Corporación de Investigaciones Económicas para Latinoamerica, Santiago), no. 14 (September).

Maxwell, A. E. 1977. *Multivariate Analysis in Behavioural Research*. London: Chapman and Hall.

Méndez, J. C. 1979. *Chilean Economic Policy*. Santiago: Budget Office.

Monckeberg, M. A. 1988. "Aceleración Privatizadora: Las Amarras del Poder." *La Epoca* (September 25).

Morandé, F. 1988. "Domestic Currency Appreciation and Foreign Capital Inflows: What Comes First, Chile, 1977–1982." Working Paper, Department of Economics, University of Santiago.

National Electricity Company (ENDESA). 1980 to 1989. *Memorias*. Santiago.

National Energy Commission (CNE). 1989. *El Sector Energía en Chile*. Santiago.

Pearson, K. 1990. "Mathematical Contributions to the Theory of Evolution in the Inheritance of Characteristics Not Capable of Exact Quantitative Measurement, VIII." *Philosophical Transactions of the Royal Society* (ser. 4) 195 (1):79–150.

Pérez, F. 1987. "Necesidades de Inversión para los Fondos de Pensiones." Documento de Trabajo no. 92. Centro de Estudios, Santiago.

Ramos, J. 1986. *Neoconservative Economics in the Southern Cone of Latin America, 1973–1983*, Baltimore: Johns Hopkins University Press.

Rao, C. R. 1952. *Advanced Statistical Methods in Biometric Research*. New York: John Wiley and Sons.

Riveros, L. A., and R. Paredes. 1989. "Political Transition and Labor Market Reforms in Chile." Word Bank, Washington, D.C. Processed.

Rosende, R., and A. Reinstein. 1986. "Estado de Avance de Programa de Reprivatización en Chile." Central Bank of Chile, Santiago. Processed.

Sapelli, C. 1989. "Ajuste Estructural y Mercado de Trabajo: Una Explicación de la Persistencia del Desempleo en Chile, 1975–1980." Annual Meeting of Economists, Santiago, November.

Short, P. T. 1984. "The Role of Public Enterprises: An International Statistical Comparison." In *Public Enterprise in Mixed Economies: Some Macroeconomic Aspects*, edited by R. Floyd, C. Gray, and R. Short. Washington, D.C.: International Monetary Fund.

Tokman, V. 1984. "Reactivación con Transformación: El Efecto Empleo." *Colección Estudios* (Corporación de Investigaciones Económicas para Latinoamerica, Santiago), no. 14.

Valdés, S. 1988. "Ajuste Estructural en el Mercado de Capital: La Evidencia Chilena." Central Bank of Chile, Santiago. Processed.

Vickers, J., and G. Yarrow. 1988. *Privatization: An Economic Analysis*. Cambridge, Mass.: MIT Press.

Vuylsteke, C. 1988. "Techniques of Privatization of State-Owned Enterprises." Vol. 1. World Bank Technical Paper no. 88. Washington, D.C.: World Bank.

Wagner, G. and C. Williamson. 1988. "Análisis Institucional y Económico de la Industria de Aeronavegación Comercial en Chile." Institute of Economics, Pontifical Catholic University of Chile, Santiago. Processed.

About the Authors

Dominique Hachette de la Fresnaye is a professor in the Institute of Economics of the Pontifical Catholic University of Chile. He received an M.A. and a Ph.D. in economics from the University of Chicago. Hachette is coauthor of several books, including *Chile 2010; Liberalizing Foreign Trade: Chile; Desarrollo Económico en Democracia;* and *Financiamiento de la Educación Superior: Antecedentes y Desafíos.* He also serves as a consultant to the World Bank and the U.S. Agency for International Development. His current research interests are privatization, trade policy, economic integration, and urban development.

Rolf Lüders is a professor of economics and research program director of the Institute of Economics at the Pontifical Catholic University of Chile. He received an M.B.A. and a Ph.D. in economics from the University of Chicago. He has been dean of the Faculty of Economics and Social Sciences at the Pontifical Catholic University (1968–1971), director of the Capital Market Development Program of the Organization of American States (1971–1974), chairman of the Morgan-Finansa Bank in Chile, a member of a legislative commission (1974–1981), and secretary of the economy and secretary of finance of Chile (1982–1983). He is coauthor of several books and has written numerous journal articles. He occasionally serves as a consultant to the World Bank and the United Nations and is chief economist of the International Center for Economic Growth.

INDEX

ICEG Academic Advisory Board

P-MX